Lindsey Bareham h...
taurants, food and ...
hotels for fifteen yea...
Design, Good Housekeep... ...*en, Caterer and Hotelkeeper*, the *O*... ...*nd The Times*. She is the author of *Mood Food* (with Stan Hey), *The London Shopping Guide, In Praise of the Potato*, an international potato recipe book, and *A Guide to London's Ethnic Restaurants* (also published by Pan Books). She has also contributed to all manner of other books on London restaurants, food and drink shops, and markets. She was *Time Out*'s food and restaurant editor for ten years, and editor of their consumer section for fifteen years. She is now the restaurant critic for *Taste* magazine and LBC's *Update*, restaurant columnist for the *Sunday Telegraph* and a freelance writer. She lives in London with her two sons.

LINDSEY BAREHAM

PAUPERS' LONDON

PAN ORIGINAL
PAN BOOKS
LONDON, SYDNEY AND AUCKLAND

First published 1990 by Pan Books Ltd
Cavaye Place, London SW10 9PG

1 3 5 7 9 8 6 4 2

Copyright © Lindsey Bareham 1990

ISBN 0 330 30729 0

Designed by Peter Ward
Photoset by Parker Typesetting Service, Leicester
Printed and bound in Great Britain by
Richard Clay Ltd, Bungay, Suffolk

CONTENTS

CONTENTS

ACKNOWLEDGEMENTS

Almost everyone I know and have known over the 25 years that I've lived in London has contributed in some way to this book. The bulk of the foot-slogging research was undertaken by James Millar and Stephen Devine and the unwieldy task of editing was done with patience by Judith Hannam.

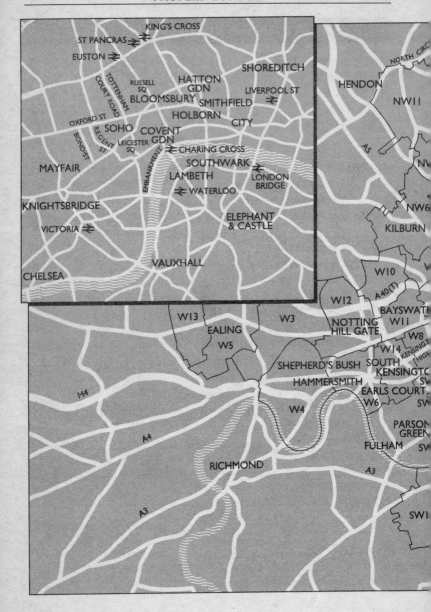

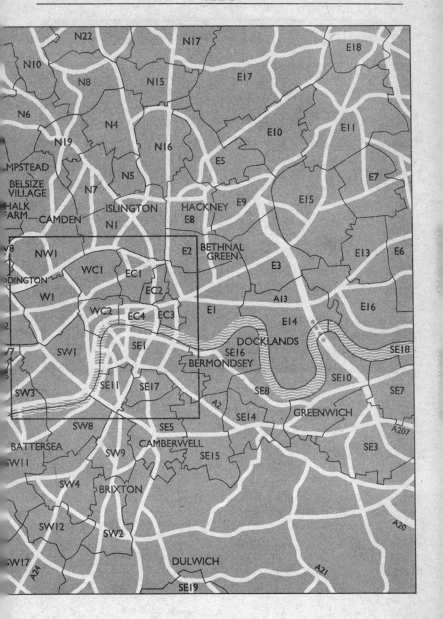

INTRODUCTION

London, like all cities, exists on many levels. If you've got money to burn, it won't take long to discover where to do so.

Finding out how to survive well on a shoestring takes a lot longer. The aim of this book is to take the slog out of learning about London's bargain-basement and to give the reader an insight into all that's good value. It isn't a tourist guide, but rather a useful companion for anyone who likes a bargain, be they a seasoned Londoner, a visitor or someone moving to an unfamiliar part of the city.

Paupers' London touches on all aspects of living in London. On a practical level, it tells you how to get the best value out of public transport, suggests cheap places to stay, gives a breakdown of London's shopping, with an extensive directory of cut-price shops, and dispels the myth that you have to be rich to eat well in London's restaurants. Turning to culture, it guides you round the city's free and cheapest museums, galleries, sporting facilities and tells you how to get cheap, sometimes free, film and theatre tickets. It also tells you the cheapest places to boogie.

A large part of the book is devoted to being a tourist, but while it tells you a little about all the obvious places, it also concentrates on those attractions where you can escape other tourists.

Another vital component of living happily in London is knowing where to turn for help in an emergency and not getting fleeced in the process. *Paupers' London* lists information about a wide range of emergency services and information help lines.

Readers should note that prices in this book were correct in December 1989. Our unstable economy and rampant inflation are bound to result in price increases in the shops, hotels and restaurants listed. However, unless they are forced out of business, they will remain some of London's best buys.

Lindsey Bareham
December 1989

HOW TO USE THIS GUIDE

Paupers' London is a practical guide to getting the best value out of London. Consult it before you do anything that involves spending money!

A NOTE ABOUT RESTAURANT PRICES

It is quite possible to eat very well at every restaurant mentioned in this guide for under £10. Many, though, will feed you for less than £5. As a guideline I have used a £ symbol to mean under £5, and ££ to mean under £10.

A NOTE ABOUT LONDON TELEPHONE CODES

On 6 May 1990 all London telephone numbers will change, the 01-code being replaced by either 071- or 081-. Which code a telephone number takes will depend on the first three digits of the number. For example, 01-434 0000 will become 071-434 0000, and 01-666 0000 will become 081-666 0000. Below is the new list of numbers and codes.

1st 3 digits of no.	The new code	1st 3 digits of no.	The new code	1st 3 digits of no.	The new code	1st 3 digits of no.	The new code	1st 3 digits of no.	The new code	1st 3 digits of no.	The new code
200	081	217	071	229	071	241	071	253	071	266	071
202	081	218	071	230	071	242	071	254	071	267	071
203	081	219	071	231	071	243	071	255	071	268	071
204	081	220	071	232	071	244	071	256	071	269	071
205	081	221	071	233	071	245	071	257	071	270	071
206	081	222	071	234	071	246	071	258	071	271	071
207	081	223	071	235	071	247	071	259	071	272	071
208	081	224	071	236	071	248	071	260	071	273	071
209	081	225	071	237	071	249	071	261	071	274	071
210	071	226	071	238	071	250	071	262	071	276	071
214	071	227	071	239	071	251	071	263	071	277	071
215	071	228	071	240	071	252	071	265	071	278	071

1st 3 digits of no.	The new code	1st 3 digits of no.	The new code	1st 3 digits of no.	The new code	1st 3 digits of no.	The new code	1st 3 digits of no.	The new code	1st 3 digits of no.	The new code
279	071	330	081	381	071	438	071	487	071	539	081
280	071	332	081	382	071	439	071	488	071	540	081
281	071	335	081	383	071	440	081	489	071	541	081
283	071	336	081	384	071	441	081	490	071	542	081
284	071	337	081	385	071	442	081	491	071	543	081
286	071	339	081	386	071	443	081	492	071	544	081
287	071	340	081	387	071	444	081	493	071	545	081
288	071	341	081	388	071	445	081	494	071	546	081
289	071	342	081	389	071	446	081	495	071	547	081
290	081	343	081	390	081	447	081	496	071	549	081
291	081	345	081	391	081	448	081	497	071	550	081
293	081	346	081	392	081	449	081	498	071	551	081
294	081	347	081	393	081	450	081	499	071	552	081
295	081	348	081	394	081	451	081	500	081	553	081
297	081	349	081	397	081	452	081	501	081	554	081
298	081	350	071	398	081	453	081	502	081	555	081
299	081	351	071	399	081	455	081	504	081	556	081
300	081	352	071	400	071	456	081	505	081	558	081
301	081	353	071	401	071	458	081	506	081	559	081
302	081	354	071	402	071	459	081	507	081	560	081
303	081	355	071	403	071	460	081	508	081	561	081
304	081	356	071	404	071	461	081	509	081	562	081
305	081	357	071	405	071	462	081	511	071	563	081
308	081	358	071	406	071	463	081	512	071	564	081
309	081	359	071	407	071	464	081	514	081	566	081
310	081	360	081	408	071	466	081	515	071	567	081
311	081	361	081	409	071	467	081	517	081	568	081
312	081	363	081	420	081	468	081	518	081	569	081
313	081	364	081	421	081	469	081	519	081	570	081
314	081	365	081	422	081	470	081	520	081	571	081
316	081	366	081	423	081	471	081	521	081	572	081
317	081	367	081	424	081	472	081	523	081	573	081
318	081	368	081	426	081	473	071	524	081	574	081
319	081	370	071	427	081	474	071	526	081	575	081
320	071	371	071	428	081	475	081	527	081	576	081
321	071	372	071	429	081	476	071	529	081	577	081
322	071	373	071	430	071	478	081	530	081	578	081
323	071	374	071	431	071	480	071	531	081	579	081
324	071	375	071	432	071	481	071	532	081	580	071
325	071	376	071	433	071	482	071	533	081	581	071
326	071	377	071	434	071	483	071	534	081	582	071
327	071	378	071	435	071	484	071	536	081	583	071
328	071	379	071	436	071	485	071	537	071	584	071
329	071	380	071	437	071	486	071	538	071	585	071

1st 3 digits of no.	The new code	1st 3 digits of no.	The new code	1st 3 digits of no.	The new code	1st 3 digits of no.	The new code	1st 3 digits of no.	The new code	1st 3 digits of no.	The new code
586	071	640	081	687	081	743	081	801	081	561	081
587	071	641	081	688	081	744	081	802	081	863	081
588	071	642	081	689	081	745	081	803	081	864	081
589	071	643	081	690	081	746	081	804	081	866	081
590	081	644	081	691	081	747	081	805	081	868	081
591	081	645	081	692	081	748	081	806	081	869	081
592	081	646	081	693	081	749	081	807	081	870	081
593	081	647	081	694	081	750	081	808	081	871	081
594	081	648	081	695	081	751	081	809	081	874	081
595	081	650	081	697	081	752	081	820	071	875	081
597	081	651	081	698	081	754	081	821	071	876	081
598	081	653	081	699	081	755	081	822	071	877	081
599	081	654	081	700	071	756	081	823	071	878	081
600	071	655	081	701	071	758	081	824	071	879	081
601	071	656	081	702	071	759	081	826	071	881	081
602	071	657	081	703	071	760	081	828	071	882	081
603	071	658	081	704	071	761	081	829	071	883	081
604	071	659	081	706	071	763	081	831	071	884	081
605	071	660	081	707	071	764	081	832	071	885	081
606	071	661	081	708	071	766	081	833	071	886	081
607	071	663	081	709	071	767	081	834	071	888	081
608	071	664	081	720	071	768	081	835	071	889	081
609	071	665	081	721	071	769	081	836	071	890	081
618	071	666	081	722	071	770	081	837	071	891	081
620	071	667	081	723	071	771	081	839	071	892	081
621	071	668	081	724	071	773	081	840	081	893	081
622	071	669	081	725	071	776	081	841	081	894	081
623	071	670	081	726	071	777	081	842	081	897	081
624	071	671	081	727	071	778	081	843	081	898	081
625	071	672	081	728	071	780	081	844	081	900	081
626	071	673	081	729	071	783	081	845	081	902	081
627	071	674	081	730	071	785	081	846	081	903	081
628	071	675	081	731	071	786	081	847	081	904	081
629	071	676	081	732	071	788	081	848	081	905	081
630	071	677	081	733	071	789	081	850	081	906	081
631	071	678	081	734	071	790	071	851	081	907	081
632	071	679	081	735	071	791	071	852	081	908	081
633	071	680	081	736	071	792	071	853	081	909	081
634	071	681	081	737	071	793	071	854	081	920	071
635	071	682	081	738	071	794	071	855	081	921	071
636	071	683	081	739	071	796	071	856	081	922	071
637	071	684	081	740	081	798	071	857	081	923	071
638	071	685	081	741	081	799	071	858	081	924	071
639	071	686	081	742	081	800	081	859	081	925	071

1st 3 digits of no.	The new code	1st 3 digits of no.	The new code	1st 3 digits of no.	The new code	1st 3 digits of no.	The new code	1st 3 digits of no.	The new code	1st 3 digits of no.	The new code
927	071	937	071	949	081	961	081	978	071	988	081
928	071	938	071	950	081	963	081	979	081	989	081
929	071	940	081	951	081	964	081	980	081	991	081
930	071	941	081	952	081	965	081	981	081	992	081
931	071	942	081	953	081	968	081	983	081	993	081
932	071	943	081	954	081	969	081	984	081	994	081
933	071	944	081	958	081	974	081	985	081	995	081
934	071	946	081	959	081	976	071	986	081	997	081
935	071	947	081	960	081	977	081	987	071	998	081
936	071	948	081								

MONEY MATTERS

See also Shopping: Paying Now or Later.

KEEPING IT SAFE

What not to do, banks, building societies and the Post Office

The slogan 'Watch out, there's a thief about' should be taken seriously. Petty thieving, with and without violence, is on the increase in London.

Don't carry lots of cash around, and especially not in coat pockets or in shoulder-slung bags. Do invest in a money-belt or pouch, and wear bags with shoulder straps across the body. It makes sense, also, for girls and women to carry a shriek alarm when going about alone at night.

Don't keep big wads of cash at home, instead open a bank account. There's not a lot to choose between the different high street banks but our research showed Midland to be the most helpful generally of all the major banks.

In the case of tourists, Barclays, Midland and Lloyds all require new customers who want to open a current account to be staying in this country for six months, to give references and ID. They do, however, offer immediate action with an Instant Option account that pays interest and a cash dispenser card; to get a cheque book takes a couple of weeks. Midland quite rightly point out that all most foreign visitors require is a facility to store their money and to get cash out. They suggest a Saver Plus account, which gives a cash card and pays interest on monies over £100.

Building Society Accounts tend to give a higher interest rate than high street bank accounts; the best rates are had from premium investment accounts but these require a minimum £500 deposit. All building society accounts facilitate the use of cash dispensers.

The Post Office operate a National Giro Account that is like any high street bank or building society account with a cheque book and cheque guarantee card, but also a simpler Savings Account and Savings Investment Account. The Savings Account is merely a way of keeping money safe and allows withdrawals of up to £50 a day at any post office. After six months, it's possible to make a special arrangement with one particular branch to draw up to £200 a day. This account pays a very low interest.

The Savings Investment Account requires a month's notice to withdraw money, also from any branch, but pays a base rate linked interest rate. The advantage of a Post Office account is their opening hours (9am–5.30pm Mon to Fri and until noon Sat) are longer than the banks (9.30am–3.30pm Mon to Fri), but they don't offer the facility of cash cards.

GETTING IT OUT OF HOURS

There are 24-hour banks at Gatwick and Heathrow airports. *Bureaux de change* cash traveller's cheques, buy and sell foreign currency and are usually open very long hours. They are though, expensive and their exchange rate is never as beneficial as a high street bank. Use them for emergencies. There are hundreds of *Bureaux de change* dotted throughout London and many of them are rip off artistes. The following are all approved by The London Tourist Board.

THE WEST END

Chequepoint 41 Cranbourn St, Leicester Sq, WC2, tel 437 4069. Open 8.30am–midnight Mon to Fri and Sun, and until 2am Sat.

Thomas Cook 1 Marble Arch, W1, tel 723 7516. Open 8am–7pm Mon to Fri, 8.30am–5.30pm Sat and 10am–1pm Sun.

Chequepoint 548 Oxford St, Marble Arch, W1, tel 723 2646. Open 24 hours daily.

Chequepoint 37 Coventry St, Piccadilly Circus, W1, tel 839 3772. Open 24 hours daily.

Deak International 15 Shaftesbury Ave, Piccadilly Circus, W1, tel 734 1400. Open 24 hours daily.

3 Coventry St, Piccadilly Circus, W1, tel 437 7167. Open 24 hours daily.

NORTH LONDON

Deak International Station Forecourt, King's Cross Station, NW1, tel 837 8416. Open 7.45am–9pm daily.

SOUTH LONDON

Deak International 426 Victoria Buildings, Terminus Place, Victoria, SW1, tel 828 0137. Open 8am–8.30pm daily.
Chequepoint 236 Earls Court Rd, SW5, tel 370 3239. Open 24 hours daily.

WEST LONDON

Chequepoint 126 Bayswater Rd, Queensway, W2, tel 792 8634. Open 24 hours daily.
Deak International 22 Leinster Terrace, Queensway, W2, tel 402 6305. Open 7.45am–9pm daily.

ACCOMMODATION

WHAT TO EXPECT

A bed for the night in London doesn't come cheap and it doesn't come easy. The greatest availability and choice is in the upper price range, which starts at £25 for a single bed.

Foreign students are the luckiest when it comes to accommodation. At the Tonbridge Club in King's Cross, £2.50 buys them a mattress, blanket and a hot shower in the morning. For anyone else, the cheapest bed for the night in London is under canvas in a large dormitory at Tent City, West London. There £4 a night buys a bed, gives access to a free baggage store, parking and hot showers. Similar accommodation at a hostel or hotel costs just over double that, and you pay more for privacy. Single or double rooms put the price up to around £15 a night per person, with marginally better deals for three or four to a room. The rooms are almost always charged by the bed and person; there's no scope for two to a single bed or sneaking a child in free. At these sorts of prices the facilities are reduced to a bare minimum. Bathrooms are rarely en suite and there won't be a TV; there might be a kettle in the room, but certainly no fridge or telephone.

London's cheap hotels vary enormously from the downright seedy, where there are often dubious security arrangements, to family-run gems. Most tend to be converted Victorian houses (sometimes several that are inter-linked) with tiny rooms or rooms crammed with bunk beds. The best guarantee of cleanliness and value for money (within various price guidelines) are those vetted by the London Tourist Board (LTB), who supply stickers to advertise their authorization.

Despite the fact that most London hotels are full most of the time, it is worth asking for a discounted rate on stays of three days or more, especially if it's a group booking. Prices are usually for bed and English or continental breakfast. Incidentally, a British breakfast is worth looking out for; it's worth about £2.

Highly recommended are the **Youth Hostel Association's** five hostels (plus two that are only open for the summer season), where charges are made according to a sliding price scale that depends on age as well as the number of people in a room. There is also a small charge to join the YHA. All the hostels are brilliantly located, efficiently run by friendly folk, and beds are highly sought after. Prices are generally under £10 a night.

Similarly good value are **University Halls of Residence** attached to London colleges, which are let to non-students during the holidays. Facilities vary, but tend to be for single rooms with shared facilities such as laundry, cooking and washing. Also worth contacting is the **International Students House** (229 Great Portland St, W1, tel 631 3223) which has 11 family flats, single and double rooms with shared hostel-style facilities.

The National Council for YMCAs (640 Forest Rd, E17, tel 520 5529) run 18 hotels which offer hostel and hotel accommodation at very keen prices (between £10 and £15) considering their location.

London Hostels Association (54 Eccleston Square, SW1, tel 828 1545 for information, 828 3263 for reservations) acts as a central reservation centre for several mixed and single sex London hostels.

Less anonymous, but sometimes better value – the prices are an average £12–£15 per night for a single room and £20–£25 for a double – is staying *en famille*, either bed and breakfast or renting a spare room. Newsagents' windows in the area of your choice (*see* Which Part of Town below) and local papers (*see* Useful Publications p.6) are the best way of finding such accommodation. The following agencies will do the booking for you and require a 20 per cent deposit in advance. Each agency specializes in a different part of London:

Aunties (Great Britain) Ltd 15 Albemarle Ave, Potters Bar, Herts, tel 0707 58811. Nothing central.
American British Connection 75 Swinson House, Highview Gdns, N11, tel 368 1009. North and North-west London.
Host and Guest Service 592A King's Rd, SW6, tel 731 5340. Greater London.

London Home to Home 19 Mount Park Crescent, Ealing, W5, tel 567 2998. West and South-west London.

London Homestead Services 154 Warwick Road, W14, tel 371 1411. Central and outer London.

World Wide Bed and Breakfast Association PO Box 134, SW5, tel 370 7099. All areas.

WHICH PART OF TOWN?

Greater London is an area of nearly 610 square miles made up of Inner London (124 square miles) and Outer London (486 square miles). Inner London is the core of the city and is composed of the Cities of London and Westminster and 13 boroughs. Since the abolition of the GLC (Greater London Council) in 1986 each borough is responsible for running and publicizing its attractions. Many borough information offices publish broadsheets listing community events, concerts and other cultural activities as well as leaflets on local facilities such as tennis courts, museums and places of interest for children. They are only too happy to send out their brochures or give information over the phone, which can be helpful in deciding where to stay in London. Some also keep lists of accommodation. Local libraries and civic centres (consult the telephone directory or ask at the council offices listed below) often keep a Viewdata System of all this information.

City of London City of London Information Centre, St Paul's Churchyard, EC4, tel 606 3030. Also Clerkenwell Heritage Centre, 35 St John's Sq, EC1, tel 250 1039.

City of Westminster Westminster City Hall, Victoria Street, SW1, tel 828 8070.

Camden St Pancras Library, 100 Euston Road, NW1, tel 278 4444.

Greenwich Tourist Information Centre, Cutty Sark Gdns, SE10, tel 854 8888.

Hackney Town Hall, Mare St, E8, tel 986 3123.

Hammersmith and Fulham Town Hall, King St, W6, tel 748 3020.

Hounslow Civic Centre Lampton Rd, Hounslow, TW3, tel 570 7728.

Islington Town Hall, Upper St, N1, tel 226 1234.

Kensington and Chelsea Town Hall, Hornton St, W8, tel 937 5464;
373 6099 for parks and sports.
Lambeth Town Hall, Brixton Hill, SW2, tel 274 7722.
Lewisham Town Hall, SE6, tel 690 4343.
Newham Town Hall, East Ham, E6, tel 472 1430.
Southwark Town Hall, Peckham Rd, SE5, tel 703 6311; 703 3499
for leisure and amenities.
Tower Hamlets Town Hall, Patriot Sq, E2, tel 980 4831.
Wandsworth Town Hall, SW19, tel 871 6000.

Prices for rooms will be higher in the most central and fashionable
parts of town and in areas close to railway stations. The greatest
concentration of hotels is in *Earls Court* and *Gloucester Road*; *Victoria*;
Bayswater, Paddington and *Lancaster Gate*; *Bloomsbury/Euston* and *King's
Cross*; *Kensington* and *Hammersmith* and *The West End*, all areas which
are considered to be very central. Better value is found slightly further
outside the centre. Anywhere close to a tube station, ideally the
Piccadilly, Victoria and Jubilee lines which are fast and frequent, has a
quick link to the centre and is worth considering.

Less fashionable areas such as *Islington* and *Finsbury Park* (Piccadilly and Victoria lines) in North London; *Vauxhall, Stockwell* and
Brixton (Victoria line) in South-West London; *Acton* (Central line),
Stamford Brook and *Turnham Green* (District line) in West London are
recommended for discerning paupers.

DUMPING LUGGAGE

It costs an average £1 per item to leave luggage for the day. Rates
aren't uniform and vary slightly depending on the size of the item.

Heathrow Airport tel 759 4321. Terminal 1, tel 745 5301, open
6.15am–11pm daily; Terminal 2, 745 6100, open 7am–10pm
daily; Terminal 3, tel 745 5143, and Terminal 4, tel 745 7460,
both open 6.10am–10.20pm daily.
Gatwick Airport tel 668 4211. Open daily 24 hours.
Charing Cross BR tel 922 6061. Open 6.30am–10.30pm daily.

Euston BR tel 928 5151 ex 40528. Open daily 24 hours.
King's Cross BR tel 928 5151 ex 40528. Open daily 24 hours.
Liverpool Street BR tel 247 7600. Open 7am–10pm daily.
Marylebone BR tel 928 5151. Open 8am–7pm Mon to Fri except Bank
 Holidays.
Paddington BR tel 928 5151. Open 7am–midnight daily.
St Pancras BR tel 922 6478. Open 7am–10.30pm daily.
Victoria BR tel 928 5151 ex 27514. Open 7.15am–10.30pm daily.
Waterloo BR tel 928 5151 ex 22833. Open 6.15am–11pm Mon to Sat;
 6.30am–10pm Sun.

HELP AND ADVICE

The place for advice on accommodation is **The London Tourist Board
(LTB)**. Their central office is at Victoria Station Forecourt, SW1, tel
734 3450, open daily 9am–8.30pm Easter to Nov and 9am–7pm Mon to
Sat and 9am–5pm Sun for the rest of the year). The staff are both
helpful and knowledgeable and their comprehensive collection of information on London includes leaflets (some free, some they will give
advice from and some for which there is a small charge) about the
various types of accommodation available. They also offer a hotel
booking service. Their bookshop is stocked with all the latest up-to-date
London guides.

The LTB annually revise their booklet, *London Budget Hotels*, which
carves London up into five central areas and is especially useful for West
End hotels in the £20 to £30 a night price range. An expanded version of
this guide is the LTB's *Where to Stay in London*, published towards the
end of the year (on the assumption that bookings are made early for the
peak summer period) at a price of around £2. It's widely available at all
the LTB Information Offices, which can be found at:

Harrods Fourth Floor, Knightsbridge, SW1, tel 730 1234. Open store
 hours 9am–6pm Mon to Sat, and until 7pm Wed.
Heathrow, Terminals 1, 2 and 3 Underground Station Concourse,
 Heathrow Airport. Open daily 9am–6pm. Also Terminal 2,
 Arrivals Concourse. Open daily 9am–7pm.

Selfridges Services Arcade, 400 Oxford St, W1, tel 629 1234. Open store hours 9am–6pm Mon to Sat, and until 7.30pm Thur.

The Tower of London West Gate, EC3. Open daily 10am–6pm Apr to Oct.

LTB Telephone Information Service 730 3488. Open 9am–6pm Mon to Sat; on an automatic queuing system. Staffed by genuinely helpful and knowledgeable people.

By Post A free LTB information pack is available by post.

USEFUL PUBLICATIONS

Information about hotels changes fast for numerous reasons. It is virtually impossible for guide books (*see* London Guide Books p.19) to do other than provide guidelines. London's evening paper the *Evening Standard* is on the streets at 10am and is one of the best sources of cheap hotel rooms, bedsits, flat shares and flats. Unfortunately *everyone* knows this and bargains are snapped up fast.

London's entertainment listings magazines *Time Out* and *City Limits* are published on Wednesday and are good for cheap hotels, temporary accommodation and rooms in flats.

London's local newspapers, sold only by local newsagents, are very good sources of rooms in small hotels who can't afford or see no point in advertising in the *Evening Standard*.

London is also awash with free newspapers and magazines that have a local interest and carry local advertising. The best for accommodation adverts are: *Law*, a weekly listing/advertising magazine aimed at Australasians which is published on Mondays and is widely available throughout London from high street stands, as is the similar *TNT Magazine*. Also worth checking are the classified advertisement newspapers *Dalton's Weekly* and *London Weekly Advertiser*, both published on Thursday, and the bi-weekly (Monday and Thursday) *Loot*.

Capital Radio, Euston Tower, Euston Rd, NW1, also gives out a flatshare list every Tuesday at 11am.

6

RECOMMENDATIONS

Prices are intended as guidelines; always check exactly what you are getting for your money and ask what facilities are available. Before you make your short list of suitable accommodation, think carefully about what you need apart from a bed and a roof over your head. Make bookings as far in advance as possible and be specific about any additional demands such as the need for a table and chair in the room or access to an iron or telephone. Very few cheap hotels accept credit cards but most are happy to be paid with traveller's cheques.

THE WEST END
HOSTELS

Carr-Saunders Hall 18–24 Fitzroy St, W1, tel 580 6338. Contact The Hall Bursar. 124 beds available March to April and July to September. Car parking, ironing and shared washing facilities. B and B from £12.

John Adams Hall 15–23 Endsleigh St, Euston, WC1, tel 387 4086. During December to January, March to April and June to September there are 126 single and 22 twin rooms in the group of Georgian houses that comprise this hall of residence. Facilities include a swimming pool, ironing room and TV lounge. B and B from £15.

Passfield Hall 1 Endsleigh Place, Euston WC1, tel 387 7743. There are 34 twin, ten family rooms (for three or more) and 100 single bedrooms, all with wash-basins, at this University hall of residence. From £12 a night B and B; car parking available, sports facilities and use of iron.

Ramsay Hall 20 Maple St, close Warren St, W1, tel 387 4537. 400 beds (mainly single study rooms with private basins) are available in December and January, March and April and June to September. From £14 a night B and B.

Tonbridge Club 80 Judd St, King's Cross, WC1, tel 837 4406. The Tonbridge is a youth sports club (mainly martial arts) by day and doubles as a hostel at night. The facility of a mattress and blanket

7

for the night (book in between 10pm and midnight) is only available to foreign students (proven with an NUS card or passport). A hot shower in the morning is included in the price, but otherwise there are no frills and everyone must be out by 10am. A canteen serves soft drinks and crisps and is part of the youth club. The cost is £2.50 a night.

CHEAP HOTELS

Gloucester Court 47 Gloucester Place, W1, tel 935 8571. There are basins in all 14 rooms at this clean, simply decorated and pleasantly run hotel. Some rooms have *en suite* bathrooms and prices range from £10.50 a head, four to a room; £11.50 for threesomes; £25 for a double room and £16 for a single. Prices are for B and B, English breakfast. No credit cards.

Gower House Hotel 57 Gower St, Fitzrovia, WC1, tel 636 4685. Small friendly B and B hotel handy for the British Museum and environs. Best bargains are the family rooms; from £15 a head; singles from £20.

Langland Hotel 29–31 Gower St, Fitzrovia, WC1, tel 636 5801. Family-run small hotel. Rooms from £20 a head B and B. Good shared facilities.

Repton House Hotel 31 Bedford Place, Russell Square, WC1, tel 636 7045. One of the few modestly priced hotels in hotel-dense Russell Square. Best bargains are for rooms with three beds (of which there are 12); B and B from £15. TVs in some rooms, for others there's a TV lounge.

Hotel Strand Continental 143 The Strand, WC2, tel 836 4880. Not to be confused with the nearby giant Strand Palace Hotel. This Strand is small and friendly and remarkably cheap considering its central location. B and B from £20 a head.

Wyndham Hotel 30 Wyndham St, W1, tel 723 7204/9400. This converted house has 11 rooms which cost £18 for a single room, £28 for a double and £36 for a triple. All rooms are centrally heated, have TVs and showers. The location is brilliant – tucked away off Marylebone Road it is quiet but very central.

NORTH LONDON
UNDER CANVAS

Picketts Lock Sport and Leisure Centre, Picketts Lock Lane, Edmonton, N9, tel 803 4756. Take your own tent (or caravan) only. Grass site with 200 pitches and access to full range of facilities. Especially good location because it is within the Sport and Leisure Centre. Open all year, nightly charge for two around £5. Must be over 18 or accompanied by someone who is.

HOSTELS

Hampstead Heath Youth Hostel 4 Wellgarth Rd, NW11, tel 458 9054. Actually Golders Green, very des res, adjacent to the Golders Green end of Hampstead Heath and located in a former nursery nurse college. 846 beds, most in rooms for three or more, which cost from £5 to £8. There's a car park, shops, washing machine and café. Open all year.

Highgate Youth Hostel 84 Highgate West Hill, N6, tel 340 1831. Delightful Georgian house close to Hampstead Heath, Kenwood House (wooded grounds and art collection), Highgate Cemetery (where Karl Marx is buried) and Highgate Ponds. Open all year, the 74 beds cost from £5 to £8 with breakfast included; additional charge for heating.

Ifor Evans Hall Max Rayne House, 109 Camden Rd, NW1, tel 485 9377. Purpose-built hall of residence for the University of London. 200 single and 50 small twin rooms available March to April and June to September. Sports facilities, TV lounge, car parking and shared bathrooms. B and B from £12.

James Leicester Hall Polytechnic of North London, Market Rd, Holloway, N7, tel 607 5417. 156 single bedrooms available March to April and July to September. Communal facilities; B and B £12.50.

Kent House 325 Green Lanes, N4, tel 802 0800. Age limit of 45 for one of the 34 beds here. Self-catering and usual shared facilities, nearest tube Manor House. Bed only from £8 (cheapest in rooms for three) £2 for breakfast.

9

ACCOMMODATION

Tufnell Park Hall Polytechnic of North London, Huddleston Rd, N7, tel 272 4649, but contact Bookings Officer, James Leicester Hall, Market Rd, N7, tel 607 5417. 210 single study rooms with shared bathrooms are available March to April and July to September. B and B from £12.

Westfield College (University of London) Kidderpore Avenue, Hampstead, NW3, tel 435 7141. 506 single and 85 twin/double rooms are available March to April and July to September at this great hostel set in its own spacious gardens and within easy walking distance of Hampstead Heath. Shared bathrooms and all the usual facilities; B and B from £15, special rates for full board.

CHEAP HOTELS

Five Kings Guest House 59 Anson Road, Tufnell Park, N7, tel 607 3996. Pleasant small hotel (16 rooms) in a quiet leafy lane location with single rooms £12 to £15, doubles £22 to £26. Exceptional English breakfast.

Marios Guest House 2 Dalmeny Rd, Tufnell Park, N7, tel 607 2875. Functional guest house offering 15 rooms at £12 single, £24 double. No *en suite* bathrooms, no credit cards but facility for ironing. Quiet des res location.

Moss Hall Hotel 10–11 Moss Hall Crescent, West Finchley, N1, tel 446 8210. A friendly Indian family runs this nine-room hotel and prices include the choice of English or continental breakfast. All rooms are centrally heated and have a kettle; bathrooms are shared. Single rooms from £12, double from £20 and three to a room £33.

White Lodge 1 Church Lane, Hornsey, N8, tel 348 9765. Small family-run hotel where the staff are unusually helpful. Cheapest rooms are for four, of which there are four, with prices starting at £12.

10

EAST LONDON

UNDER CANVAS

Eastway Cycle Circuit Temple Mills Lane, E15, tel 534 6085. Take your own tent (or caravan) only. 50 tent pitches, 20 caravan. Grass site in landscaped parkland within Lee Valley Park. Full range of facilities. Open April to October; nightly charge for two around £5. 1 mile walk to Leyton tube; 4 miles from central London. Must be over 18 or accompanied by someone who is.

Hackney Camping Millfields Rd, E5, tel 985 7656. Run by Tent City but bring your own tent only. 200 pitches plus ten pitches for caravans. Level grass site within large canal-side park. Full range of facilities. Open June 18 to August 25; nightly charge for two around £5. 38 bus into town; 4 miles from central London. Must be over 18 or accompanied by someone who is.

Sewardstone Caravan Park Sewardstone Rd, Chingford, E4, tel 529 5689. Bring your own tent only. 242 pitches on grass and hard site within Lee Valley Park. Full range of facilities except restaurant. Open Easter to October; nightly charge for two around £5. 12 miles from central London. Must be over 18 or accompanied by someone who is.

HOSTELS

Finsbury Hall City University, Bastwick St, EC1, tel 251 4961. 320 single and 50 twin rooms are available during April, June to October and December to January. Shared bathrooms, TV lounge, sports facilities and irons. From £15 a head. Handy for the Barbican and Camden Passage antiques centre.

Northampton Hall City University, Bunhill Row, EC1, tel 628 6661. Bookings through The Conference Office, The City University, Northampton Square, EC1, tel 253 4399. 558 beds are available between February and June, March, October and December at this hall of residence, located in a peaceful City backwater. Parking, TV lounge, ironing facilities and shared bathrooms. B and B from £15.

Queen Mary College Halls of Residence 98–110 High Road,

South Woodford, E18, tel 504 9282. Contact The Conference and Booking Secretary. 635 single, 38 twin/double beds and shared TV lounge, laundry, washing, etc facilities. Bed only £9, with breakfast £11. Available March to April and July to September.

Rosebery Avenue Hall 90 Rosebery Avenue, Clerkenwell, EC1, tel 278 3251. Contact The Hall Bursar. 161 beds available during March to April, June to September. Rooms from £12 (with breakfast) and shared laundry, TV lounge and washing facilities (but basins in all rooms).

CHEAP HOTELS

Barbican YMCA Hotel 2 Fann Street, Barbican, EC2, tel 628 0697. Modest comfortable accommodation for 240 people in a choice of single or twin-bedded rooms. Prices from £15 a night include breakfast with very reasonable rates for week-long stays with evening meal (from £50).

Grangewood Lodge Hotel 104 Clova Road, Forest Gate, E7, tel 534 0637. Quiet and comfortable small hotel in listed building. B and B from £12.

London City YMCA 8 Errol Street, EC1, tel 628 8832. Worth checking short-stay single rooms during summer months; prices from £15 a night, which includes breakfast, with evening meal available if required.

SOUTH LONDON

UNDER CANVAS

Caravan Harbour Crystal Palace Parade, SE19, tel 778 7155. Bring your own tent only. 'I've got a bit of grass on which I stick tents, when I'm full, I'm full; the number of pitches depends on the size of the tents.' Tent and electricity charges are separate but there's a full range of facilities except food. Open all year; nightly charge for two around £6, more with a car. Crystal Palace BR.

Co-operative Woods Caravan and Camping Site Federation Rd,

Abbey Wood, SE2, tel 310 2233. Bring your own tent (or caravan) only. 330 pitches. Full range of facilities except food shop and restaurant. Open all year; nightly charge for two around £6. BR to Abbey Wood, 12 miles from central London but handy for Greenwich and river bus to Charing Cross, Tower and Westminster Piers; for more information about river travel tel 730 4812.

HOSTELS

O'Callaghan's 205 Earl's Court Rd, SW5, tel 370 3000. On the dingy side but cheap: bunk beds (usually four to a room) cost £9 a night. A kettle is provided for tea/coffee making.

Earl's Court Youth Hostel 38 Bolton Gardens, SW5, tel 373 7083. Bang in the fray of cosmopolitan Earl's Court in an old town house in a residential street. 111 beds, overnight charge from £5 to £8 depending on age. Very handy for a wide range of cheap places to eat although there's also a café on the site.

Field Court House 32 Courtfield Gardens, Gloucester Road, SW5, tel 373 0152. Prices range from £9.50 to £14 for a bed in a room with seven others. Single rooms start at £19, double at £29, and all rooms have a basin; bathrooms are shared. Good clean rooms. All prices B and B.

Halliday Hall King's College, 64–67 Clapham Common South Side, SW4, tel 673 2032, but enquiries to Conference Administrator, King's College, 552 King's Rd, SW10, tel 351 6011. Halls of Residence overlooking Clapham Common with their own lawned gardens. Rooms available April, July to September and December. Communal TV rooms, laundry facilities, shower and bathrooms. 202 beds; best bargains for three or more but double and single rooms available. Prices from £12.50 for B and B.

Imperial College 15 Prince's Gardens, SW7, tel 589 5111. Dead handy for the museums, Albert Hall, Knightsbridge and Hyde Park and therefore highly sought after. Accommodation is cheapest for double rooms (they sometimes have triple rooms available which are cheaper) at £47 per week, singles £50; minimum stay one week. Shared facilities include games room, TV room, kitchen and bathrooms.

Ingram Court King's College, Chelsea Campus, 552 King's Road, SW10 and **Lightfoot Hall**, King's College, Manresa Rd, SW3, both tel 351 2488. Contact Conference Administrator, tel 351 6011. Terrific location in the heart of Chelsea. 107 singles and seven twin/doubles available during April, July to September and December. Share facilities. B and B from £15 a night.

International House Brookhill Rd, Woolwich, SE18, tel 854 1418. Purpose-built student hostel with 101 beds in total; 83 single, 9 twins and various self-contained flats. Available April, July to September and December. Prices from £8 B and B.

King George's House YMCA Stockwell Rd, SW9, tel 274 7861. Age limit of 35 for one of the 300 beds here. Cheapest is in rooms for three or more but 230 single rooms and 15 twins. Prices from £15 for B and B.

King's College Hall King's College, Champion Hill, SE5, tel 733 2166, but bookings to Conference Administrator, 552 King's Rd, SW10, tel 351 6011. Peaceful place in quiet grounds with 446 single rooms and a few twin/doubles available April, July to September and December. Communal TV rooms, laundry facilities, shower and bathrooms. B and B prices £14.

Malcolm Gavin Hall King's College, Beechcroft Rd, SW17, tel 767 3119, but bookings to Conference Administrator, 552 King's Rd, SW10, tel 351 6011. 150 single bedrooms with shared bathrooms available April, July to September and December. Communal TV rooms, laundry facilities, shower and bathrooms. The Hall is modern, set in lawned grounds with plenty of parking space. B and B £12.50.

Victoria Youth Hostel Ambrosden Ave, SW1, tel 834 1451. Accommodation with sheet and sleeping bag from £12 a night; £2 extra for breakfast.

CHEAP HOTELS

Aaron House 17 Courtfield Gardens, Gloucester Road, SW5, tel 370 3991. Despite not having central heating, Aaron House is friendly, clean and in good condition. Rooms (B and B) are a standard £15 rate for single; doubles £24 without *en suite* bath, £28 with.

Boka Hotel 35 Eardley Crescent, Earl's Court, SW5, tel 373 2844 or 370 1388. This is a typical B and B hotel but has good clean rooms and central heating. Of the 70 rooms, five have *en suite* bathrooms and prices range from £16 to £22 for a single and £22 to £30 for a double. Cheapest rooms are for three or more when the prices come down to around £11 per person. They accept Visa cards.

Colliers Hotel 97 Warwick Way, Victoria, SW1, tel 834 6931. There are basins and TVs in all the 18 rooms at this pleasant but rather noisy hotel. Triple rooms cost £12 a head, singles £18 to £20 and doubles £28 to £30. All major credit cards accepted.

Curzon House Hotel 58 Courtfield Gardens, Gloucester Road, SW5, tel 373 6745. There is a fully equipped kitchen for the use of guests and duvets on all the beds at this friendly hotel run by an Australian. Rooms are quiet and some have a view across Courtfield Gardens. Cheapest of the 20 rooms are those with three beds, when it works out at £11 each. Single rooms range from £15 to £22 depending on the season, doubles vary from £24 to £33.

Flaxman House 104 Oakley St, Chelsea, SW3, tel 352 0187. Small guest house handy for King's Road. B and B from £15 single, £25 double. All major credit cards accepted.

Hotel St Simeon 38 Harrington Gdns, Gloucester Road, SW7, tel 373 0505. Good, clean and spacious hotel with 32 rooms. Cheapest rooms are for four when the charge can be as low as £7; single rooms are £15 or £18 depending on the season and doubles £24/30. All rooms have radios and basins and the hotel is centrally heated. All prices are for B and B; the breakfast is English.

Luna and Simone House 47 and 49 Belgrave Road, Victoria, SW1, tel 834 5897. It is wise to specify a back room at this pleasant, friendly hotel as front rooms can be noisy. All 36 rooms have an intercom and a basin, and most have a bath or shower. Best prices are for four-bed rooms with their own shower and toilet which work out at £15 a head. Singles are good value, too, at £14 to £16; doubles £22 to £38. Prices are for B and B, English breakfast. No credit cards.

Manor Hotel 23 Nevern Place, Earl's Court, SW5, tel 370 6018. This is a pleasant and friendly hotel in the heart of Earl's Court. All rooms have TVs and some have bath or shower. Prices range from £15 to £22 for a single, £24 to £30 for doubles.

WEST LONDON

CANVAS

Tent City Old Oak Common Lane, W3, tel 743 5708. Dormitory-style tents (£4 a night) and space for 130 tents (no caravans or motor caravans) on this huge site on Wormwood Scrubs. Full range of facilities. Open June 2 to September 9. East Acton tube, 6 miles central London but very handy for Heathrow.

Riverside Caravans Thorney Mill Rd, West Drayton, Middx, tel 0895 446520. Bring your own tent (or caravan) only. Instant cash payment required and no admission after 6pm. 30 pitches on grassy site and very handy for Heathrow, but note that minimum summer stays are two nights. Open all year; nightly charge of around £6 for one. Full range of facilities except food and restaurant.

HOSTELS

Centre Français 61–69 Chepstow Place, Bayswater, W2, tel 221 8134. 200 beds for age range 16 to 30; 25 single bedrooms, ten twin/doubles and 23 rooms sleeping three or more; the majority of accommodation is in 12-bed dormitories. Prices for B and B from £15 for a single, £13 for a double and from £10.75 for triples. French-run and with good restaurant in the basement.

Holland House YHA Holland House, Holland Walk, Kensington, W8, tel 937 0748. Beautiful, spacious, modern hostel incorporating part of a Jacobean mansion and set in Holland Park with its woodlands, lawns and playing fields. 190 beds, café facilities, but no on-site car parking. Bed only charges from (approximately) £5 to £8; with bed linen and breakfast £8 to £10.

Queen Elizabeth Hall King's College, Campden Hill Road, Kensington High Street, W8, tel 937 5411, but bookings through

Conference Administrator, King's College, 552 King's Rd, SW10, tel 351 6011. 250 beds are available during April, July to September and December. Share communal facilities. Rooms from £15 for B and B.

CHEAP HOTELS

Acton Town Hotel 109–11 Gunnersbury Lane, Acton, W3, tel 993 2477. Small hotel in residential area but close to tube and very convenient for Heathrow. 12 rooms; four with private bathrooms. Prices from £20 per person. All major credit cards.

Ashley Hotel 15 Norfolk Square, Bayswater, W2, tel 723 3375. Run by two brothers who are friendly and keep their hotel clean. 52 rooms, 18 with showers, but all with basins. Prices from £15.50 per person.

Christine's Guest House 26 Kenilworth Road, Ealing, W5, tel 579 5569. Small and personally run guest house in residential up-market 'village' of Ealing. Handy for tube (about 30 minutes into the West End) and Heathrow. Rooms from £20.

Continental Hotel 40 Norfolk Square, Bayswater, W2, tel 723 3926 or 262 1582. Four houses comprise this pleasant hotel that has 70 rooms and overlooks gardens in a quiet-ish square. Rooms for four are a bargain at £8.50 each; triples cost £23.50, doubles £19.50 and singles £13.50. The hotel is centrally heated, has a TV lounge and accepts all major credit cards. B and B; continental breakfast.

Foubert's Hotel 162 High Road, Chiswick, W4, tel 994 5202. A friendly Italian family run this modest hotel famous locally for its ice cream and cheap bistro and wine bar (with live music). Rooms from £20 for a single, £35 for a double.

Glendale Hotel 8 Devonshire Terrace, Paddington, W2, tel 262 1770. More of a hostel than a hotel with rooms for four (£8.50 a head), three (£9.50 a head) and two (from £12 a head). Bathrooms and other facilities are shared except for a few more expensive rooms that have private bathrooms and TV. Quiet, pleasant and run by friendly, helpful people. B and B; continental breakfast.

Hyde Park House 48 St Petersburgh Place, Bayswater, W2, tel 229

17

1689/9652. All rooms have basins, central heating, TVs and are recently decorated. Set back from the road with a front garden, the hotel is quiet yet conveniently close to the tube. Prices for the 18 rooms are standardized; £15–£17 for singles; £25 for doubles; £35 for triples, and £40 for quads. No credit cards.

Kingsway Hotel 27 Norfolk Square, Bayswater, W2, tel 723 7784. Quiet but within a stroll of Hyde Park, Paddington and Bayswater. 32 rooms, 15 with private bathrooms. Prices average £20 for single rooms and approximately double for twins. Their four family rooms get snapped up quickly. B and B. All credit cards.

Ruddimans Hotel 160 Sussex Gardens, Paddington, W2, tel 723 1026. Small, pleasant yet modest B and B hotel with 16 family rooms, seven doubles, eight twins and four singles. Rooms from £22 for a single; £32 for a double. Extra for *en suite* bathroom/ shower. No credit cards.

St Peter's Hotel 407–11 Goldhawk Road, Stamford Brook, W6, tel 741 4239. Family-run small hotel in residential area close to the river, Heathrow and 30 minutes by tube (opposite) to the West End. 15 rooms, 11 with *en suite* bathroom; prices from £25 for a single, £35 for a double. Access and Visa accepted.

Topaz Hotel 15 Lexham Gardens, Gloucester Road, W8, tel 373 3466. Conveniently located just off Cromwell Road with standard prices all the year round: £16 single, £25 double and £28.50 triple. Share bathrooms. B and B; continental breakfast.

GETTING AROUND

MAPS AND MAP SHOPS

The best investment any visitor or newcomer to London can make is to buy a set of up-to-date maps. When you consider that it takes a London cabby a minimum of two years to qualify to take their licensing body's street test (the Knowledge), the reality of the size of London begins to register. London is Europe's largest capital city and supports sales of hundreds of different maps and street atlases of various sizes, deception and usefulness. Most newsagents, bookshops and some petrol garages stock a small selection but it is worth a visit to a specialist map shop to tailor the selection to your exact needs. At the very least you will need a single sheet map (mount it on cardboard and post it opposite your loo seat or somewhere very accessible) and a paperback street index. The best single sheet map is the *Ordnance Survey Map of London Central*, scale 1:10,000. There isn't much to choose between *The London A–Z Street Atlas* (the de-luxe version is well worth the extra) and Nicholson's *London Streetfinder*.

London's comprehensively stocked map shops are: **Stanford's**, 12–14 Long Acre, Covent Garden, WC2, tel 836 1321 (Leicester Square or Covent Garden tube) and **Geographia Map Shop**, 58 Ludgate Hill, EC4, tel 248 3554 (Chancery Lane tube).

WALKING

London is on the brink of having no such thing as a rush hour. Traffic jams caused by too much traffic are becoming a fact of life and increasingly the fastest, most hassle-free and safest way to travel around the capital is by foot.

Fortunately, London is a very green city (one of the greenest in Europe) with lots of parks and open spaces which provide fume-free short cuts linking as they do one part of town with another. For example, it is just as quick and far more pleasant to walk from Piccadilly to Victoria through Green Park or from Kensington to Hyde Park Corner through Hyde Park than it is to take the tube.

It also isn't essential to arrive at Covent Garden from Covent Garden tube; Charing Cross, Trafalgar Square, Leicester Square and Tottenham Court Road stations are all only a few minutes walk away. Thoughtful journey planning co-ordinating a central London at-a-glance map with a bus and tube map is becoming vital to avoid both traffic jams and being herded like cattle. The very worst time to travel is from 7.45am–9.45am and 4.45pm–6.30pm Mon to Fri.

HITCHING

About 15 years ago when I wrote about consumer matters for *Time Out* magazine a young Irish man made an appointment to discuss hitching in London. He arrived with what he called his Rule of Thumb. This was a large board crudely shaped like a hitch-hiking hand made out of white, wipe-clean melamine. He explained his theory that most people driving about in inner London are just going on short journeys. His idea was to break any given journey up into short trips and to change the destination on the wipe-clean board between lifts. As anyone who has ever hitched knows, it is vital to stand somewhere where drivers can pull in without difficulty or danger.

The next day my boss Tony Elliott and I put his theory to the test. We got ourselves to Archway (north) and set about crossing London with Richmond (south-west) as the final destination. Our progress was monitored by a photographer and although the article was never published because we felt the question of insurance was too problematic, it was a very successful journey devoid of any hiccups.

That is the only time I have ever tried hitching in London and I have never seen anyone else attempting it.

The pitfalls are of course obvious and should there be an accident in which you are injured you will not be able to claim against the driver's insurance policy.

BICYCLES

Although cyclists risk their life, limbs and lungs on the roads of London, cycling has never been more popular. The disadvantages of pot-holed roads, punctures from broken glass, fumes (buses are worst), grime and dust, taxis (they stop quickly and without warning), roundabouts (Hyde Park Corner, Highbury and Islington and Shepherds Bush are particularly fast and frightening), right-hand turns and the chauvinist attitude of most cars are outweighed by the advantages of cycling. Most importantly it is free. It also enables exact journey times to be calculated, gives a new-found freedom and flexibility and (in theory) keeps you fit. A high proportion of London cyclists wear safety helmets (American research shows that these reduce the incidence of head injuries by as much as 85%) and some form of eye protection (sun glasses are better than nothing). Getting yourself noticed is vital, so fluorescent arm bands or bright coloured clothing is sensible.

Another major consideration for bike owners is guarding against theft. Solid steel D and U locks are the most dependable and worth the £20, but an insurance policy is strongly advised too. Lights and saddle bags should be removable.

Only use main roads when essential and look out for special cycle paths. **The London Cycling Campaign** (Tress House, Stanford St, SE1, tel 928 7220) publish an irregular guide to cycling in London called *On Your Bike*, which costs £2.50. Each edition has a detailed map of cycle routes throughout London and is invaluable to anyone considering doing a lot of inner London cycling. Contact them direct or pick up a copy from one of the following central cycle shops: **Covent Garden Bikes**, 2 Nottingham Court, WC2, tel 836 1752; **Dial A Bike**, 18 Gillingham St, Pimlico, SW1, tel 828 4040 or **Savilles**, 97/99 Battersea Rise, SW11, tel 228 4279. LCC also publish route maps to North-east London (£1), North-west London (50p) and South London (66p).

London's cycle shops are many and marvellous and staffed by helpful enthusiasts. All stock some security and safety equipment but the following are particularly recommended and competitively priced:

Bike 53 Pimlico Rd, SW1, tel 730 6668.

Bike Peddlers 50 Calthorpe St, WC1, tel 278 0551.
On Your Bike 52–54 Tooley St, SE1, tel 407 1309.
South Bank Bicycles 194 Wandsworth Rd, SW8, tel 622 3069.
Stuart Bikes 309–11 Horn Lane, W3, tel 993 3484.

HIRING

Theft and the cost of maintenance has curbed the number of cycle shops prepared to offer a hire service but the shops listed here have plenty of well-tended bikes on their books. Bike hire costs between £5 and £10 a day and £20 to £25 a week with negotiable rates for longer hires. Deposits range from £15 to £50 and are rarely required in cash. A passport or driving licence is also needed as ID. Always ask for a lock and lights and if they aren't included in the hire you must buy a lock. It is a wise precaution to check insurance details too.

Bike UK Vault 11, Lower Robert St, WC2, tel 839 2111 (branches 40 Clapham High St, SW4, tel 622 1334 and 242 Pentonville Rd, N1, tel 833 3917).
Chelsea Cycles Park Walk, off the Fulham Road, SW10, tel 352 3999.
On Your Bike 52–54 Tooley St, SE1, tel 407 1309.
Porchester Cycles 8 Porchester Place, W2, tel 723 9236.
Portobello Cycles 69 Golborne Rd, W10.
Savilles 97–99 Battersea Rise, SW11, tel 228 4279.

BUYING

NEW

The cheapest basic, three-gear bikes cost between £80 and £150 from:

Bike 53 Pimlico Rd, SW1, tel 730 6668.
Bike UK 40–42 Clapham High St, SW4, tel 622 1334; Lower Robert St, WC2, tel 839 2111; 242–44 Pentonville Rd, N1, tel 833 3917; 296–98 Upper Richmond Rd, SW15; and 273–79 High Street, Acton, W3, tel 992 2877.

Camden Bikes 3 Camden Rd, NW1, tel 485 1372.
Cycle and Mower 143 Fortress Rd, NW5, tel 482 2255.
Edwardes 221–25 Camberwell Rd, SE5, tel 703 3676.
Fudge 564–66 Harrow Rd, W9, tel 969 5991.
Stuart Bikes 309–11 Horn Lane, Acton, W3, tel 993 3484.

SECOND-HAND

A decent second-hand adult bike with gears is pretty hard to come by in London. Many bike shops are loath to bother with the second-hand trade but occasionally come by bikes as part of a trade-in sale. All bike shops have a workshop and should be prepared to give their s/h bikes the once-over before a sale, but don't be surprised if they are 'too busy'. Many bike shops with good workshops offer a general overhaul service for around £10. A list of these places together with those shops that offer a speedy repair service are listed at the end of the bike section.

Keener bargains are had through private sales; scan local papers, *Exchange and Mart* (the weekly 'for sale' newspaper) or your local newsagent's window. It also often pays dividends to post your own advert. The following shops specialize in second-hand bikes. Prices start at £50 but are more often £80+. The fashionable mountain bikes with their sturdy, thick wheels and extensive gear system are ideal for coping with London's roads but they rarely appear for sale second-hand.

Bike Peddlers 50 Calthorpe St, WC1, tel 278 0551.
Dave Martin Golborne Rd, end Portobello Rd (street market), W11, Sat only.

SPEEDY REPAIRS AND OVERHAULS

Bell Street Bikes 73 Bell St, NW1, tel 724 0456.
Camden Bikes 3 Camden Rd, NW1, tel 485 1372.
Cycle and Mower 143 Fortress Rd, NW5, tel 482 2255.
On Your Bike 52–54 Tooley St, SE1, tel 407 1309.
Stuart Cycles 1 Ascot Parade, Clapham Park Rd, SW4, tel 622 4818.

Yellow Jersey Cycles 62 Drayton Park, N5, tel 359 1971.

TRANSPORT

London's buses and underground tube train system are run by London Regional Transport (LRT) who operate a 24-hour, seven-day phone enquiry service for route information on 222 1234. LRT also up-date a recorded information service every 24 hours on 222 1200.

Leaflets and maps galore, advice about travel passes, routes and timetables of bus, tube and London overland train routes operated by British Rail are available from **LRT Information Centres** located in the following underground stations: *Oxford Circus* (open 8.15am–6pm Mon to Sat); *Piccadilly Circus* (open 8.15am–6pm daily); *Victoria* (open 8.15am–9.30pm daily) and *Euston* (open 7.15am–6pm Mon to Thurs and Sat, 7.15am–7.30pm Fri and 8.15am–6pm Sun). Also useful is Judy Allen's *London by Bus and Tube*, published by Nicholson, which is full of helpful pointers about getting the best out of London's public transport system.

TRAVEL PASSES

Bus and tube ticket prices are worked out on a zone system with a different price rating for different zones. This means that a short journey that crosses several zones can cost more than a longer one within one zone. Passes are valid for unlimited travel and can be bought for the day, week, month or year. A *Travel Card* pays for itself within a couple of journeys, saves time on queuing to buy tickets and can be bought at any tube station. Travelcards can be used on the tube and most buses in all zones, and can be used from 9.30am until the end of the service Mon to Fri and all day Sat and Sun. By the day it costs (from) £2, by the week £15.90, and by the month £64.60.

The similar *Capitalcard* can also be used on British Rail trains and costs (from) £2.60, £16.80 and £64.60. Weekly and monthly cards for both Travelcards and Capitalcards require a passport-sized photo.

Children travel free until the age of five and at reduced rates up until the age of 14. 14- and 15-year-olds can also travel at a discount with a *Child Rate Photocard* (for the tube) and *Child Bus Pass*; proof of age and a passport-sized photo will be required. Senior citizens (over 60 for women and 65 for men) can apply for a free Travelcard.

BUSES

There are 569 bus routes throughout Greater London and a limited night service that runs on 34 routes. The daytime service runs between (approximately) 5.30am and midnight, at which point the night service takes over and continues until 6am. Detailed bus map routes are available from **LRT Information Centres** (*see* separate entry above).

Bus Passes can be bought for the day, week, month or year and give great savings if you intend a lot of bus travel; they are priced according to zone travel; a day card costs the equivalent of a return journey.

NIGHT BUSES

The 34 routes that constitute the night service operate between midnight and 6am with an estimated 40,000 people using the service on Saturdays. A leaflet called *Night Owls Guide* gives full details of routes. Travelcards cannot be used on the night service.

THE UNDERGROUND (TUBE)

London's underground system is the oldest and deepest of the world's subway train systems, with a network of lines between 248 stations throughout the Greater London area. 815 million people use the system every year (an average 3 million a day) and it is operating at maximum strain.

The newest addition to the system is the Docklands Light Railway, which only appears on recently printed maps. Modernization and cosmetic facelifts are under way, but escalators break down every day and long train delays are common. Overcrowding at peak travel times (7.45–9.45am and 4.45–6.30pm Mon to Fri) seems unbearable until you get used to it. There are plans for more lines (between Hackney and Chelsea; Liverpool Street and Paddington and a link between Victoria, Euston and King's Cross), but £165 million has just been spent on a new ticket system and automatic gates that are intended to ease congestion.

Theft and violence in the Underground is increasingly common and much is organized by gangs called steamers. There is now a greater police presence on the platforms but I think twice about travelling alone after 10.30pm. Smoking is illegal.

OVERLAND TRAINS

Network SouthEast is part of the nationwide British Rail system. It has several stations strategically placed in London linking parts of the city not well served by LRT. Most useful is the North London Link, which connects Richmond, Kew and Gunnersbury with Hampstead, Canonbury (Highbury and Islington) through Dalston and Hackney to Docklands and across the Thames to Woolwich. A map inter-linking the network with tube trains is available.

THE RIVER

A speedy, efficient boat service is run by **The River Bus Partnership**, tel 376 3676 (Chelsea Harbour) and 987 0311 (Docklands), which links Chelsea Harbour (where there is plenty of parking and a Hoppa bus service from Sloane Square) with Greenwich Pier. It stops at Charing Cross Pier (by the Festival Hall), Swan Lane Pier (north-side London Bridge), London Bridge City Pier (south side at Hays Galleria), West India Pier (for London Docklands), Greenland Pier (for Surrey Docks) and finally Greenwich. The fare is £3 for the entire journey; short trips are £1 and medium trips £2. Mon to Fri the service operates every 20 minutes between 7am–10am and 4pm–7pm and every 30 minutes between 10am–4pm and 7pm–10pm. At the weekend the service operates between 10am–6pm every 30 minutes and doesn't call at Swan Lane.

For information about other sailings ring **LTB River Service**, tel 730 4812 for 24-hour recorded information. Alternatively, ring **River Rides** at Westminster Pier, tel 839 2349/930 0970 and **Thames Cruises**, tel 930 0971 at Charing Cross Pier.

MOTORBIKES

HIRING

Scootabout 59 Albert Embankment, SE1, tel 582 0055. This is London's only motorbike hire company and they offer 50cc mopeds and small motorbikes. Hire includes a helmet and is for unlimited mileage; rates from £10.95/£12.95 a day, £54.50/£64.50 per week, plus VAT at 15 per cent. The deposit is between £50 and £100.

BUYING

Motorcycle City 533–35 Staines Rd, Bedfont, Feltham, Middx, tel 890 1849, is a vast showroom specializing in new and nearly new bikes of all sizes. Although not bargain basement (there is no such thing; buying a reliable, cheap motorbike is impossible), Motorcycle City offers a month's warranty and will arrange finances to bridge sales. There is rarely anything under £700.

RECOVERY

Streetfinders, tel 906 3668, provide a 24-hour recovery service for an all-in £15 (plus VAT). They will travel anywhere within the London postal area. Streetfinders also offer a puncture repair service for £20 (plus VAT).

CARS

AUCTIONS

Apart from a lucky private sale (it is worth getting the AA to check over the vehicle, they charge from £54 depending on engine size: ring 891 4444) buying at auction is the cheapest way of buying a second-hand car. Sales are no-nonsense affairs mainly attended by the trade. Cars are sold as seen, often without the opportunity to inspect under the bonnet or to start the engine. Business is cash and payment is generally a 10 per cent deposit and full settlement within 24 hours. Some auction companies offer an indemnity option which can be as little as £12 and as much as £50 (against outstanding HP payments but not for stolen vehicles) and others give a one-hour warranty on newer vehicles. Admission is never less than £10.

British Car Auctions 620 Great Cambridge Rd, Enfield, Middx, tel 388 1144. Sales 11am Tue, Thur and Sat. Viewing 9am on day of sale.

City Motor Auctions Evelyn St, SE8, tel 691 0066. Sales 7pm Tue, noon Thur and 11am Sat. Viewing one hour before the sale.

London Car Auctions Wandsworth Bridge Rd (on left by petrol station just before the bridge), SW6, tel 736 0086. Sales 7.30pm Tue and Fri. Viewing from 10.30am on day of sale.

Motor Auctions (London) Harlequin Ave, Great West Rd, Brentford, Middx, tel 560 0303. Sales 11am Tue and Sat, noon Wed, 11am and 6pm Thur. Viewing from 9am on day of sale.

Whitechapel Cars and Commercial Auctions Car Park, Fulbourne St, E1, tel 377 1422. Sales 7pm Tue, Thur and 11am Sat. Viewing from 9.30am on day of sale.

HIRE

The prices quoted are for the cheapest (ie smallest) car. Be sure to check that prices are for unlimited mileage and that there are no insurance extras. You will need your driving licence and credit card (for deposit). The advantage of the more expensive, big companies such as **Avis** (central reservations, tel 848 8733) and **Hertz** (central reservations, tel 679 1799) is that cars can be hired in one part of the country and left in another. All-found prices start at around £30 per day. The cheapest companies are:

Damn Cheap Car Hire 24 Martello St, Hackney, E1, tel 254 3072. £12.50 per day, £47 per week. £75 deposit.
Portobello Mini Hire 317 Westbourne Park Rd, W11, tel 221 4455 and 2 Metropolitan Arcade, Beadon Rd, W6, tel 741 4458. £21.53 per day, £99 a week. Full insurance included.
Team Cars 327 King St, Hammersmith, W6, tel 748 8465. Rates are seasonal and start at £14 per day, £72 per week, with an additional daily insurance rate.

PETROL

By operating a cash-only system and so saving on credit card charges, **Hills**, 588 High Rd, Leytonstone, tel 556 1362, sell the cheapest petrol in London. Not worth crossing town for, but worth remembering if you are in this area and need to fill the tank; prices are a minimum 10p per gallon cheaper than other garages. Open 24 hours.

PARKING

It is crazy to take a car into the West End at any time during the day. If you must, be forearmed with the National Car Park list and map of car parks. It can be collected directly (or by post with a stamped addressed envelope) from their offices at NCP, 21 Bryanston St, W1, tel 499 7050 (Marble Arch tube).

Illegally parked cars are clamped and later scooped up and taken to one of several police car pounds dotted around London. To get the car back costs £12 for a parking ticket, £25 to be de-clamped, £57 for the police removal charge and £5 per day for storage. The following companies will do it all for you.

Car Clamp Recovery Club 160 Vauxhall Bridge Rd, SW1, tel 235 9901. Membership £25, declamp £8, delivery £15.
Clamp Rescue 148 King's Cross Rd, WC1, tel 837 7342. Membership £25. First clamp free, thereafter £10.

TAXIS AND MINICABS

All black cabs are licensed and have to display their fare charge. Drivers must also have completed the Knowledge, a rigorous test on the streets of London about the shortest, quickest way of getting around them. The fare is clocked up on a meter and charges are worked out on time and distance. Drivers can generally give a reasonable estimate of journey cost and have a good overall reputation for being honest and helpful. Complaints can be reported to the Carriage Office, tel 278 1744, in which case be sure to note down the cabbie's number which will be displayed beneath the fare table.

Black cabs can be hailed in the street (only when their light is on) but can also be ordered by phone. The largest reliable firm is **Radio Taxis**, tel 286 0286/272 0272/272 3030 and 235 5000. They specialize in instant bookings (within a few minutes) from their 2,500-strong fleet and arrive with a small charge on the clock.

All black cabs require cash payment and though it's not obligatory, they expect a 10–15 per cent tip.

Mini-cabs are far more hit-and-miss. They have no licensing body, rarely use meters or have adequate insurance provisions. It is illegal for them to solicit trade in the street (they often kerb crawl in the West End late at night) and it is only advisable to use a well established firm. Always ask for a price quote in advance and take the precaution of checking your route beforehand and discuss it with the driver. It is very common for drivers to ask passengers for directions and/or waste time consulting an A–Z.

Reputable companies with large fleets who operate all over London are **Addison Lee**, tel 431 4444 and **Abbey Car Hire**, tel 727 2637. Both operate 24 hours and give preferential service to account holders.

SHOPPING

I began writing about shopping in London in the early 70s for *Time Out* magazine. Being a consumer columnist then was a constant voyage of discovery, there was so much happening, such variety and individualism.

At that time, each area of London had a strong sense of identity, which was based not only on tradition but reflected concentrations of cultures. Covent Garden, for example, used to be home to craftsmen servicing the ballet and theatre, as well as the fruit, vegetable and flower market. The King's Road used to be full of one-off boutiques, antiquarian book dealers and modest antique traders, whereas Soho was thick with authentic French and Italian family-run food shops.

In the 80s the specialist and family-run shop is something of a rarity. As gentrification creeps all over London and new areas are adopted as fashionable the everyday shops selling the essentials of life such as hardware, haberdashery, drapery, food and chemist requisites get nudged out in favour of boutiques. Increasingly the high street shops are multiples selling identical goods from identical shops all over London. Shopping malls and arcades have replaced the department store as the mecca for out-of-towners. Street markets remain relatively unchanged, but where the developers can get their hands on adjacent land, hey presto the area is on its way to becoming another Covent Garden and a centre for expensive fashion and trendy giftware. Smithfield, the area around the wholesale meat market, is evolving thus and Camden Lock market in north London is about to emerge homogenized like Covent Garden.

Despite the evolution, London still remains one of the most interesting shopping cities in the world and there are pockets of character and plenty for the pauper. I am a great believer in planned shopping. If, for example, you are going to Soho for some fresh pasta it is as well to know that you can also buy cheap second-hand records there too. I also think that it is useful to have all the great shopping assets of an area listed together as a reference should you move or go to stay there. At the beginning of each area I have given a thumbnail sketch of the character of the shopping and mentioned shops that aren't of particular use to paupers. An index at the end of the book annotates all the shops by subject as well as alphabetically.

SHOPPER'S RIGHTS: THE LAW

Shoppers are protected by the Sales of Goods Act 1979 and the Trade Descriptions Act 1968. Despite any disclaimers the shop may care to post you are entitled to a replacement or cash refund if the goods bought aren't 'fit for their purpose' or 'of merchantable quality'. Fit for their purpose means that goods must perform the function for which they are commonly used; for example, a pen must write and a saucepan must not leak. Merchantable quality means that the goods are in pristine condition and complete: for example, a roof rack must contain all the necessary parts and a suit should not be in need of dry cleaning. Goods must also be what they say they are: for example, china must be china and cotton must be cotton.

Should you need to complain and get no joy with the shopkeeper, then you have redress with the Trading Standards Officer or Consumer Protection Department at your local Town Hall. The only time when your rights are waived is at sale time when attention is drawn to defects which reflect knock-down prices. If you decide you don't like a purchase when you get home you rely on the shop's goodwill to change it for you. If you are in doubt about a purchase or need a second opinion, explain your predicament; any sensible shopkeeper will agree to a cash refund.

A leaflet explaining the two Acts is available from the **Citizen's Advice Bureaux** (*see* telephone directory for your local branch) or by post from **The Office of Fair Trading**, Field House, Room 310C, 15–25 Breams Buildings, EC4, tel 242 2858.

PAYING NOW OR LATER

All shopkeepers prefer cash and many who are locked into expensive concessions with credit card companies give discounts for cash. Using a *credit card* (Visa and Access) sensibly (which means paying their bill within their settle-by date before they can charge you interest) gives you interest free credit or cash (up to a pre-determined limit based on your financial status) for a month. Similarly *charge cards* (American Express, Diners Club) have to be bought (£32.50/£27.50), but have no limit and are billed each month. Interest is charged at a percentage of the outstanding amount (1.5 per cent/3 per cent). *Shop option cards* work like credit cards and can be used at any branch of a chain. Interest charges are rarely below 2 per cent of the bill. Some chains like Marks and Spencer and John Lewis only accept their own credit cards.

See also Money p.xvi.

SALES

Traditionally, end of season sales are held at London's department stores, fashion outlets and any shops that sell seasonal or fashion-tied goods. Although the seasons are increasingly blurred and there is always a sale of something at any time during the year, the bulk of the sales begin after Christmas (but are known as the January sales) and at the beginning of July. The sales last one or two weeks and often drag on and on; the best bargains happen on the first couple of days. The best sales are at the most exclusive shops; Harrods sale, for example, is famous and so, too, are the sales at designer fashion shops in South Molton Street and Sloane Street, Knightsbridge. Sales are always advertised locally and in the *Evening Standard*. Ring to check exact sale dates in advance and try to get yourself on their mailing list. Don't forget that a bargain is only a bargain if you want it; best buys are in linen, lighting, cookware, classic knitwear, beds and toys.

OTHER BARGAINS

One man's rubbish is another man's treasure and the most accessible place to find useful cast-offs for the home is **The Skip**. Skips are great big dustbins that are parked in the street by builders to collect their rubbish. While debris from a house gut can offer all manner of useful objects, it is the cast-offs (from other people using the skip as a bin) that appear when the builders have gone home that are the most useful. Skip scavenging is an art form at which paupers excel.

Jumble sales are advertised in local papers and tend to take place in middle-class areas in church halls and cub/scout/girl guide huts on Saturday afternoons. They are good sources of old and hardly worn contemporary clothes for all the family, toys, books, bric-à-brac and occasionally bicycles and small pieces of furniture. Always arrive early with carrier bags for booty, plenty of loose change and an open mind. There is generally a small admission charge.

Charity shops are good sources of cheap clothes, books and objects. Most charities list their branches under their name in the telephone directory. The most common are Oxfam and The Spastics Society. Neither takes credit cards and relies on voluntary helpers. Oxfam shops tend to be open 10am–4pm; those of The Spastic Society 9am–5pm Mon to Sat.

Buying at **auction** puts drama into shopping and is a hit and miss yet fun affair. First timers are advised to go and watch a sale before joining the fray. There are auction houses selling everything from office and trade stock, catering equipment and lost property as well as the more usual antiques, books and furniture, and all of them offer a viewing in advance of the sale. The lots (as they're called) are often job lots and include a lot that you don't want. If you make a successful bid be prepared to have to pay cash and to take your goods away there and then. Auction houses most useful to paupers are listed on pp.37, 55, 70, 79, others are advertised in the quality press and the *Antique Trade Gazette*.

Watch out for adverts for **Car Boot Sales**, which are a cross between a jumble sale and a flea market. Some are advertised in local papers and in newsagents' windows, but most often a hand-written poster goes up in and around the venue a couple of days in advance.

Buying **wholesale** or **in bulk** saves money if you need a lot of something or can share your purchase with friends. London's wholesale markets are accessible to the general public but all happen in the early hours of the morning and are run on a business-like basis; traders are not amused by sightseers or dithering purchasers. Billingsgate (for fish) and New Covent Garden at Nine Elms (for fruit, vegetables; cut flowers and plants) and Spitalfields (for fruit and vegetables) are more accommodating than the meat market at Smithfield.

Hiring electrical tools, a lawn mower or home decorating/ building equipment makes a lot of sense. **HSS Hire Shops** have branches all over London and hire out by the hour, day, weekend or week. Contact their head office at 25 Willow Lane, Mitcham, Surrey, tel 640 1115 for details of your most convenient branch. For more details *see* North London shopping section.

THE WEST END

Oxford Street, Bond Street, Tottenham Court Road, Regent Street, Soho and Leicester Square

Oxford Street is still London's most famous shopping centre. Apart from the mecca of the Marble Arch branch of Marks and Spencer (which holds the world record for the fastest turnover of goods sold annually for every square foot of the store!), it is also home to all the leading fashion, footwear and children's multiples. It is probably best known, however, for its department stores – Selfridges, John Lewis, D. H. Evans, BHS, House of Fraser and Debenhams. Its shopping arcade, The Plaza, stays open until 8pm every night but has little to offer paupers.

More interesting shops can be found in Oxford Street's side streets, the most notable being St Christopher's Place, which rivals South Molton Street for high fashion.

Bond Street is the place for couture clothes and footwear, expensive jewellery and antiques, while Regent Street is famous for the enormous children's toy shop Hamleys.

Piccadilly is now dominated by two shopping arcades, The London Pavilion and Trocadero, and a mammoth branch of Tower

Records, but in its back streets, that lead into Soho, there are plenty of small specialist shops that haven't yet succumbed to pressure like much of the rest of Soho and become fashion boutiques. Food and drink shopping have always featured strongly in Soho (there is also a greater concentration of restaurants, wine and sandwich bars, pubs and cafés here than in any other part of London) but increased rents due to the area's new-found trendiness are forcing them out.

Its food street market in Berwick Street is a great haunt for paupers, as, too, are the shops and markets of Chinatown, which centres around Gerrard Street.

Charing Cross Road is famous for its specialist, second-hand and antiquarian bookshops, while Tottenham Court Road is the place for hi-fi, photographic and electrical goods.

Specialist food shops proliferate in Charlotte and Goodge Street (also good for cheap restaurants and sandwich bars).

STREET MARKETS

Berwick Street Market Berwick St, leading into Rupert St, Soho, W1. Open 9am–5pm Mon to Sat. There's been a market on this site since the early 19th century and there are plans to clean it up and instill order with pitches paved into the ground and numbered. Until then, stalls are crammed together down both sides of the road and there's a constant barrage of repartee between stallholders. Fruit and veg is the mainstay of the market, but quality and prices vary enormously making it essential to have a good look before parting with money. The market is especially good for seasonal gluts and there are several specialist stalls too; personal favourites include the British cheese and mushroom stalls. Several butchers in Berwick Street sell cheap meat. As the market approaches Rupert Street food stalls give way to those selling cut-price new clothes, household goods, etc.

Gray's Antique Market 58 Davies St and **Gray's Mews** 1–7 Davies Mews, W1, tel 629 7034. Open 10am–6pm. Credit negotiable with individual stallholders but cash preferred. Get here early on Monday for best buys is the advice of my deep throat in the antique business. There are 200 stalls which deal mainly in small antiques and bygones; jewellery, tin toys and games and oriental rugs predominate. Most traders are experienced dealers and few major bargains slip through their net.

AUCTION HOUSES

Frank G. Bowen 15 Greek Street, Soho, W1, tel 437 3244. No credit cards or cheques. Sales 10.30am and 1pm on alternate Thurs with viewing 9am–4.30pm the day before and from 9am on the day. Bowen's is an old established company specializing in bankrupt office stock from desks to calculators. A catalogue of sales for the year is available at £15 or 60p per sale.

CLOTHES, FOOTWEAR AND ACCESSORIES

Blackout 33 Gt Windmill St, W1, tel 439 1998. Open noon–7pm Mon to Wed and Fri, until 8pm Thur, and 11pm–6pm Sat. Access, Amex, Visa. Great source of American 40s clothing for men and women. *See* entry for Siren in North London section for full details. Also evening wear hire service.

C&A Modes 501–19 Oxford St, Marble Arch, W1, tel 629 7272. Open 9.30am–7pm Mon to Wed and Fri, until 8pm Thur, and 9am–6pm Sat. Access, Amex, Visa. Enormous store well stocked with clothes for men, women (including maternity wear) and children. Careful hunting produces great bargains in plain, sensible everyday wear. Especially good for trousers, jackets and jerseys.

Denny's 39 Old Compton St, W1, tel 437 1654. Open 9am–5pm Mon to Fri. Access, Visa. This is where chefs, waiters and the catering trade buy their uniforms, some of which make very acceptable fashion alternatives. Navy and white check cotton trousers, spotted cotton handkerchiefs, towelling socks, white overalls, butcher's stripe aprons and much more. Delightfully shambolic, old fashioned shop.

Department X 189 Oxford St, W1, tel 494 3646. Open 9.30am–6pm Mon, Tue and Sat; until 7pm Wed and Fri, and until 8pm Thur.

All major credit cards. The flagship of the floundering Next empire which contains the whole Next collection on a rotating racking system, the idea being that you make a mental note of clothes that particularly interest you before making for the appropriate department where an assistant will call up a sample. While not bargain basement, Next clothes are well made and priced very low considering their style and quality. Especially good for men's suits and casual wear.

Eastern Bazaar 131a Tottenham Court Rd, W1, tel 387 4605. Open 9.30am–6pm Mon to Sat. All major credit cards. Great stock of cheap cotton clothing, mainly imported from India. Dresses (£8 to £25), embroidered shirts (£4.99 to £7.99) and skirts (£9.99). Also women's underwear.

The Gap 208 Regent St, W1, tel 434 2091; 395 Oxford St, Marble Arch, W1, tel 408 2400 and 315 Oxford St, opposite John Lewis, W1, tel 493 3316. Open 9.30am–7pm Mon to Sat, until 7.30pm Thur. All credit cards except Diners Club. Casual, functional, well made and well designed day-wear from the States for males and females. All natural fabrics, good colours, simple styles and realistic prices. For example, pocketed long-sleeved T-shirt £8, blue jeans £24, paisley cotton polo top £24, suede waistcoat £48, wool and chino trousers around £24.

Hennes 481 Oxford St, W1, tel 493 8557. Open 10am–6.30pm Mon to Wed and Fri; 10am–8pm Thur and 9.30am–6pm Sat. All major credit cards. Budget-priced, reasonably fashionable, mainly day-wear clothes for men, women, children and babies. I have many friends who swear by Hennes but I've never succeeded in finding the right size or colour in any garment I've been after. Stock changes frequently and it's a shop that deserves regular checking over.

Marks and Spencer 458 Oxford St, W1, tel 935 7954. Open 9am–8pm Mon to Fri and 9am–6pm Sat. Their own credit card only. Great for men and women's underwear, knitwear, men's shirts and, occasionally, children's wear. Very, very busy and often hopelessly understaffed and irritating to shop at.

Mash 73 Oxford St, W1, tel 434 9609. Open 10am–7pm Mon to Wed, Fri and Sat; 10am–8pm Thur. All major credit cards. A good source of cheap, worn Levi 501s; otherwise followers of high street fashion.

Off the Cuff 93 Regent St, W1, tel 437 3870. Open 9.15am–6pm Mon to Wed, Fri and Sat; 9.15am–7pm Thur. All major credit cards. Similar in concept to the Sock Shop and Tie Rack, this shop specializes in men's cotton shirts in a wide range of fabric designs (from £12 to £25), braces, cuff links, scarves and button covers.

Paramount Stores 114 Tottenham Court Rd, W1, tel 387 7503. Open 9am–6.30pm Mon to Sat. No credit cards. Discount bag shop which is particularly good for leather, vinyl and fibreglass briefcases. Prices from £20.

Salisbury's Handbags 68 Oxford St, W1, tel 580 7225. Open 9am–6pm Mon to Wed, Fri and Sat, until 8pm Thur. All major credit cards. Since this high street chain of travel goods (purses, wallets, handbags, holdalls and suitcases in every imaginable material) was bought by Next, there has been a noticeable improvement in their designs. Prices are comparatively low but this is not a source of the exceptional or the stylish. Leather handbags from £20; good range of cheap leather purses.

Shelly's 159 Oxford St, W1, tel 437 5842. Open 9.30am–6.30pm Mon to Wed, Fri and Sat; 9.30am–7.30pm Thur. All major credit cards. Branch of a small long established chain that specializes in very cheap fashion shoes for both sexes. DMs, suedes, spiv and winkle-pickers, biker boots and huge range of gibsons all under £30.

Sonico Jean Centres 49 Oxford St, W1, tel 734 7958. Very cheap new jeans. *See* North London section for details.

Warehouse 27 Duke St, W1, tel 486 5270. Open 9.30am–5.30pm Mon to Wed and Fri; 10am–8pm Thur and 9.30am–6pm Sat. All major credit cards. Excellent source of well designed, simple and fashionable women's clothes. Fast turnover and limited stocks so regular visits essential. This is the place to buy a working wardrobe at a fraction of the normal cost.

What She Wants 50 Oxford St, W1, tel 636 8428. Open 9am–6.30pm Mon and Tue; until 8pm Thur and 7.30pm Fri and Sat. Access and Visa. Shopping at WSW is like permanent sale time.

Clothes are piled high in bargain bins and you sift through until you find what you want. Cheap and cheerful day-wear; jeans, jerseys, T-shirts and skirts in moderately fashionable designs, usually man-made fabrics but rock bottom prices.

HOUSEHOLD, ELECTRICAL AND RECREATIONAL

Charlotte Robinson's Bookshop Great Pulteney St, Soho, W1, tel 437 3683. Open 11am–6pm Mon to Fri. Access, Visa. Unusual shop in that five dealers operate under one roof. Keen prices on second-hand and rare books, mostly modern first editions. Also children's books, illustrated books and detective fiction.

Freeway Elite 84 Tottenham Court Rd, W1, tel 580 4946. Open 9am–6pm Mon to Sat. Amex, Visa, Access. General hi-fi/audio visual shop that claims to 'beat any price in the UK'.

Hi-Way Hi-Fi Ltd 67 Tottenham Court Rd, W1, tel 637 9787. Open 9am–6pm Mon to Sat. Also 242 Tottenham Court Rd, W1, tel 636 1752. All major credit cards. Good prices on the more sophisticated Walkmans.

House Bros 85 Brewer St, W1, tel 437 3857. Open 9am–5.45pm Mon to Fri, 11am–3pm Sat. Access, Visa. Old-fashioned shop that stocks a wide range of cooks' knives, including the chefs' favourite Victorinox and Granton range, and the only London stockist of the Opinel range of French wooden-handled pen-knives. Also stocks saws from all the leading makers, wood carving and jewellers' tools, plus screws, nails and miscellaneous bits and bobs. Also tool grinding, saw setting and knife sharpening service.

Kingsley Photographic 93 Tottenham Court Rd, W1, tel 387 6500. Open 9am–5.45pm Mon to Fri and 9.30am–4pm Sat. Amex, Visa, Access. New cameras from £14, but cut-price leading brands such as Olympus XA2 £59, Ricoh FF 3 Auto Focus £69 and Kodak Retinette £30.

The Linen Cupboard 21 Gt Castle St, W1, tel 629 4062. Open 9am–6pm Mon to Wed, Fri and Sat, until 8pm Thur. Visa. Great source of cheap bed linen which is arranged in big piles directly on the floor. (They also sell top quality Irish linen sets of double sheets for £199 – £250 is the cheapest I've come across elsewhere

– while white Egyptian cotton double sets cost £46 with pillow slips costing £7.99 each.) Limited range of not particularly cheap duvet covers. This little shop also offers a made-to-measure service for unusual sizes.

Material World 4 Berwick St, W1, tel 494 3272. Open 9.30am–6pm Mon to Sat. Access, Visa and most foreign currencies. There are 5,000-odd fabrics in stock at this eccentric, long established shop that used to be called Fabrics. They specialize in the unusual but also keep several well known ranges, including Liberty prints and Armani fabrics at great discounts. Students can get a further discount.

Reckless Records 30 Berwick St, Soho, W1, tel 437 4271. Open 10am–7pm daily. Access, Visa, Mastercard, Eurocard. Second-hand records. *See* North London section for details.

Ries of Holborn 242 High Holborn, WC1, tel 242 7721. Open 8.30am–6pm Mon to Fri and 10am–4pm Sat. All major credit cards. Over 200 yarns are sold from this supermarket for knitters. Very cheap prices.

Russell and Chapple 23 Monmouth St, Covent Garden, WC2, tel 836 7521. Open 8.30am–1pm and 2pm–5pm Mon to Fri. No credit cards. Much frequented by art students, artists and theatre set designers because R & C specialize in cotton sail-cloth, linen and calico (amongst other things). Fabric is sold by weight and colour. Delightful, old fashioned shop.

Video City 233 Tottenham Court Rd, W1, tel 631 1491. Open 9am–6pm Mon to Sat. All major credit cards. Particularly good for Walkmans, plus keenly priced general audio visual stocks, including TVs, hi-fis, cassette radios, computers, calculators, etc.

Vintage Magazine Company 39 Brewer St, Soho, W1, tel 439 8525. Open 12.30pm–7pm Mon, 10am–7pm Tue to Sat, and 2pm–7pm Sun. All major credit cards. Marvellous shop that is well stocked with an enormous selection of vintage magazines and comics at a wide range of prices. Everything from a 1933 copy of *Hotspur* to a 1953 edition of *Picture Post* and a July 1966 *Playboy*. Also big selection of movie star photos and new and repro movie posters.

Morgan Computer Company 179 Tottenham Court Rd, W1, tel 636 1138. Cut-price computers and software. *See* Bloomsbury for full details.

Morgan's Stationery Supermarkets 22 Goodge St, W1, tel 636 0935. Open 9am–6pm Mon to Fri and 9am–5.30pm Sat. Cheap stationery, office and arts supplies, office furniture and computer software. *See* Bloomsbury for full details.

FOOD

See also Street Markets and Restaurants

Algerian Coffee Stores 52 Old Compton St, Soho, W1, tel 437 2480. Open 9am–5.30pm Mon to Sat. All major credit cards. This 100-year-old shop is a Soho landmark, and still run on a very personal basis. They sell 25 blends of coffee (which is ground to order), 90 teas, spices in the pod and a full range of coffee and tea machines. Their own blends are the most competitively priced; mail order service and free local deliveries.

I. Camisa and Son 61 Old Compton St, Soho, W1, tel 437 7610. Open 9am–6pm Mon to Sat. My favourite of the small clutch of Soho's Italian delis. It's tiny, cramped and you often have to queue, but their salamis, wafer-thin Parma ham, prosciutto and other cured meats are both superb and keenly priced, so it's well worth it. A further attraction for paupers is their cut-price meat trimmings. They also sell freshly made pastas, mozzarella, Parmesan and other Italian cheeses, home-made sauces, fresh sausages, dried mushrooms and, of course, olive and truffle oils, plus some breads and wines.

Fratelli Camisa 1a Berwick St, Soho, W1, tel 437 7120, and 53 Charlotte St, W1, tel 255 1240. Open 9am–6pm Mon to Sat; 2pm closing Thur at Berwick St. Access. The parent Berwick Street shop has been selling Italian foods for nearly 50 years and at the newer shop the stock is greatly expanded. Cheeses, oils, vinegars, dried beans, fresh and dried pasta, superb olives, dried mushrooms, salamis, prosciutto and Parma ham and all manner of tinned and dried groceries. Also their own breads, made with olive oil, which are almost a meal in themselves!

International Cheese Centre 21 Goodge St, W1, tel 631 4191. Open 8am–6.30pm Mon to Wed and Fri, until 7.30pm Thur, and 9am–6.30pm Sat. Access, Amex. A proper cheese shop, where the cheeses are in good condition and so have pronounced flavours. Everything is labelled with origin and price and grouped by country; there's also a special section for vegetarian cheeses. Much better value than pre-packaged supermarket cheese.

Lina Stores 18 Brewer St, W1, tel 437 6482. Open 8am–6pm Mon to Sat, until 1pm Thur, and 5pm Sat. Tiny, old-fashioned Italian grocery now in its 50th year, which is run by Giovanni and Rose Filippi. Hams are sliced to order, Parmesan is sold in big chunks and their daily made pasta sells out fast (in the autumn their king-sized pumpkin ravioli called *tortelloni di zucca* is a major treat). They also sell pulses and rice from big sacks, mozzarella in various grades, terrific bread, home-made *pesto* and a big range of Italian groceries, coffee and oils.

Loon Fung Supermarket 42–44 Gerrard St, Soho, W1, tel 437 7332. Open 10am–7pm, sometimes later, daily. No credit cards. Chinatown's oldest supermarket, and a veritable treasure trove of oriental fresh, dried and frozen fish, meat and vegetables. Also herbs and spices, ready prepared frozen and dried meals (watch out for the MSG content!), noodles, rice (in big sacks), as well as beers, *sake* and other wines, spirits and teas.

Loon Moon 9 Gerrard St, Soho, W1, tel 734 9940. Open erratic hours but essentially 10am–7pm daily. No credit cards. My favourite Chinese supermarket, which is as good for its wide range of food as it is for its cooking equipment and china. A wonderful place to browse; don't forget the back basement room which has the deep freezers and a wide range of dried produce.

Maison Bertaux 28 Greek St, Soho, W1, tel 437 6007. Open 9am–7pm Tue to Sat, 9.30am–1pm and 3.30pm–6.30pm Sun. No credit cards. An authentic French patisserie, now in its 117th year, where everything is made on the premises. Drool over the window display of whole gâteaux, fruit flans, elaborate cakes, patisserie and cream confections and order to take away or enjoy

43

with tea or coffee at one of their cramped and sought after tables.

Markus Coffee Co. 13 Connaught St, W2, tel 723 4020. Open 8.30am–5.30pm Mon to Fri, and 8.30am–1pm Sat. No credit cards. Small and atmospheric coffee shop where the beans are stored in big open sacks. Despite its prestigious address, there are some surprisingly cheap blends sold here. They offer a mail order service.

Patisserie Valerie 44 Old Compton St, W1, tel 437 3466. Open 8am–7pm Mon to Sat, 10am–6pm Sun. No credit cards. This Belgian patisserie has been a fashionable haunt for over 40 years and rivals Maison Bertaux for the best patisserie in Soho. Take away or eat on the premises with tea or coffee. Wonderful chocolate truffle cake, fruit tarts, choux and puff pastry, stuffed gâteaux and all manner of patisserie. Also brioche and croissants, *petit fours* and a cake-making service.

BOOZE

Del Monico's 64 Old Compton St, Soho, W1, tel 437 2738. Open 9am–6.30pm Mon to Fri, until 5pm Sat, and noon–2pm Sun. No credit cards. A reliable source of bin ends and other cheap wines. Famous, though, for its range of vodkas.

Oddbins 47 Brewer St, Soho, W1, tel 437 6371; 25 Charlotte St, W1, tel 636 5526; 7 George St, W1, tel 935 6727; and 32 Marylebone High St, W1, tel 935 7266. Open 10am–9pm daily. All major credit cards. Part of a vast chain which is able to pass on great savings thanks to bulk purchases. Well chosen wines in all price brackets, but a very large part of their extensive stock is at the cheaper end of the market. Helpful, amusing tasting notes accompany their catalogue (illustrated by Ralph Steadman) and there are further reductions on case purchases and free local delivery.

Soho Wine Market 3 Greek St, W1, tel 437 9311. Open 9am–6pm Mon to Fri and 9.30am–5pm Sat. All major credit cards. Not a market at all, but a small shop stuffed full of booze. It's a browser's paradise for wine and whisky fans (over 200 varieties including Irish whiskey and unusual malts) and is a good source of bin ends and other bargains. They publish a list, offer discounts on cases and deliver in London; free on orders of two cases or more.

The Vintage House 42 Old Compton St, W1, tel 437 2592. Open 9am–11pm Mon to Sat, noon–2pm and 7pm–10pm Sun. No credit cards. One of Soho's finest off-licences (and there are many!), which is particularly good on cheaper wines. Also over 100 whiskies and fair range of beers. Discounts are negotiable on decent sized orders and they offer free glass loan and sale or return for party orders.

BLOOMSBURY

Covent Garden, Russell Square, Bloomsbury and Holborn,
King's Cross and Euston.

Traditionally, Bloomsbury is synonymous with the literary and publishing worlds and the many narrow streets surrounding the British Museum and London University house more specialist and academic bookshops than anywhere else in London. There are also some eccentric, long established, specialist shops in Bloomsbury, such as Smith's, the umbrella and walking stick shop, Davenport's, the professional conjurer's shop, and Mel Calman's cartoon Workshop. Sicilian Arcade, a little pedestrianized street that is close to the main high street (Southampton Row), is home to several rather special à la mode clothes shops. Food shopping centres around Tavistock Place, Marchmont and Red Lion Street and the enormous, but fairly useless, Brunswick Shopping Centre.

When London's wholesale fruit, vegetable and flower markets decamped from Covent Garden to Nine Elms in the early 70s the empty warehouses were snapped up by designers and advertising agencies. The area became trendy and very soon the shopkeepers who'd serviced the market trade and supplied the ballet, music and theatricals associated with the area, couldn't afford the new high rents. Initially, the newcomers were interesting one-offs like the Kite Store, the Hat Shop, the Bead Shop and the Neal's Yard Wholefood Warehouse, and wacky, eccentric young fashion designers like PX, Yes?No! and Flip, the first shop to make American second-hand clothes fashionable.

Many of these shops, however, are now being nudged out by very slick, expensive fashion houses and by successful high street multiples who are increasingly the only shops who can support the high rents. Covent Garden is still fun to visit but it is full to bursting with tourists and people who work in the area. This can make shopping there pretty unbearable. Half term and school holidays are the worst.

King's Cross is the next area poised for a similar re-development. Ambitious plans for a major clean-up of the area include a mega shopping centre in the bowels of King's Cross Station: the station ear-marked as the main outlet to the Channel Tunnel. For the moment, it remains seedy (it's famous for its hookers!), with little of interest to keen shoppers.

STREET MARKETS

The Apple Market The Piazza, Covent Garden, WC2. Open 9am–5pm Mon to Sat. Located in what was the central market building, stalls are arranged in the middle of what is now a trendy shopping mall. On Mondays the market is devoted to (small) antiques, but the rest of the week stalls are wide ranging. Most things are hand-made with a predominance of jewellery, knitwear and leather bags. Prices tend to be high and bartering isn't expected.

The Courtyard St Martin's Church Yard, St Martin's Place, WC2. Open 11am–6.30pm Mon to Sat. Anything and everything that has been made by hand is sold here: clothes, knitwear, patchwork, wooden toys, jewellery, pottery, leatherwork, etc. Terrific home-made food is available in their café.

Earlham Street Market Earlham St, Covent Garden, WC2. Open 10am–5pm Mon to Fri. There's been a small mixed market here for years; fruit and veg, second-hand books, records and comics and bric-à-brac. Cheap and variable quality.

Jubilee Market Jubilee Hall, between the Piazza, Tavistock and Southampton St. Open 7am–5pm daily. This large, covered market has lost its edge since it moved into a new building. On Mondays it is still a good place to go for antiques and old clothes (get there early for best buys) and during the week it is a mixed clothing, houseplants, records and household market. At the weekends the emphasis is more tourist orientated, with lots of craft and gifty, novelty items, much of which is trash. Hot food (bagels, pizza, ribs, etc) is available upstairs.

CLOTHES, FOOTWEAR AND ACCESSORIES

Boules 22 James St, Covent Garden, WC2, tel 379 7848. Open 11am–7.30pm Mon to Fri, 10.30am–7pm Sat, and 1pm–6pm Sun. All major credit cards. Own-label, casual, easy-to-wear clothes for women in a price range centred around £20.

Cenci 31 Monmouth St, Covent Garden, WC2, tel 836 1400. Open 11am–7.30pm Mon to Sat. Good quality American 50s to 70s clothing. Particularly good for jerseys and cardigans £12 to £20. Small range of dresses from £20 to £40. Especially good sales, when they give a 50 per cent discount.

City Bag Store 434 Strand, WC2, tel 379 7762. Open 9am–6pm Mon to Sat, and until 7pm Thur. All leading credit cards. Extensive and constantly changing stock of brightly coloured bags made from rip-proof nylon, canvas and vinyl. All sizes, from belt pouches to roomy travelling bags. Also stylish imitation leather range. Prices from £8.

Fleurrose 112 Southampton Row, WC1, tel 631 5348. Open 9am–8pm Mon to Sat, and 11am–6pm Sun. All major credit cards. Good multi-purpose luggage shop, particularly recommended for its range of cheap, lesser known brands. Large suitcases from £20. Also briefcases, rucksacks (£17), wallets, handbags and umbrellas.

Flip 125 Long Acre, Covent Garden, WC2, tel 836 7044. Open 11am–7pm Mon to Sat, until 9pm Thur, and noon–6pm Sun. Access, Diners Club, Visa. Originator of the boom in US-imported second-hand clothes, services clothing and sports wear. Two floors of generously stocked rails that necessitate plenty of time for searching. Loads of dross, but plenty of good bargains, too. T-shirts, flannel and lumberjack shirts, sweaters, jeans and more jeans.

The Gap 30 Long Acre, Covent Garden, WC2, tel 379 0779. Open 11am–9pm Mon to Sat, and 1pm–7pm Sun. All major credit cards except Diners Club. Casual, functional, well-made and well designed men's and women's day-wear from the States. All natural fabrics, good colours, simple styles and realistic prices. For example, pocketed, long sleeved T-shirts £8, blue jeans £24, paisley cotton polo top £24, suede waistcoat £48, wool and chino trousers around £24.

Omran 5 Sicilian Ave, off Southampton Row, WC1, tel 405 4563. Open 9am–6.30pm Mon to Sat. All major credit cards. Cut-price new men's clothes shop with jeans from £12.99, shirts from £4.99, T-shirts (including their own designs) from £2.99 and contemporary casual clothes.

Sam Walker 41 Neal St, Covent Garden, WC2, tel 240 7800. Open 10am–7.30pm Mon to Sat. All major credit cards. Go here for the quality end of the vintage clothing boom; great leather jackets, suede and silk waistcoats, great ties, 50s suits, etc. Mainly for blokes. A girls' branch selling similarly stylish 20s to 50s clothes, can be found at **Rebecca**, 66 Neal St, Covent Garden, WC2, tel 379 4958.

70,70 Lamb's Conduit St, WC1, tel 430 1533. Open 10am–6.30pm Mon to Fri, and until 5.30pm Sat. All major credit cards. 70,70 specialize in discontinued lines and samples from top fashion designers and leading labels. Hence Armani, Polo, Jean-Paul Gaultier, Retour, etc, at a fraction of their 'real' price. Worth regular perusal; stock changes fast. For both sexes.

A Shop Called Sale 28 Bedfordbury, Covent Garden, WC2, tel 240 9730. Open 11am–7pm Mon to Sat. No credit cards. The rails are crammed with junk and great finds at this permanent sale shop that deals in end of season designer clothes. Wide range of labels, styles and prices, but little under £20, most often from £75.

Westaway and Westaway 62 Gt Russell St, WC1, tel 405 4479. Open 9am–5.30pm Mon to Sat. All leading credit cards and most foreign currencies. London's cheapest source of good quality Scottish knitwear; most particularly Shetland, lamb's wool, Aran and cashmere. It's a delightful, chaotic shop on several floors with rooms leading off rooms and an essentially foreign staff who can cope with the hordes of tourists who find their way here. Also great tartan children's trousers, children's equivalents of most knitwear, hats, gloves, scarves, tartan dressing gowns and, next door, kilts (from adjoining shop).

Any Amount of Books 62 Charing Cross Rd, WC2, tel 240 8140. Open 10.30am–7.30pm daily. Access, Visa. Antiquarian and second-hand books and a regular basement sale.

The Bead Shop 43 Neal St, Covent Garden, WC2, tel 240 0931. Open 1pm–6pm Mon, 10.30am–6pm Tue to Fri, and 11.30am–5pm Sat. The place for everything to make your own bead jewellery. Bags of glass, metal, stone, wood and plastic beads; clasps and findings, wires and threads.

The Button Box 44 Bedford St, Covent Garden, WC2, tel 240 2716. Open 10am–7pm Mon to Fri, and until 6pm Sat. Buttons, buttons and more buttons. All shapes, sizes and types, and in most materials. Far cheaper than its classy inspiration The Button Queen in Marylebone.

Charing Cross Road Bookshop 56 Charing Cross Rd, WC2, tel 836 3697. Open 10.30am–7.30pm daily. All major credit cards except Diners. Antiquarian and second-hand books from 40p.

Henry Pordes Books 58–60 Charing Cross Rd, WC2, tel 836 9031. Open 10am–7pm Mon to Sat. All major credit cards. Second-hand books bought and sold; big stocks of remaindered books at below half price. Basement sale of hardbacks.

Runaway Records 42 Shorts Gardens, Covent Garden, WC2, tel 497 2118. Open 11am–7pm Mon to Sat. Second-hand records, tapes, CDs and videos bought, sold and exchanged. Also posters and T-shirts. Albums from £2.

Skoob Books Ltd 15 Sicilian Ave, off Southampton Row, WC1, tel 404 3063. Open 10am–6.30pm Mon to Sat. All cards except Diners. 10 per cent discount to students and UB40s. Nearly new second-hand books bought and sold; this is a shop rated as the best of its type by the *Spectator*. Wide range of subjects and helpful, knowledgeable staff. Incidentally, they publish a helpful and detailed directory of second-hand book shops all over the British Isles which costs £5.

Walters World Cameras 1 Victoria Colonnade, Southampton Row, WC1, tel 242 7182. Open 9.30am–6pm Mon to Fri, and 9.30am–1pm Sat. All major credit cards. Used cameras bought and sold, also part-exchange deals and reasonably cheap new cameras. Halina Super Mini Pocket Camera with film and flash £10.95 is a typical bargain. Also cheap watches with 25 per cent off display watches (which start at £29.95) and 25 per cent discount off Parker pens.

OFFICE AND STUDIO

Morgan Computer Company 64–72 New Oxford St, WC1, tel 255 2115. Open 9am–5.30pm Mon to Fri, and 9am–5pm Sat. Access, Visa. Cut-price computers and software with a limited stock of second-hand equipment. The cheapest goods are the demonstration models in the window; examples on offer are NEC PC–881E, including twin drives and monitor £199; new Apricot PC 256K twin drive, mono £275 and Amstrad 8256 Word Processor with printer £275. Second-hand Apple disc drive £50.

Morgan's Stationery Supermarkets 102 Southampton Row, WC1, tel 405 0027. Open 9am–6pm Mon to Fri, and 9am–5.30pm Sat. Access, Visa. Wide range of cut-price stationery supplies, including pads, folders, envelopes, pens, diaries, binders, typewriter ribbons, masking tape, arts materials, maths equipment, office chairs (at a third off the marked price) and computer software. Special offers include ten A4 ruled pads with 80 sheets per pad £5.99; 50 manila envelopes £1.15; 50 white envelopes £1.89; 1000 white envelopes £19.95 and leather-look filofax-style personal organizers £19.99.

FOOD

See also Street Markets and Restaurants

Golden Orient Spice Centre 17 Earlham St, Covent Garden, WC2, tel 836 5545. Open 10am–6pm Mon to Sat. Visa. Having run a small ramshackle Indian grocery round the corner in Shorts Gardens for 20 years, Mr Undeem moved here to concentrate on his spice trade. He grinds the spices himself and they are sold without fancy packaging, in large quantities, so keeping prices down. He also sells large bags of rice and a big range of teas.

Monmouth Coffee House 27 Monmouth St, Covent Garden, WC2, tel 836 5272. Open 9.30am–6.30pm Mon to Fri, 9.30am–6pm Sat, and 11am–5pm Sun. No credit cards. The cheapest coffee beans in London (they do not grind) can be bought here and the larger the quantity (up to 12lb bags), the lower the price per lb; beans are even cheaper when bought unroasted (the shop will give advice about roasting at home). There is a small coffee bar/tasting room adjoining the shop where all the coffees can be sampled. Incidentally, beans keep freshest in the fridge (they can also be frozen and ground directly from the freezer).

Neal's Yard Dairy 9 Neal's Yard, Covent Garden, WC2, tel 379 7646. Open 9.30am–5.30pm Mon to Sat, and 9.30am–6pm Thur and Fri. No credit cards. In France, every cheese shop worth its salt employs an *affineur*. He is the equivalent of a cellar master and he is responsible for looking after cheeses while they mature. The boss of this shop, Randolph Hodgson, is one of a small number of British *affineurs* and he specializes in British and Irish cheeses. He has a list of 50-odd cheeses, which he stores and matures himself, and he can tell you about the farm, the type of field and the cattle which made them. The shop looks like a store room, with whole cheeses piled high around the place. Everything can be tasted. Whole cheeses work out far cheaper and can be successfully stored, and – *sacre bleu* – even frozen!

Neal's Yard Wholefood Warehouse 21–23 Shorts Gardens, Covent Garden, WC2, tel 836 5151. Open 10am–6.30pm Mon to Sat, until 8pm Thur, and 5pm Sat. No credit cards. Enormous health food emporium that was the first of the Neal's Yard food shops to open 15 years ago. The shelves (made from old railway sleepers) groan with dried pulses and beans, nuts, Bombay mix, organic muesli, peanut butter, honey, cooking oils and juices. The prices are very competitive anyway, but get cheaper with bulk purchases. Also worth a visit, although it isn't exactly a pauper's shop, is **Neal's Yard Bakery Bread Shop**, 8 Neal's Yard, tel 836 1082, which sells a range of delicious, traditional breads made with fine flours.

BOOZE

Oddbins 318a High Holborn, WC1, tel 405 0071; 78 Southampton Row, WC1, tel 405 1452; and 23 Earlham St, Covent Garden, WC2, tel 836 6331. Open 9am–9pm Mon to Sat, noon–2pm and 7pm–9pm Sun. All major credit cards. Part of a vast chain which is able to pass on great savings thanks to bulk purchases. Well chosen wines in all price brackets, but a very large part of their extensive stock is at the cheaper end of the market. Helpful, amusing tasting notes accompany their catalogue (illustrated by Ralph Steadman) and there are further reductions on case purchases and free local delivery.

Peter Dominic 449 Strand, WC2, tel 836 0704. Open 9am–7pm Mon to Sat. All major credit cards. The selection of wines for the Peter Dominic chain is chosen with value for money in mind. Bulgarian, Chilean, Italian and French country wines under £3 and discounts offered on case purchases.

NORTH LONDON

Islington, Camden and Chalk Farm, Hampstead and Belsize Village and Kilburn.

Islington's shopping focuses around its famous antique centre, Camden Passage, and Chapel Market, which sells food and general items. Upper Street, the main thoroughfare, is changing from being a home to useful shops to being one for outposts of style and estate agents. Wide, busy, scruffy Holloway Road is good for builders' merchants and junk furniture shops and is home to the area's only department store, a branch of John Lewis called Jones Brothers.

The core of Camden Town is the Lock and its flea market, but the area is dense with interesting furniture and home related shops, as well as some notable food shops that reflect the tastes of cosmopolitan inhabitants.

Traditionally, Hampstead is home to the literary set and the shops reflect it. There are sophisticated food shops, numerous book and antique shops and expensive fashion shops.

By contrast, Kilburn is very down to earth and its high street is full of cheap hardware and new clothes shops.

Camden Lock Commercial Place, Camden High St, NW1. Open air market Sat and Sun; workshops and new covered market open at individuals' discretion, and according to the weather, but approximately 10am–6pm daily. Camden Town on Saturday and Sunday is a mecca for young tourists and Londoners and the entire area between Camden Town tube, over the bridge and past the Lock (and views of Eggcup House; TVam) and Round House up to Chalk Farm tube is one elongated market. Stalls are contained within various covered and open air markets (Electric Ballroom, Canal Market, Chalk Farm Market and The Old Stables), but many are impromptu. The area is currently being 'cleaned up' and the market area around the Lock given a new lease of life with York stone paving (instead of mud and puddles) and what was The Black Shed will emerge as a retail hall (with market stalls) with three storeys of workshops above it.

When Dingwalls Market (as Camden Lock market used to be called because it was associated with the adjacent Dingwalls Dance Hall) first started some 20 years ago it provided the perfect location for cheap artists' and craftsmen's workshops (the new development will increase them twofold) which was complemented by a weekend market for craft, leatherware and musical instruments, home-made foods, stained glass, period clothes and clothes imported from China, Mexico and Guatemala. As it expanded, the diversity of stallholders increased, shops opened that reflected the post-hippie culture (posters, pine furniture, left-wing bookshops) and additional markets opened that concentrated more on bric-à-brac, junk and antiques. The area comes alive at the weekend and while it is no longer somewhere to find real bargains, it's a great place to visit and home to many young commissionable craftsmen.

Until the renovation work is completed, a ship has been sunk in the Lock (of Camden Canal) to make a temporary home for the street market traders, which is known as **The Canal Market**.

Camden Passage Islington High St, N1. Open from 9.30am Wed morning and 9.30am–5.30pm Sat. The Passage, the streets that run off it, and much of this end of Essex Road are dense with antique, junk and curios shops. On Wednesday morning and Saturday various parts of the Passage become small street markets and on fine days the entire passage is full of impromptu stalls, often people selling their own collection of bric-à-brac. There are also several huge malls or indoor markets where the goods are likely to be far cheaper than the shops and more specialized than the outdoor stalls. Jewellery, glass, silver, clothes, porcelain, books, furniture, clocks, lights and much more.

Chapel Market Chapel Street, Islington, N1. Open Tues to Sun 9.30am–4pm, with trade dwindling by mid-afternoon; weekends are best. This well established market, which has been here since 1866, sells both food (fruit, veg, fish, eggs and cut-price meat from many market-style shops) and cut-price new clothes. Flowers, records, electrics also have a presence.

Electric Ballroom 184 Camden High St, NW1. Open 9am–5.30pm Sun. Basement indoor market specializing in second-hand clothing (dinner jackets, waistcoats, ties, T-shirts, etc), plus some streetwise new fashions.

Hampstead Community Market Hampstead High St, NW3. Open Mon to Sat 9.30am–6pm. This is a small hall that houses an almost country Women's Institute-style food market with home-made cakes, fruit and veg and cut flowers. The bulk of the stallholders sell pictures, antiques and junk, books, crafts and new and second-hand clothes.

Inverness Street off Camden High St, NW1. Open daily, 9am–5pm, but best Wed, Sat and Sun am. This is a great little market that is essentially fruit and veg with a regular cheese and dairy produce stall, pet foods and requisites (leads, toys etc) and flowers. On Saturday and Sunday, the rear end of the market is devoted to small junk and bric-à-brac and has always been a notable source of old working tools, art deco and other old lighting and old kitchen equipment.

Kilburn Square Kilburn High Rd, NW6. Open Thur and Sat 9am–4.30pm. Located at the mouth of and within a shopping precinct this is a good, small, general market that is especially good for cut-price new clothes. Much of the food and clothing reflects the West Indian, Irish and Asian population of the area.

Nag's Head Seven Sisters Rd, Holloway, N7. Open 8.30am–4.30pm Wed, Fri and Sat. On Friday and Saturday this is a good general market trading in fruit and veg, household goods and cut-price men's and women's clothes. On Wednesday it becomes a bric-à-brac, flea and antique market which is far less well known (and thus has better bargains and fewer tourists) than nearby Camden Lock, Bermondsey Market in the East End or Portobello Road in West London. Sadly it may close.

The Old Stables Market Chalk Farm Rd, NW1. Open 8am–6pm Sat and Sun. Set back from the road, the market consists of a courtyard and an indoor market. The courtyard sells cheap junk, bric-à-brac and old clothes and army surplus. The indoor market is in a long loft that is reached by climbing up some old wooden stairs. The stalls here sell antiques and bygones and range over old kitchen equipment, clothes, cameras, lighting (there's a particularly good 1930s to 1950s lighting and china stall) and ethnic goods.

Picketts Lock Antique Fair Picketts Lock Leisure Centre, Picketts Lock Lane (off Montagu Rd), N9. Open 11am–5pm (usually) every first Sun in the month from Sept–June: details contact 0444 400570. Furniture, kitchen equipment, prints, militaria and jewellery stalls line up inside the roller skating hall. Good bargains if you get there early.

Swiss Cottage Market by Swiss Cottage Sports Centre, 88 Avenue Rd, NW3. Open 8am–4pm Sat and Sun. Good, small, general market with fruit and veg, household goods, cheap new clothes and a few second-hand clothes and junk stalls.

AUCTION HOUSES

North West London Auctions Lodge House, 9–17 Lodge Lane, N12, tel 445 9000. No credit cards. Sales 5pm Mon, viewing 9am–1pm Sun and 9am–5pm Mon. Specializing in antiques and modern furniture, this auction house has a reputation for lower prices than similar West End houses. Also silver, jewellery, art deco and prints.

Southgate Auction Rooms rear of Southgate Town Hall, Green Lanes, N13, tel 886 7888. Sales 6.30pm Fri, viewing from 10am. There's an easy, unintimidating atmosphere at this general household goods and furniture auction house run by husband and wife June and David Motts. Sales are well attended and prices keen.

CLOTHES, FOOTWEAR AND ACCESSORIES

American Rag Company 2a Jamestown Rd, NW1, tel 482 1948. Open 10am–6pm daily. Access, Visa. Men, women and children's second-hand 1950s American classic workwear clothing. Wide selection of quality stuff in good condition: jeans from £3 to £20, baseball or football leather or suede jackets from £15 to £25, suits that look virtually new from £25, cotton and wool lumberjack shirts from £3 to £5, shorts and boxer shorts from £5. Also army and navy surplus.

Within the shop are two mini-shops: *Hanes US Activewear*, for smart sportswear and superior cotton T-shirts, and *Utopia*, for hip-hop skateboard clothes and swimwear.

Bostonian 66 Parkway, NW1, tel 267 5605. Open 9.30am–5.30pm Mon to Sat. Tiny shop whose shelves are stuffed with inexpensive knitwear (lambswool sweaters £10 and cashmere cardigans £65). Styles are classic, the quality first class and they stock a wide range of colours.

Cobwebs 60 Islington Park St, N1, tel 359 8090. Open 11am–6pm Mon to Sat. No credit cards. Good selection of men's and women's second-hand and antique clothing encompassing the 20s to 1960s. Dinner jackets, shirts (from £8–£12), slacks and trousers (£8–£25), suits (from £25) and 20s to 50s frocks and ball gowns (from £15). Prices depend on age and condition.

Cloud Cuckoo Land 6 Charlton Pl, N1, tel 743 9868. Open 9.30am–5.30pm Tue to Sat. No credit cards. Good quality and good condition ladies' period clothing from Victorian to 50s. Best buys are from the later years: 50s day dresses from £15 going up to £400 for a beaded Victorian gown. Blouses from £14.

Designs 60 Rosslyn Hill, NW3, tel 435 0100. Open 10am–6pm Mon to Wed, Fri and Sat; 10am–8pm Thur. Access, Visa. At Designs they sell posh, nearly-new clothes; in fact this one sells second-hand (white ticket) and new (blue ticket) designer gear at a fraction of normal prices. Stuff that doesn't sell within a month is slashed in price by a further 25 per cent.

Gateway Trading 4–5 Chalk Farm Rd, NW1, tel 485 2560 (ask for the shop). Open 10.30am–6pm Tue to Sun. Cheap streetwise footwear with special offers for purchases of more than two pairs: espadrilles £1.99; buy two pairs and get one free. DM shoes £21.95, DM boots £26.95 and brogues for both sexes £35. Canvas and rubber Palladium shoes £19.95, boots £24.95.

The Glorious Clothing Company 60 Upper St, N1, tel 704 6312. Open noon–6pm Mon and 11am–7pm Tue to Sat. No credit cards. Mostly women's original clothing and accessories from 1920s to 1990s (!). About 90 per cent is period clothing ('chosen with current fashions in mind') and the other 10 per cent is futuristic and new. Price depends on age, condition and style with dresses from £10–£250; blouses from £4–£35, hats and shoes from £4–£50. Also jewellery, sunglasses, gloves and handbags. All clothes are available for hire at approximately one-third the sale price.

High Society 46 Cross St, N1, tel 226 6863. Open 10.30am–6.30pm Mon to Fri, 10am–6pm Sat. Access, Visa, Mastercard. A major attraction of this shop is its £5 rail that is always jammed but requires a lot of sifting. Otherwise good range of men's and women's second-hand period clothes with 1950s and 1960s styles predominating.

Humana 69 Kilburn High Rd, NW6, tel 328 1453. Open 10am–6pm Mon to Sat, 1pm–6pm Sun. All major credit cards. Third world charitable second-hand clothes shop. With plenty of sifting there are bargains in shirts (£2–£5), dresses (£3–£6), jeans (£3–£7), coats (£4–£12) and T-shirts (£1.50–£4). Mainly for adults but some children's clothes.

Laurence Corner 62–64 Hampstead Rd, NW1, tel 388 6811. Open 9am–5.30pm Mon to Sat. Amex, Visa. Now over 30 years old, this was the first army surplus shop to make its clothing fashionable and while not the bargain basement, it is well run and careful rummaging will be rewarded. The bargain rail is especially fruitful.

Miracles 190 Kilburn High Rd, NW6, tel 624 5746. Open 10am–6pm Mon to Sat. Access, Visa, Diners. Asian and Western new cut-price clothes: men's briefs 99p a pair, £1.75 two pairs; socks 99p or £2.50 for three pairs; boxer shorts £1.99 or £5 for three pairs; cotton shirts £4.99 or £8 for two; baggy T-shirts £2.99 each or £5 for two, surfing shorts £3.50 and dresses from £10.

Shirts For Less 189 Kilburn High Rd, NW6, tel 328 8381. Open 9.30am–6pm Mon to Sat. All major credit cards. Mainly men's shirts in a general price range of £3–£15. Short-sleeved £3 each or £5 for two, sweatshirts £5 each and T-shirts £2 each.

Siren 285 Camden High St, NW1, tel 482 4300. Open 10am–6pm daily. Access, Visa. Up-market men's and women's second-hand and vintage clothing sold by pleasant people in a nice atmosphere. Wide-ranging stock includes jackets and blazers from £5–£25, suits from £15–£65, dinner jackets at £32, trousers £12–£25, shoes from £12–£25 and ties from £3–£20. Hire facility for ball gowns and wedding dresses from £15–£40.

Sonico Jean Centres 106 Camden High St, NW1, tel 267 5268 and 99 Kilburn High Rd, NW6, tel 328 3187. Open 9.30am–5.30pm Mon to Sat. All major credit cards. Along with Dickie Dirts (*see* West London) this is the cheapest place for good quality brand name jeans in London. The price range is £9.99 to £31.99 with regular Levis at £16.50, blue Levi 501s £21.99 to £24.99 and black £24.99; Lee Roughriders gold star £19.99 (black) and £21.99 (blue); Wranglers £16.99 to £19.99. Also a decent range of casual shirts from £4.99.

Tumi Latin-American Craft Centre 23 Chalk Farm Rd, NW1, tel 485 4152. Open 10am–6pm daily. Clothes (all made in natural, often hand-woven, fabrics), jewellery and crafts from Latin-American countries, including brightly coloured cotton shirts from Guatemala (£25) and multi-coloured jumpers from Bolivia and Ecuador.

HOUSEHOLD, ELECTRICAL AND RECREATIONAL

Acu-Medic Centre/East Asia 101 Camden High St, NW1, tel 388 6704. Open 10am–5.30pm Mon to Sat. Centre for equipment for, textbooks on, charts about and herbs related to the oriental disciplines of acupuncture, acupressure and moxibustion (a form of heat treatment applied to the skin). Also a range of 300 herbs used in Chinese medicine. Complementing the Centre, East Asia is an oriental health bookshop and source of natural cosmetics, oils and remedies.

Aston-Matthews 143–47a Essex Rd, N1, tel 226 7220. Open 8.30am–5pm Mon to Fri, 9.30am–2pm Sat. Access, Visa. A trade-style shop that is extremely busy with trade and 'knowing' customers. Their stocks of taps, basins, baths, lavatories and various seats, shower units and all the paraphernalia that goes with them is extensive and amongst the cheapest in town. Terrifically patient staff.

Bartletts Hi-Fi 175–77 Holloway Rd, N7, tel 607 2296. Open 9.30am–6pm Mon to Wed, Fri and Sat. Access, Amex, Diners, Visa. Specializes in British equipment, but has a decent range of international names; all equipment chosen for value for money in the mid to lower price range.

Beller's 193 Upper St, N1, tel 226 2322. Open 9am–6pm Mon to Wed, Fri and Sat, 9am–1pm Thur. Old-style drapery shop with bargains in towels, cotton sheets and pillowcases.

Cambridge Furniture Shop 8a Cambridge Ave, Kilburn, NW6, tel 624 8868. Open 10am–6.30pm Mon to Sat. Access, Visa, Eurocard, Mastercard. They advertise themselves as the cheapest place for sofabeds, three-piece suites, beds and bedroom furniture. Their sofabeds (from £99) are the best value and the least naff.

The Cane Store 207 Blackstock Rd, N5, tel 354 4210. Open 10am–7pm Mon to Fri. Visa. Delightfully shambolic shop with good supplies of cheap split bamboo blinds, furniture, rush matting and even radiator covers.

Cloth Shop 130 Royal College St, NW1, tel 485 6247. Open 9.30am–6pm Mon to Fri and 10.30am–5.30pm Sat. Wide range of fabric for home and clothes. Short lengths of designer fabric (including

Jasper Conran), cottons, linens, Indian cotton, wool and cashmere suiting, wools and tartans.

Denny's 6 Parkway, NW1, tel 485 1677. Open 9.30am–5pm Mon to Sat, 9.30am–2pm Thur. Extremely cheap bedding: double duvet covers with pillowcases £18 and cotton pillowcases 99p.

Discount Carpet Company 290 West Green Rd, N15, tel 889 6366 and 614 High Rd, Tottenham, N17, tel 808 1955. Open 9am–5.30pm Mon to Wed, Fri and Sat, 9am–1pm Thur. Access, Visa. Multi-purpose floor covering company who deal with the commercial and domestic market. They are especially good at the cheaper end of the range – coconut matting, vinyl and cut-loop pile carpeting.

Discount House 148 Kilburn High Rd, NW6, tel 328 4306. Open 9am–5.30pm Mon to Thur, 9am–6pm Fri and Sat. Access, Amex, Visa for big purchases. General houseware wholesale-style shop that bursts at the seams with medium-sized aluminium saucepans £3.99, tea towels 79p, wastepaper-baskets £2.49, kettles from £2.49, 12in × 12in mirrors £1.10, vinyl suitcases from £9.99 to £24.99, plain white plates 39p, espadrilles 89p, umbrellas from £1.99 and much more besides.

Foam Plan 164 Holloway Rd, N7, tel 609 8569. Open 9.30am–5.30pm Mon to Sat. Access, Visa. Fire-retardant and combustion modified foam can be cut to size here; a single bed would cost around £30. Also bunk beds, sofa-beds, mattresses and mattress re-covering service.

Functional Furniture Factory 56 Chalk Farm Rd, NW1, tel 485 1000. Open 11am–5.30pm Wed, Thur, Sat and Sun, noon–5.30pm Fri. Previously, and now incorporating **The Reject Pot Shop**, this is a useful source of plain though stylish china: 30-piece white dinner service £17.50 and white teapots £2.99. Also cheap roll-up Japanese futon beds: base £95, covers £22 and bolsters £25.

Garden Centre at Alexandra Palace Alexandra Palace, N22, tel 444 2555. Open 9.30am–5.30pm Mon to Fri, 9.30am–6pm Sat and 10am–6pm Sun and Bank Holidays. Access, Visa. Extensive, environment-aware garden centre with stunningly planted areas displaying their products. Teak furniture, organic gardening products and ozone-friendly packaging. Extensive range of indoor and outdoor plants with climbers a speciality. Also garden furniture. Good prices and a very pleasant place to visit.

House of Steel 400 Caledonian Rd, N1, tel 607 5889. Open 10am–5.30pm Mon to Fri and by appointment Sat. No credit cards. Salvaged and repro (of original casts) steel staircases, balconies, tables and other furnishings.

HSS Hire Shops 53–55 Kilburn High Rd, NW6, tel 328 1798. Open 8am–5.30pm Mon to Fri and 8.30am–5pm Sat. Access, Visa, Eurocard, Mastercard. Home decorating, garden, car maintenance tools and building equipment for hire by the hour, day, weekend, week or longer. Two sets of ID (banker's card, credit card or driver's licence) are needed and a damage waiver scheme for accidental damage to equipment is available. Two-speed electric drill costs £5 for the weekend, £8 the week; wallpaper stripper £10 a week; Flymo electric mower £10 for the weekend and a power saw costs £20 for the week.

Jessop Photo Centre 11 Frognal Parade, Finchley Rd, NW3, tel 794 8786. Open 9am–6pm Mon, Wed to Fri, 9.30am–6pm Tue and 9am–5pm Sat. Access, Visa. One of the cheapest places in London for photographic equipment. Wide range of Kodak and Ilford film, Paterson chemicals and extensive range of darkroom requisites. Price list available.

Julie's Bargain Centre 86 Kilburn High Rd, NW6, tel 624 6780. Open 9am–6pm Mon to Sat. No credit cards. Market-price hardware store with good buys in glass, china and kitchenware. Mugs 69p, bath towels £4.99, medium-sized stainless steel saucepans £4.99, cutlery 30p a piece, Addis bins £6.99 and Addis squeeze mops £5.99.

Ian Mankin 109 Regent's Park Rd, NW1, tel 722 0997. Open 10am–5.30pm Tue to Fri and 10am–4pm Sat. Ian Mankin is a leathersmith by trade and fabric man by inheritance. His father had a delightful old fabric and haberdashery shop in Charlotte Street that Ian updated and moved here. The fabric has taken over from leather, such has been the demand for Ian's beautiful, natural and very cheap selection. Specialities are ticking and Indian cottons.

Wide fabrics are also a speciality.

Material World 104 Camden High St, NW1, tel 482 2548. Open 9am–6pm daily. There are thousands of different fabrics in all styles on sale here, keenly priced from £1.50 to £60 per metre.

MFI 92 Stamford Hill Rd, N16, tel 806 1297. Open 10am–8pm Mon, Thur and Fri, 10am–6pm Tue and Wed, 9am–6pm Sat. Access, Amex, Diners, Visa. Cheap, functional and (with careful searching) acceptable self-assembly pine or melamine furniture for the kitchen (in particular) and rest of the home. The finished products are installed in showrooms for viewing.

S. and M. Myers 100 Mackenzie Rd, N7, tel 609 0091. Open 10am–5.30pm Mon, Wed and Fri, 9.30am–2pm Sat and by appointment Tue and Thur. No credit cards. Run by Mr Myers senior and his two sons, this 170-year-old company is more like a warehouse than a shop. It is without doubt the cheapest source of decent carpeting in London. Ordering is done against exact measurements and you either collect or arrange a carpet fitter (booked through Myers) to collect and then fit for you. All the carpet is plain.

Old Woodworking Tools 228 Upper St, N1, tel 359 9313. Open 9.30am–6pm Mon to Fri, 10.30am–6pm Sat. Crammed with old tools, all in working order and ranging over trades of woodcarving, carpentry, ship building and musical instrument making. Allow plenty of time for a good snoop; bargain basement in boxes outside the shop.

Reckless Records 79 Upper St, N1, tel 359 0501. Open 10am–7pm Mon to Sat. Access, Visa, Mastercard, Eurocard. Second-hand records bought (from £2), sold and exchanged. Also cassettes and new CDs.

Rhythm Records 281 Camden High St, NW1, tel 267 0123. Open 10.30am–6.30pm daily. Access, Visa, Mastercard, Eurocard. New and second-hand records, tapes and CDs. Wide-ranging stock includes jazz, reggae, rock 'n' roll, soul, country, punk, new wave, heavy metal, blues, latin and new pop chart. Prices from £1.99. Knowledgeable staff.

Smith and Sons Anvil House, Mathias Rd, N16, tel 254 1200. Open

8am–5.30pm Mon to Fri, 10am–5pm Sat. Access, Visa. Cheap and functional, as well as a range of sophisticated bathroom suites with a full back-up of brackets, sealants, valves, tubing and other necessary DIY equipment. This is a builder's merchant rather than shop so it's rough and ready but thoroughly professional.

Techno Cameras 326 Euston Rd, NW1, tel 388 2871. Open 9am–5.30pm Mon to Fri, 9am–5pm Sat. Access, Visa. Terrific bargains in discounted cameras; all leading names. Also camera repair and 24-hour film processing.

Thomas Brothers 798 Holloway Rd, N19, tel 263 1536. Open 8.30am–5.30pm Mon to Fri, and 9am–5.30pm Sat. Access, Visa. Cut-price good quality hand and power tools; up to 20 per cent discount on Makita, Bosch and Elu. Also tool and equipment (lawn-mowers) sharpening service.

Townsends 3a Prowse Place, NW1, tel 485 8611. Open 10am–6pm Tue to Sat. This is the door, stained glass, staircase, cast-iron work, floorboard, radiator, fireplace, shop-counter and stone-work department of the Townsends empire of architectural salvage. Keen prices and helpful staff.

Tumi 23 Chalk Farm Rd, NW1, tel 485 4152. Open 10am–6pm daily. Access, Visa. South American arts and crafts but beautiful white or brightly coloured cotton single and double hammocks. Prices from £25.

Uneek Enterprises 359 Kilburn High Rd, NW6, tel 624 9121. Open 10am–7pm Mon to Sat. No credit cards. Second-hand Calor gas heaters (from £25), fridges and cookers (from £30 to £70). Occasionally hi-fis and TVs.

Warren Evans 1a Hawley Rd, NW1, tel 267 5354. Open 10am–6.30pm Mon and Wed, 10am–5.30pm Thur to Sun. I first wrote about this man some 15 years ago when he first started up at Camden Lock. He remains one of the best and cheapest wood-working craftsmen who happens to specialize in beds. Double beds from £45.

FOOD

See also Street Markets and Restaurants

Ambala Sweet Centre 112 Drummond St, NW1, tel 387 3521. Open 10am–8.30pm daily. No credit cards. Asian sweets are very sweet and come in fluorescent, lurid colours. This pristine factory-style shop is the most highly regarded of its type in London (it's used by many top Indian restaurants) and its huge turnover keeps prices sweet too.

Camden Coffee Shop 11 Delancey St, NW1, tel 387 4080. Open 9.30am–6pm Mon to Wed, Fri and Sat; 9.30am–1pm Thur. Along with the Monmouth Coffee House (*see* West End section) this shop sells the cheapest quality, freshly ground coffee in London. From £3.20 per lb; coffees from all the top producers: Costa Rica, Ethiopia, Kenya, Brazil and Columbia.

Cheeses 134 Fortis Green Rd, N10, tel 444 9141. Open 9.15am–6pm Tue, Wed, Thur and Sat, 9.15am–6.30pm Fri. There are over a hundred cheeses from France, Britain, Ireland, Italy, Scandinavia and Switzerland on sale at this tiny lock-up shop with hardly enough room to swing a cat. Great cheeses in fine condition and keen prices.

Solopasta 26 Liverpool Rd, N1, tel 359 7648. Open 2pm–9pm Mon to Thur, noon–9pm Fri, and 10.30am–9pm Sat. No credit cards. This is mainly a fresh pasta café/restaurant (*see* Restaurants) but they sell their pasta and sauces at a dispensing bar. Prices are a steal, quality is great and everything is freshly prepared daily. Also cheeses and bread.

Steve Hatt 88–90 Essex Rd, N1, tel 226 3963. Open 7.15am–5pm Tue, Wed, Fri and Sat, 7.15am–1pm Thur. No credit cards. Steve Hatt is quite simply the best fishmonger in North London (there are other good ones such as Talby's in Camden High St; Sam Stoller and Yoshimo in Temple Fortune, NW11) and offers the best fish, shellfish and smoked fish from our own and foreign waters. All pockets catered for.

Yassar Halim Patisserie 495 Green Lanes, N4, tel 340 8090. Open 8am–10pm daily. No credit cards. Go here for freshly baked (on the premises) Turkish/Cypriot breads, pastries and sweets; keenly priced and unbeatable!

BOOZE

Bibendum Wine 113 Regent's Park Rd, NW1, tel 586 9761. Open 10am–8pm Mon to Sat. Access, Visa. Wine by the case only. This is not a bargain basement but wines are chosen for quality value for money, best buys are in the Italian range. Wine list available, sale or return and free London delivery.

The Beer Shop 8 Pitfield St, N1, tel 739 3701. Open 11am–7.30pm Mon to Fri, 10am–4pm Sat. Owned by the Pitfield brewery, which is just around the corner, it sells minipins, polypins and firkins of quality brews such as Adnams, Arkells, Green King, Youngs, plus their own beers. Also fully equipped brew-your-own section. Local delivery service.

Grape Ideas Wine Warehouse 2a Canfield Gdns, NW6, tel 328 7317. Open 11am–8.30pm Mon to Fri, 10am–8.30pm Sat, noon–2pm Sun. Access, Visa. Wine warehouse specializing in South American wines which are great quality and value for money. Sells by the bottle as well as by the case. Delivery service and list on request.

Jack's 178a Stroud Green Rd, N4, tel 272 2431. Open 12.30pm–11pm Mon to Sat, noon–3pm and 7pm–10.30pm Sun and Bank Holidays. No credit cards. A specialist beer off-licence which is stocked with beers from all over the world: Macabbe from Israel, Gulder from Nigeria, Golden Eagle from India and Broken Hill Big Barrel from Australia. Also obscure ciders and wines.

Le Nez Rouge 12 Brewery Rd, N7, tel 609 4711. Open 10am–7pm Mon to Fri and 10am–4pm Sat. Access, Visa. There are bargains on this list but they tend to be in the mid-price and steep end of the market. The list of wines is an idiosyncratic choice by the owner who is a great expert on Burgundy and Beaujolais. He is the *négociant* for Duboeuf wines and the entire range can be bought here. There are regular bin end sales and a great try before you buy facility. Discounts on cases and great reductions for members of Le Nez Rouge Club (£11.75 a year). Mail order service, list by request and delivery service.

Oddbins 101 Upper St, N1, tel 359 3747; 64 Upper Street, N1, tel 226 2200; 68 Highgate Village, N1, tel 340 7957; and 64 Belsize

Lane, NW3, tel 435 6862. Open 10am–9pm daily. All credit cards. Part of a vast chain which is able to pass on great savings thanks to bulk purchases. Well chosen wines in all price brackets, but a very large part of their extensive stock is at the cheaper end of the market. Helpful, amusing tasting notes accompany their catalogue (illustrated by Ralph Steadman) and there are further reductions on case purchases and free local delivery.

Wine On The Green 35 Fortune Green Rd, NW6, tel 794 1143. Open 8.30am–5.30pm Mon to Fri and 9am–1pm Sat. Visa. Specializes in Spanish wines, but always has bin ends (all sorts) at bargain prices. They offer a 5 per cent case discount and delivery service.

EAST LONDON

Hatton Garden, Smithfield and City, Hackney, Shoreditch, Bethnal Green and Docklands.

Hatton Garden is London's jewellery centre and the streets that radiate around it are full of long established shops associated with the silver, jewellery and clock trades. Leather Lane is the area's famous street market. Smithfield, the home of London's wholesale meat market, is located on the edge of the City and is slowly evolving into something akin to the Paris Left Bank. The two very different communities of market folk and artists, designers and architects who live and have studios here is reflected in the mixture of shops, cafés and restaurants. Many pubs here serve a great traditional British breakfast – with a pint of beer!

The City is not associated with shopping and London's centre of commerce is a virtual desert on Saturdays. Hays Galeria in Tooley Street is a mini Covent Garden-style shopping mall and boasts leading fashion names, several wine bars and restaurants. Food shopping centres on Leadenhall market, but there are also specialist food shops such as The Champagne and Caviare Shop, a cheese shop, a fishmonger and several high class game butchers.

The river sweeps through the East End, the catch-all name that refers to anywhere east of the City of London. The revitalized Docklands is now home to various newspaper empires, as well as Billingsgate,

Britain's wholesale fish market. Terence Conran's Design Museum, which is surrounded by a growing number of shopping malls, is at Tobacco Dock. Markets are a great feature of the East End, the most famous being the flea markets of Petticoat Lane and Brick Lane, the cut-price new fashions market on Roman Road and the flower and plant market on Columbia Road. Shopping centres around the markets, most of which are open on Sunday mornings, and reflect the culture clashes of Bengali and Jewish rag trades and young trendies who've moved to the area.

STREET MARKETS

Brick Lane E1. Open 8am–1pm Sun. Less commercial and less well known than its neighbour Petticoat Lane (10 minutes away) Brick Lane is a proper flea market. It spills into surrounding streets, including Sclater (pets, groceries, electrical goods and junk) and Cheshire (new and second-hand clothes and bric-à-brac of wildly diverse quality), as well as other side streets and derelict courtyards. The atmosphere is friendly and the market full of unexpected surprises. Don't miss the traditional seafood stall (whelks, eels, cockles and prawns) or the one selling freshly baked bagels. Look out also for a stall selling smoked salmon scraps at almost giveaway prices. This market is much frequented by antique dealers.

Bermondsey Market, also known as **New Caledonian Market** Bermondsey St/Abbey St, SE1. Open 7am–noon Fri. This is where dealers sell to each other and much of the trading is done before the official opening time; as one dealer friend said, 'If you see anything by the time it's light, presume it's repro'. The market takes place in a big open space crammed with stalls (you need a torch in the winter) and the diversity of small antiques, jewellery, silver, porcelain and ceramics, clocks, old toys, books, etc is enormous. There is little leeway for bartering these days, but 10 per cent off the price is the norm; 15 per cent if you're lucky.

Bethnal Green Market Bethnal Green Rd, E1, Open 9am–5pm Mon to Sat and 8am–1pm Sun. Useful multi-purpose market with fruit and veg, fish and shellfish; children's toys, cut-price lingerie, pet food and supplies, and household goods.

Billingsgate 87 West India Dock Rd, E14. Open 5.30am–10am Tue to Sun. This 13-acre, custom designed riverside warehouse is home to this country's wholesale fish market. An average 160 tons of fish pass through the market every day and business is brisk and conducted to time honoured traditions. Although there is no admission charge (except for a 50p parking fee) and no rules about entry, visitors must respect the business of the market. Bulk purchases (by the crate) are permissible, but be sure to know exactly what you want, and be prepared to cart it away immediately and to have cash in hand. The best way of getting a market price is to try to follow on after a sale as prices are not displayed; haggling will not go down well from someone not in the trade.

Columbia Road Market Columbia Rd, E2. Open 8am–1pm Sun. It is very difficult to park close to this busy plant and flower market. Prices are rock bottom and go down throughout the morning, but be careful to check what you're buying carefully – some plants can be diseased or damaged. The market is particularly good for bedding plants, bulbs and more common plants like roses and clematis. The best bargains are bulk purchases.

Farringdon Road Market Farringdon Rd, EC1. Open 11.30am–2pm Mon to Fri and 9.30am–1pm Sat. This eccentric and shambolic market is devoted to old books and original manuscripts. There are great bargains to be had from the six or seven stalls that turn up; where they get their stocks from and how they make a living is a mystery.

Hackney Wick Car Boot Market Hackney Wick Greyhound Stadium, Waterden Rd, E15. Open 6am–2pm Sun. Traders pay £10 to open their boot which might include a wardrobe turnout, household appliances, toys, new clothes, books and is most usually a combination of the lot. Bartering is part of the game.

Kingsland Waste Kingsland Rd, Dalston, E8. Open 9am–2pm Sat. Traditionally (since its mid-19th-century beginnings) this has been a spare parts market and there are still stalls selling electrical and mechanical bits. Nowadays, though, the mix is more eclectic, and includes fruit and veg and other food (there is far more at nearby Ridley Road Market), second-hand books and magazines, bric-à-brac and cut-price tools.

Leadenhall Market Whittington Ave, off Gracechurch St, EC3. Open 7am–3pm Mon to Fri. Delightful covered food market that is housed in an elegant Victorian arched hall built in 1880 and with a history that dates back to the 14th century. Good quality fruit and veg, game and meat, fish and shellfish, cheese and eggs. Not for paupers, but do check out the Champagne and Caviare Shop.

Leather Lane Market Leather Lane, EC1. Open noon–2.30pm Mon to Fri. This is a famous lunchtime bits and bobs market. It is especially good for plants (best bargains just before they pack up), and also has some specialized stalls, most notably the chamois leather lady. Also fruit and veg and cut-price new clothes – mainly for men.

Petticoat Lane Market Middlesex St, E1. Open 9am–2pm Sun. Petticoat Lane is the name for a complex of streets that include Middlesex, Goulston, New Goulston (now a separate market called **Petticoat Lane Designer Fashion Market** selling clothes made by young designers and including jewellery, knitwear and a great second-hand Levi 501s stall), Toynbee, Wentworth, Cobb, Leyden, Strype, Old Castle and Cutler (silver), and Bell Lane that heaves with activity on Sunday mornings. New and old clothing predominates on the stalls but just about everything is sold here, including fruit and veg, cut-price leather goods, household goods, jewellery, antique and junk. Best bargains are gone by 10am.

Ridley Road Market Ridley Rd, Dalston, E8. Open 9am–3pm Mon to Wed, 9am–noon Thur, 9am–5pm Fri and Sat. This is a smashing multi-purpose market that is as good for fruit and veg as it is for exotic fish and all the ingredients for Caribbean cookery. Also good for cheap fabric by the yard and new casual clothes. All this and constant reggae too.

Roman Road Market Roman Rd, E3. Open 8.30am–2pm Thur and 9am–5.30pm Sat. Famous for its 'cabbages' (designer clothes made with fabric left-overs when an order has been completed), samples and seconds from leading fashion houses. Go here for bargains in all styles of cut-price new clothes, but remember that the old maxim 'buyer beware' was probably invented with Roman Road in mind. Men's, women's and children's cut-price new clothes, bed linen, plants (in one of two indoor markets), also fabrics and household goods.

Spitalfields Market Commercial St, E1. Open 3am–11am Mon to Fri. Spitalfields is London's other horticultural wholesale market (the main one being New Covent Garden, *see* South London section, p.78) with 12 acres of stalls selling fruit, vegetables and cut flowers. While the public are free to visit and buy, sales are by the case or box only.

Smithfield Market London Central Markets, West Smithfield, EC1. Open 5am–10.30am Mon to Fri. Smithfield is Britain's largest meat market and it takes place on a 10-acre site in three buildings devoted to meat, poultry and meat produce (sausages and bacon). The open plan of the buildings means that it's possible to see the rows of whole carcases hanging waiting for butchering; not a pretty sight! The market is a very friendly one, and they are used to domestic 'deep-freeze-fill-up' purchases. At Christmas this is a good place to buy the turkey as they are auctioned off at way below retail prices. Smithfield porters are called bummarees and they can be hired for carry-outs to the car. Many of the pubs in the area are open for breakfast, most notably The Cock Tavern, Poultry Ave, Central Markets, tel 248 2918, and Fox and Anchor, 115 Charterhouse St, tel 253 4838; big plates of wonderful sausages, bacon, liver, kidney, black pudding, eggs, tomatoes, baked beans and toast and a pint for around £3!

Walthamstow Market Walthamstow High St, E17. Open 9am–5pm Thur, Fri and Sat. Reputedly England's longest street market and certainly one of the most varied. Predominantly fruit and veg but also specialist food stalls such as a pickle barrow, dried fruit and nut stall and smoked salmon. Also lots of stalls selling cheap new clothes; there are good finds to be had amongst a lot of tat.

AUCTION HOUSES

Bethnal Green Auction 4–6 Ellsworth St, E2, tel 739 7348. Sales 11am Tue, viewing 4pm–7pm Mon and from 10am Tue. No credit cards. Household effects sales which range over carpets, furniture of all sorts, electrical goods, paintings and silver. Good bargains; catalogue 50p.

Forrest and Co. 79–85 Cobbold Rd, E11, tel 534 2931. Sales fortnightly 11am Thur, viewing 10am–5pm Wed and from 10am Thur during the week of sale. No credit cards. Regular bargains in household goods and stock from all manner of bankrupt businesses. Ring for details of forthcoming sales, but you can rely on everything and anything (houses cleared) for the home.

Hatton Garden Auctions 36 Hatton Garden, EC1, tel 242 6452. Sales 1.30pm Thur (jewellery) and 3pm Thur (silver), viewing 9am–4.30pm Mon to Fri. No credit cards. Essentially a trade sale, making it difficult to snaffle bargains, but the trade often pass over items not in pristine condition. Modern and antique jewellery, silver, coins and medals.

CLOTHES, FOOTWEAR AND ACCESSORIES

Blackman's Shoes 44 Cheshire St, E2, tel 739 3902. Open 10am–4pm Mon to Wed, 10am–1pm Thur, 10am–5pm Fri and 8am–1pm Sun. Sandwiched between two semi-derelict houses in this very run-down part of town Blackman's is the cheapest place for good quality, streetwise shoes. DM shoes for men and women £20–£22, DM brogues £22 and £25, suede desert and monkey boots £12, black Oxfords £15, leather moccasins £25 and leather sandals £15.

J. Mendel and Sons 19 Cobb St, E1, tel 247 7930. Open 9am–5.30pm Mon–Fri and 9am–2pm Sun. Access, Visa. Cheap traditional men's footwear ranging over brogues and Oxfords, Doc Martens and patent pumps. So now you know where to get shod on a Sunday.

Myshella 48 High St, E11, tel 530 3678. Open 9.30am–6pm Mon to Sat. Access, Amex, Visa. Classy contemporary jewellery with a witty line in perfect repros of serious stuff as worn by the Royals. Also plenty of great plastic and paste jewellery at rock bottom prices.

Sonico Jean Centres 404 Mare St, E8, tel 985 7388, and 16 High St, E17, tel 520 6893. Open 9.30am–5.30pm Mon to Sat. All major credit cards. Cheapest good quality new jeans in London. *See* North London section for full details.

The Surplus Centre 120 Bethnal Green Rd, E1, tel 739 7134. Open 9.45am–3pm Mon to Wed and Fri, 9am–2pm Sun. Government surplus clothing and camping equipment. Combat and donkey jackets, leather and fur-lined flying jackets, motor-cycle clothing, anoraks,gloves, socks and tents. Keen prices.

Tokki 9 Bradbury St, Stoke Newington, N16, tel 249 7705. Open 10am–6pm Mon to Thur and 10am–6.30pm Fri and Sat. Access, Visa. Women's designer clothes at normal prices with several great lines in cotton and wool skirts, dresses, blouses and jumpers.

HOUSEHOLD, ELECTRICAL AND RECREATIONAL

Chapelfield Nursery Sewardstone Rd, E4, tel 529 1840. Open 9am–5pm Mon to Fri and 9.30am–5pm Sat and Sun. No credit cards. Possibly the cheapest nursery in London; certainly a more reliable source than Columbia Road Market (*see* Markets) and more accessible than New Covent Garden, the wholesale plant market. Country-style plants include lupins, tea roses (roses are a speciality), conifers, shrubs and fruit trees.

City Print Business Centres 742 Forrest Rd, E17, tel 521 8881. Open 9am–5.30pm Mon to Fri. Access, Visa. General stationery store, but with a wide selection of new and used office furniture. Good for second-hand filing cabinets, which they will deliver free within a four-mile radius.

City Carpets 84 Goswell Rd, EC1, tel 490 0589. Open 9am–5.30pm Mon to Fri. No credit cards. Very cheap carpet, vinyls and other floor coverings. Their speciality is own design ('anything as long as it doesn't infringe copyright laws'), but only on orders over 21 sq yds.

Electrical Presentations 382–88 Hoe St, Walthamstow, E17, tel 520 8057. Open 9am–6pm Mon to Fri and 9am–5.30pm Sat. Access, Visa. General lighting shop with wide price spectrum but a good range of budget-priced shades and light fittings. Particularly recommended for their stock of cheap children's bedside lamps.

Farringdon Records 42 Cheapside, EC2, tel 248 2816. Open 9am–

5.45pm Mon to Fri, 10am–2pm Sat. Amex, Access, Visa. General record shop but with an extensive bargain section of records and tapes.

The Felt and Hessian Shop 34 Greville St, EC1, tel 450 6125. Open 10am–3pm Mon to Fri. No credit cards. Trade-style shop that sells felt and hessian in a stunning range of colours. Orders are cut from big rolls in a warehouse behind the shop and VAT is added to prices. The cheapest source in town.

Frank Martin 528 Kingsland Rd, E8, tel 254 5615. Open 10.30am–5.30pm Mon to Wed, Fri and Sat, until 1.30pm Thur. Access, Visa. Great source of cheap new and second-hand photographic equipment, film and paper at wholesale prices, plus an awful lot of free advice. Also continually changing supplies of camera-related collectables.

Handweavers Studio and Gallery 29 Haroldstone Rd, E17, tel 521 2281. Open 10am–5pm Tue to Thur and Sat, 10am–9pm Fri. Visa. The cheapest source of equipment, yarn and fleece for the home spinner, weaver and tapestry maker. Run by enthusiasts, the shop has a notice-board for details of courses and occasionally, of second-hand equipment. Also books and a mail order catalogue (send s.a.e.).

McQueen Pine 365 St John St, EC1, tel 278 6905. Open 10am–6pm Mon, Tue and Thur to Sat. Access, Visa. Uncomplicated varnished or plain pine beds at keen prices. A basic single costs £64; with drawers or as a bunk costs slightly more. Also mattresses made to order.

Potty People 302 Bethnal Green Rd, E2, tel 729 2217. Open 9.30am–5.30pm Mon to Wed, Fri and Sat. Access, Visa. Baby equipment at very keen prices. Everything from Moses baskets to car seats, pushchairs and alarms.

Roman Tiles London House, 380 Lea Bridge Rd, E10, tel 556 0904. Open 8.30am–6pm Mon, Tue, Thur to Sat, until 8.30pm Wed. Visa. There is free delivery on orders over 15 sq yds at this gem of a place. Over a million floor and wall tiles are kept in stock and prices are amongst the cheapest in London. The range is extensive but includes plain, patterned and hand-painted ceramic, marble and terracotta.

FOOD

See also Street Markets

S. Baron 9 Assembly Passage, Mile End Rd, E1, tel 790 2246. Open 9am–3pm Mon to Fri. No credit cards. Kosher delicatessen that is famous for its smoked salmon; prepared on the premises and to the same formulae as when they started over 80 years ago. Their main business is with caterers and wholesalers but retail sales are very keenly priced. Also marinated herrings, salads, etc. Catalogue and free delivery on orders over £25.

Brick Lane Beigel Bake 159 Brick Lane, E1, tel 729 0616. Open noon–6am Mon to Thur; 24 hours Fri to Sun. No credit cards. This is probably the most famous bakery in London; certainly to every cabby. Beigels are baked continually (note the opening hours!) and sold plain, poppy seeded, with crisp fried onions and filled.

Friends Foods 51 Roman Rd, E2, tel 980 1843. Open 11am–6pm Mon, 10am–6pm Tue and Wed, 10am–7pm Fri and 9.30am–6pm Sat. Health food shop run by Buddhists for the benefit of the London Buddhist Centre. Everything sold is organic and/or without involving the killing of animals. Very keen prices.

G. Gazzano and Son 167 Farringdon Rd, EC1, tel 837 1586. Open 8.30am–6pm Tue to Fri, 8.30am–5.30pm Sat and 10.30am–2pm Sun. No credit cards. Family-run (third generation) Italian delicatessen. Specialities include sausages, salamis and cured meats. Also fresh and dried pasta and peak condition Italian cheeses.

Grodzinski's Bakery 235 Whitechapel High St, E1, tel 247 8516. Open 7am–4.30pm Mon to Fri, 8am–1pm Sun. No credit cards. Old established kosher bakery famous for its bagels and cholla (plaited bread). Also highly regarded filled bagels; *the* best are the smoked salmon and cream cheese. Also rye breads.

Leonidas 110 Fleet St, EC4, tel 353 3590. Open 8.30am–6pm Mon to Fri. Possibly the cheapest real cream, hand-made Belgian chocolates (imported twice a week) in London. Extensive range of filled chocolates and truffles in milk, white and dark chocolate.

New Taj Stores 112 Brick Lane, E1, tel 377 0061. Open 9am–9pm daily. Access, Amex, Diners, Visa. Enormous Asian supermarket stocking a very wide range of native foods. There are great savings on large bags of rice and dried herbs and spices.

Rogg 137 Cannon St Rd, E1, tel 488 3386. Open 9.30am–6pm Mon to Fri, 7am–2pm Sun. The full range of kosher food and Jewish specialities can be found at this family-run, old-fashioned Jewish delicatessen and general food shop. They salt and cook their own beef and tongue on the premises and the meats can be bought piping hot. Freshly pickled cucumbers are sold from wooden barrels and they sell marvellous chopped liver, gefilte fish balls, chopped and pickled herrings, kippers, smoked salmon and haddock.

BOOZE

Majestic 60 High St, E11, tel 530 5710. Open 10am–8pm Mon to Sat, 10am–6pm Sun. All credit cards, including their own. Nation-wide wine warehouse chain that stocks over 1000 wines that are sold by the case. Free local delivery, tasting service and mix and match facility. Prices for all pockets, but plenty of bargains for paupers.

Oddbins 41a Farringdon St, EC4, tel 236 7721 and 42 King William St, EC4, tel 623 1406. Open 9am–7pm Mon to Fri, 10am–3pm Sat. Part of a vast chain which is able to pass on great savings thanks to bulk purchases. Well chosen wines in all price brackets, but a very large part of their extensive stock is at the cheaper end of the market. Helpful, amusing tasting notes accompany their catalogue (illustrated by Ralph Steadman) and there are further reductions on case purchases and free local delivery.

SOUTH LONDON

Earls Court, South Kensington, Chelsea and Knightsbridge, Fulham and Parsons Green, Victoria, Southwark, Battersea and Brixton.

Earls Court and Gloucester Road is bedsitter land and the shops reflect this transient and disordered lifestyle. Many shops, particularly in the Earls Court Road, stay open late. South Kensington and

Knightsbridge is markedly more affluent and window shopping is the name of the game for paupers, except when it's sale time at Harrods. Chelsea, and the King's Road in particular, remains good for young fashion and footwear, but bargains are few and far between. At the kink in the King's Road, known as World's End, the shops become more eccentric (this is where Vivienne Westwood's famous shop with the clock that goes backwards is situated) and towards Parson's Green and Fulham, antique and artisan shops take over. There is still a smattering of junk shops in the back streets of Fulham (Munster and Lillie Road) leading up to and radiating around the North End Road Market.

The effect of the lavish new riverside residential and business development at Chelsea Harbour, with its expensive shops and restaurants, is noticeable throughout Fulham. As leases expire on the second-hand furniture and junk shops that were the hallmark of this area, they are being snapped up and re-opened as expensive, exclusive shops servicing the booming interior design business. Over the river in south-west London, Putney, Clapham, Barnes and Wandsworth are prosperous 'villages' with sophisticated shopping. Lavender Hill, Battersea, Balham and Brixton are slowly gentrifying and there are still plenty of junk shops, second-hand furniture, cut-price and eccentric, specialist shops. Brixton is famous for its West African street market and the shops that radiate around it are heaven-sent for paupers.

South-east London is markedly different from the South-west and the shops are very down to earth. The wide and busy Old Kent Road is thick with second-hand furniture and junk shops, while Peckham has lots of cheap, wholesale-style household, clothes and toy shops.

STREET MARKETS

Battersea High Street Market Battersea High St, SW11, Open 8am–5pm Fri and Sat. Good general fruit, veg, hardware and cheap clothing market, with a notable West Indian grocer.

Brixton Market Electric Ave (also Popes Rd, Brixton Station Rd, Atlantic Rd and Coldharbour Lane), SW9. Open daily from 8am–mid-afternoon; most shops close on Sunday. Despite its anarchic reputation, Brixton Market is an easy-going, friendly place with no segregation and great vibes. Business is conducted to constant hip-hop or soul music and strong, sweet, spicy smells of food. Go here for every type of fresh and dried West Indian food. Stalls and shops are colourful and overflow with bread-fruit, okra, many different types of chillies, plantains (big bananas), yams, cassavas, *callaloo*, mangoes, hong-choi greens, West Indian herbs, bottles of Jamaican sorrel pop, seafoods like you've never seen before, the biggest pigs' trotters ever sold, first lay small duck eggs, wonderful breads, rice, flours and exotic dried foods.

Brixton Market is also famous for its West Indian fabrics, records and tapes and rasta hats. But there's also luggage, hardware, kitchenware, greetings cards, carpets, rugs, plants, cheap and second-hand clothes and records (in the area around Brixton Station Rd), toys and even wigs. The outdoor market is flanked by three arcades: Granville, off Electric Ave and Coldharbour Lane; Reliance Arcade, on Brixton Rd, and Brixton Market Row, off and running between Electric Lane and Atlantic Row.

Granville is the largest with 113 shops of all kinds (their general enquiry number is 937 1572) and is divided into eight avenues. Space prevents me from listing all the shops but the following is a selection of some of my favourites:

The Arcade Bakeries 1 Granville Arcade, tel 733 3105. There's always a queue for the fine West Indian bread, buns, bun loaves and patties baked all day, on the premises. The speciality is bun loaf.

Brixton Travel and Fancy Goods 78 Granville Arcade, tel 732 3729. The biggest trunks ever are sold here for £45.99.

Dragons Ltd 16 Granville Arcade, tel 274 1665. West Indian fishmonger with an enormous range of unusual fish, including scad, wrasse and snappers.

Nasseri Fabrics 37 Granville Arcade, tel 274 5627. Wonderful selection of very colourful, bold West Indian fabrics. Six yards of assorted tie-dye designs in bright colours cost £15.

Robinson's Self Service Grocers 50 Granville Arcade, tel 733 2405. Wide range of dried seafoods, rice, flour and herbs.

Reliance Arcade (Brixton Rd) also has a variety of shops, but there is a predominance of cheap, new clothes, hats, leatherware and shoes. There's a great second-hand camera shop and place that specializes in cheap watches and alarm clocks.

Brixton Market Row (between Electric Lane and Atlantic Row) is especially good for cheap clothes, but the following shops are particularly recommended:

The Hargoss Discount Warehouse 2 Market Row, tel 274 8770. Specializes in wholesale household hardware; stainless steel cutlery 20p–40p per piece, mugs 50p, bath towels £1.99 to £2.99, large aluminium saucepans £4.99 and a set of three Luminarc glasses £1.50.

Market Row DIY 15–17 Market Row, tel 274 1661. Cheap hardware, plumbing and electrical goods such as kettles from £3.99, swing bins £5.99 and ten black bin liners, 99p.

Remy's 26–30 Market Row, tel 274 8240. 'The cheapest for clothes in Brixton' says the owner. Kids' T-shirts £1.99, cycling shorts £3.99 and ladies' cotton trousers from £3.99.

(New) Covent Garden Market Nine Elms Lane, SW8. Open 3.30am–10.30am Mon to Fri. There is no admission charge to get into London's main fruit, veg and flower market, but entrance is only possible in a vehicle, and that costs £2! Anyone can buy here, but no trader has the time or the inclination to deal with retail; a minimum five cases is the order of the day. As at all the wholesale markets, goods are not priced, but an informal bartering system takes place that is incomprehensible to outsiders. The best advice to serious buyers is to follow on from another sale. When it comes to cut flowers, they arrive fresh on Mondays, Tuesdays and Wednesdays only; that day's blooms will be very tight.

Earls Court Sunday Market Car Park, Seagrave Rd, SW5. Open 9am–2pm Sun. There's something rather depressing about this huge open air market but, like the similar Wembley Sunday Market (*see* West London section) it is very good for cheap, new clothes. Especially notable is the children's shoe stall and several kitchen equipment stalls.

Greenwich Arts and Crafts Market Market Sq, SE10. Open 9.30am–5pm Sat and Sun. This is not a market to cross town for but nice to know about if you plan a visit to historic Greenwich.

The market is outside but is covered and stalls regularly include hand crafted wooden toys, wholefood snacks, hand-made clothes and aromatherapy oils.

Northcote Market Northcote Rd, SW11. Open 9am–5pm Mon to Sat. This is a great little general street market. Apart from several good but basic fruit and veg stalls, there's an excellent wet fish stall, British and continental cheese stall and a few cut-price women's fashion stalls.

Platts Market Station Hall, London Bridge underground station, SE1. Open 10am–4.30pm Mon to Fri. Browsing through the craft, bygones and antique stalls is a pleasant way to kill time waiting for a train. You can expect to find aspiring-designer clothes of varying quality but modest price, hand-made cushions, candles and toys.

Rye Lane Market Rye Lane, Peckham, SE15. Open 9am–5pm Mon to Sat. Like Brixton Market, Rye Lane Market takes over the whole area and there are several arcades and an indoor market as well as the outside stalls. Cheap fruit and veg and seasonal gluts are the speciality, but other notable attractions include an old fashioned haberdasher and a particularly good pet food stall.

AUCTION HOUSES

Dowell Lloyd 118 Putney Bridge Rd, SW15, tel 788 7777. No credit cards. Sales 9.30am Tue (jewellery), viewing 9am–3.30pm Mon; 9.30am alternate Sats (police lost property), viewing 9am–7.45pm Fri; and 9.30am alternate Sats (furniture), viewing 9am–7.45pm Fri. This is the main auction house for lost property from the Metropolitan Police and occasionally for London Taxis and British Airport Authorities. Their sales are very varied.

The General Auction Company 63–65 Garratt Lane, SW18, tel 870 3909. Sales 11am Mon, viewing 10am–3pm Fri and Sat. Terrific source of antique and modern furniture, household effects and bric-à-brac, garage tools and bankrupt stock of various types. General Auction also hold car sales every Monday at 7.30pm with viewing 10am until 7.30pm. Catalogue 50p.

R F Greasby 211 Longley Rd, SW17, tel 672 1100. Sales fortnightly

10am Mon, viewing 10am–4pm Sat before sale. This is a great auction house for paupers as Greasby's are the main agents for London Transport and British Airways lost property. Their mixed bag of lots also comes from county court, customs, inland revenue and bailiff hauls. Ring to check what's coming up; catalogue available by post at 80p.

Lots Road Chelsea Auction Galleries 71–73 Lots Rd, SW10, tel 351 7771. No credit cards. Sales 4pm Mon (contemporary), 6pm Mon (antiques), viewing 9am–3pm Fri, 10am–1pm Sat and Sun, and 9am–6pm Mon. The goods spill out on to the pavement at this busy, essentially non-trade sale house. Both sales are worth checking and range over furniture, pictures, carpets and rugs, glass, ceramics and objects.

CLOTHES, FOOTWEAR AND ACCESSORIES

The Army Shop 143 Peckham High St, SE15, tel 732 5155. Open 10am–5pm Mon to Sat, closed Tue and Thur. No credit cards. This is a genuine world-wide army surplus clothing store. Everything is second-hand and there's loads of it; winter greatcoats £8; khaki trousers from £4–£14; combat jackets £20–£40; berets £1–£3 and a wide range of boots from £3–£30.

Circa 147 Trafalgar Rd, SE10, tel 858 6440. Open 11am–6pm daily. No credit cards. Men's and women's period day, and (mainly) evening clothes. Prices depend on age (Victorian to 60s) and originality, but are always reasonable.

Circus, Circus 176 Wandsworth Bridge Rd, SW6, tel 731 4128. Open 10am–6pm Mon to Fri. Access, Visa. Colourful, cheerfully run, fun shop selling everything from second-hand nursery equipment to keenly priced workwear-style children's clothes. Their speciality is organized children's parties; they will do the whole thing or sell (or hire) just about everything a mum might need. Wish there were more shops like this.

Crampton's Clothiers 283 Old Kent Rd, SE1, tel 231 2340. Open 9.45am–5pm Mon to Sat. No credit cards. 'Rummage and get results' ought to be the slogan outside this second-hand clothes, junk and bric-à-brac shop run by a saucy old woman and her daughter. Jackets £4, suits from £8, trousers from £2, dresses and shirts £1, ties 20p and an antique radio, £6!

Cornucopia 12 Tachbrook St, SW1, tel 828 5752. Open 11am–6pm Mon to Sat. Access, Visa. This was one of the first shops to specialize in period clothing and it is always jam-packed with stock. Evening gowns hang from the ceiling and rails bulge with blouses and day dresses. Prices are low and the period extends from Victorian to 60s.

T. Cullum 5 Putney Bridge Rd, SW8, tel 870 3755 and 199 Wandsworth High St, SW18, tel 874 2346. Open 9.30am–5.30pm Mon to Sat, until 6pm Fri. All major credit cards. Two shops stuffed with great value, new army surplus and general outdoor clothing; the Wandsworth branch specializes in camping, hiking and Barber jackets, plus a range of very cheap rucksacks. Particular bargains include rucksacks from £3.99 up to £11.90 for a 25-litre capacity, three-pocket Wynnster Ecuador £25; regatta storm-break waterproof jackets £9.99, ex-German army sleeping bags £19.95; big heavy duty ex-Navy polyester work shirts at £2.50; combat trousers £5 and ex-army fur fabric lined or quilted parka jackets at £20.

Designers Sale Studio 241 King's Rd, SW3, tel 351 4171. Open 10am–7pm Mon to Fri, until 6pm Sat. Access, Visa. Opened by an ex-buyer for Browns, the stock here consists of end-of-lines and cancelled order designer clothes for men and women. Prices are a fraction of their original tag. It's the sort of shop that needs to be visited on a regular basis.

Eat Your Heart Out 360 King's Rd, SW3, tel 352 3392. Open 11am–6pm Mon to Sat. No credit cards. This is a delightful shop to browse in and full of surprises because they sell second-hand clothes (mainly for men), old furniture (mainly 50s) and a wide range of bags, suitcases and accessories.

Emperor of Wyoming 408 King's Rd, SW10, tel 376 3596. Open 10am–6.30pm Mon to Sat. Access, Amex, Visa. Fully run-in or 'artfully aged' clothes. Wide range of Levi 501s and other jeans (from £10), 50s cocktail and day dresses, leather and suede bomber jackets, gaberdine raincoats, and stylish coats. Allow plenty of time for searching the rails.

Four Seasons Fashions 366 Old Kent Rd, SE1, tel 703 0520. Open 9am–6pm Mon to Fri, 9.30am–6.30pm Sat and 10.30am–2pm Sun. No credit cards. This is a wholesale-style shop and not a smart boutique, where they offer a wide range of cheap cotton women's dresses. This is not high fashion, but everything is quite acceptable with a little bit of imaginative 'dressing up'. Prices from £10–£75.

Frock Exchange 450 Fulham Rd, SW6, tel 381 2937. Open 10am–5.30pm Mon to Sat. This shop was started by Gabrielle Crawford when she was married to actor Michael Crawford. I remember interviewing her when it opened and she explained that it was somewhere where she and her friends could sell the cast-offs of their high profile lifestyles. Hence, designer label second-hand clothes have always been the name of the game here, but the Kenzo, Bruce Oldfield and Saint Laurent are eked out with more down-market labels these days. Sometimes it seems like a posh jumble sale, other times prices seem outrageous.

Lewis Surplus 720b Old Kent Rd, SE15, tel 732 0258. Open 10am–4pm Mon to Sat. No credit cards. Very, very cheap government surplus clothing from all around the world; khaki army trousers from £4 and air force and naval shirts £4.

Murrays 419 Brixton Rd, SW9, tel 733 8570. Open 9am–6pm Mon to Sat. All major credit cards. Cheap luggage, handbags and leather goods with a 10 per cent discount on Delsey suitcases. Best bargains include spacious two-colour nylon rucksacks by Unicorn at £8.99, mega-size Louis Vuitton-style suitcases £24.99, large safari-style suitcases £21.99 and black leather handbags from £9.99.

Next For Men, 13 King's Rd, SW3, tel 730 7673. Open 9am–6pm Mon to Sat, until 7pm Wed. Access, Amex, Visa. Classic, well-made designer-style clothes at affordable prices. Especially good for suits and jackets.

Office Shoes 93 King's Rd, SW3, tel 351 4634. Open 9.30am–6.30pm Mon to Sat. Access, Amex, Visa. In reaction to the shoe-shop chains, Office Shoes specialize in selling unusual shoes by little known designers at high street prices.

People's Weatherman Shop 57 Atlantic Rd, SW9, tel 274 5753.

Open 9.30am–6pm Mon to Sat. No credit cards. Wide range of Rasta hats, caps and badges in traditional black with green, red and gold stripes as well as a range of keenly priced men's headgear.

R. Soles 178 King's Rd, SW3, tel 352 8798. Open 9.30am–7pm Mon to Sat. Access, Amex, Visa. The cheapest and biggest range of cowboy boots in London. Cheapest are the Spanish range, from £70.

Swallows and Amazons 40 Webbs Rd, SW11, tel 228 6909. Open 10am–5pm Mon to Fri, 10am–1pm Sat. No credit cards. Two-floor shop stuffed with dirt cheap second-hand baby and small children's clothes, nightwear and smalls.

HOUSEHOLD, ELECTRICAL AND RECREATIONAL

Ace Discount Store 187 Wandsworth High St, SW18, tel 874 0856. Open 9.30am–6pm Mon to Sat. No credit cards. Well-stocked household hardware store whose bargains include plastic dustbins at £7.99, squeeze mops at £1.99, bars of soap for 7p, sets of three glass tumblers 99p, dustpan and brush sets 99p, red-handled, stainless steel 24-piece cutlery sets £5.99, hedge shears £3.99 and large casserole pans with Pyrex lids, £34.99.

Amey's 82–84 Peckham High St, SE15, tel 639 7302. Open 9am–5.30pm Mon to Sat. Big general household discount store.

G. Austin and Sons 11–23 Peckham Rye, SE15, tel 639 3163. Open 8.30am–5pm Mon to Wed and Fri, 8.30am–1pm Thur and 8.30am–5.30pm Sat. No credit cards. Long established second-hand furniture warehouse, neatly organized by price and quality on ascending floors.

Bathroom Discount Centre 297 Munster Rd, SW6, tel 381 4222. Open 8.30am–5.30pm Mon to Sat, 8.30am–4pm Sun. No credit cards. All the leading British bathroom manufacturers are represented here and their baths and suites are sold at knock-down prices. Stock is constantly changing, although they will send a brochure.

Battersea Dogs Home 4 Battersea Park Rd, SW8, tel 622 3626. Open 10.30am–4.15pm Mon to Sat. No credit cards. This is where all London's lost dogs (that get handed in to the police) end up. If they aren't reclaimed, they are eventually put up for sale. There is a charge of 50p (adults) and 25p (children) to view the dogs for sale. It is a harrowing experience.

Best Buys 165 Peckham Hill St, SE15, tel 358 9630. Open 9.30am–6pm Mon to Sat. No credit cards. A hardware household store that used to be a feature of every high street and is now a dying breed. Go here for huge bottles of shampoo at 50p, washing-up liquid at 30p, big wooden brooms £2.50, dustpan and brush sets £1.25 and Tefal, non-stick frying pans at £5.99. The more you look, the more bargains you find.

Blue Mantle 299 Old Kent Rd, SE1, tel 237 3931. Open 10.30am–5.30pm Mon to Sat. No credit cards. The cheapest place I've found in London for antique marble and wooden fireplace surrounds. Prices from £40 (pine) and £250 for unrestored marble.

Colin's Antiques 124 Richmond Rd, SW15, tel 788 1811. Open 8.30am–5.30pm Mon to Sat. No credit cards. To call this an antique shop is a misnomer; this is more of a houses cleared/second-hand and junk shop. Apart from small bric-à-brac and a diverse collection of other people's junk, furniture is the mainstay. Large chest of drawers £45, wardrobes £75, washing machines from £100, pairs of chairs £20 and big dressing mirrors £35.

M. Coulston 218 Battersea Park Rd, SW11, tel 720 8359. Open 10am–5pm Mon to Fri, 10am–2pm Sat. No credit cards. One of the last surviving bric-à-brac shops that used to dominate this area. There's always lots of rubbish but a few gems, too, such as a recent find of a pair of Nordica ski boots in perfect condition at £20. Second-hand china, furniture, paintings and books.

Desperate Dan The Junk Man 94 New Cross Rd, SE14, tel 358 9961. Open 9am–5pm Mon to Sat. You never know what will be on offer here; recent finds have included a large wooden chest of drawers at £35, microwave oven £50, wooden wardrobe £30, small black and white TV £25, three rolls of plain carpet from £10 and a second-hand gas cooker priced at £55.

Everyman Stores 104 New Cross Rd, SE14, tel 639 5774. Open 9am–5.30pm Mon to Sat, Thur 9am–1pm. Useful do-it-yourself store selling a wide range of hardware, electrical fittings, locks, tools and paints at very keen prices.

Falcon Carpet Tiles 278 Upper Richmond Rd, SW15, tel 788 9075. Huge warehouse offering a wide range of floor coverings from carpet, terracotta, ceramic and cork tiles. Falcon get regular supplies of ex-exhibition carpeting which reduces the prices even further. Some is available immediately, other stuff has to be ordered.

Falcon Road Appliances 91 Falcon Rd, SW11, tel 228 6458. Open 9am–6pm Mon to Sat. No credit cards. The friendly, Irish bloke who runs this shop repairs and reconditions all the fridges, freezers, cookers and furniture he sells and can thus offer a six-month guarantee. Reconditioned fridges cost around £50, fridge/freezers around £100 and cookers £90 to £125. The furniture prices are more variable but are always rock bottom.

Fens Restorations 46 Lots Rd, SW10, tel 352 9883. Open 9am–5.30pm Mon to Fri, 9am–1.30pm Sat. A good source of old stripped pine doors (£15–£30) shutters (from £35), tables and original staircase parts. There are even better bargains in old brass taps, mixer taps and door furniture.

House Hospital 68 Battersea High St, SW11, tel 223 3179. Open 10am–5pm Mon to Sat. No credit cards. Previously an aeroplane factory, these vast premises are a repository for second-hand hardware and equipment for the home. Outside in the yard you will find gates, railings, roof tiles and chimney stacks and a variety of different radiators; inside there is an extensive range of bathroom antiques and bygones. Allow plenty of time for searching; most thing are 'as found', but they offer a restoration service.

W. Iles and Sons Ltd 69 Falcon Rd, SW11, tel 228 0951. Open 9am–5pm Mon to Sat, 9am–noon Wed. No credit cards. Free local delivery is offered on orders over £20 from this incredibly cheap carpet and lino shop. Offcuts and end of roll pieces of carpet are the best buys, for example 12ft × 6ft 6in grey wool mix recently cost £17. Florco Cord works out at £1.99 a sq yd, whereas cushioned lino (can't be marked by stiletto heels!) costs £2.90 sq yd.

Harry's Furniture and Ambiance Antiques 531 Old Kent Rd, SE1, tel 237 3656. Open 9.30am–6pm Mon to Sat. This is a cut above the many second-hand furniture shops on the Old Kent Road; Harry has obviously got good taste. He offers a restoration and French polishing service and most items are in good repair. Polished wooden cabinet with drawers and a mirror £50, enormous fridge freezer £90, fridges from £30, chest of drawers £20 and bureau £50.

HSS Hire Shops 282 Clapham Rd, SW9, tel 720 6524; 865 Fulham Rd, SW6, tel 736 1769. Tool and equipment hire for home and car. *See* North London section for details.

Kenon Limited 358 Old Kent Rd, SE1, tel 703 4970. Open 8.30am–5.30pm Mon to Sat. Access, Eurocard, Mastercard. Plumbers' merchants selling the cheapest, good quality new baths I've come across at £55, plus VAT.

Quality Bargains 127 Peckham High St, SE15, tel 732 5741. Open 9.30am–5.30pm Mon to Fri and 9.30am–1pm Sat. No credit cards. Anything and everything turns up here, but this shop is a good source of second-hand washing machines, cookers and fridges, furniture of all types and radios.

London Building Centre 10–20 Varco Rd, Southwark, SE16, tel 237 2426. Open 8am–6pm Mon to Fri, 9am–4pm Sat. Access, Amex, Visa. This is one of the cheapest places in London for basic, unfancy new bathroom furniture. Most leading British and some European manufacturers.

Mistakes: The Interior Designer's Sale Shop 654b Fulham Rd, SW6, tel 736 2108. Open 10.30am–5pm Mon to Sat. Amex, Visa. This is not a bargain basement but a source of cut-price fabrics from leading furnishing fabric designers. End of roll, surplus stock and end of line cottons, silks, chintzes, etc at knock-down prices.

Moriaty's Antiques 74 Brixton Hill, SW2, tel 737 4589. Open 9am–6pm Mon to Sat. No credit cards. Cheap household furniture of varying styles and grades of quality; most of it comes from house clearance sales. Don't expect antiques or anything fancy but low prices and free delivery on goods over £200.

Poundwise Discount Furniture 670–72 Old Kent Rd, SE15, tel 639 6021. Open 9am–6pm Mon to Fri and 9am–5pm Sat. No credit cards. Rock-bottom prices for basic household furniture;

sofa-beds from £75, beds from £46, three-piece suites £149 and four-drawer wooden chests £28.

Reject China Shop 183 Brompton Rd, SW3, tel 581 0737. Open 9am–6pm Mon to Sat. Access, Amex, Visa. Part of the huge Chinacraft group and able to pass on savings because of its ability to buy in bulk. This is a good place (apart from street markets) to buy a full set of matching china. Here it is quality stuff (prices from £30) in a reasonable choice of classic styles. There are even greater reductions on the defective (hence the name Reject) goods; occasionally up to 40 per cent.

Reliable Rads 551 Old Kent Rd, SE1, tel 231 0357. Open 8.30am–5pm Mon to Thur, 8.30am–2pm and 3.30pm–5pm Fri, and 9am–11.30pm Sat. A gem of a place. Reliable Rads refers to car radiators and RR offer a fitting and repair service. All makes undertaken and prices from £20.

Richer Sounds 2 London Bridge Walk, SE1, tel 403 4710. Open 10am–7pm Mon to Fri and 10am–5pm Sat. Access, Visa. Hi-fi supermarket with enormous stocks of budget and end of line stock. There is plenty of advice on building up a system (from £100). Their next door **Music Bar** specializes in similarly cheap personal hi-fis and car stereos.

Robill's Discount Warehouse 429 Brixton High Rd, SW9, tel 326 1268. Open 9am–6.30pm Mon to Sat. Access. Go here for a wide range of cut-price household hardware, garden equipment, wicker and bamboo furniture. Best buys include kettles from £3.99, brooms £2.49, dustpan and brush 99p, stainless steel medium-sized saucepans £3.99, Teflon (non-stick) pans £5.99 and Japanese paper lanterns £2.99.

Scallywag 187 Clapham Rd, SW9, tel 274 0300. Open 10am–6pm Mon to Wed, Fri to Sun, and 10am–8pm Thur. Access, Visa. Claims to be Europe's largest source of antique and reproduction pine furniture. Low prices and stripping service.

Tilling Furniture 145 New Cross Rd, SE14, tel 639 1673. Open 9am–5.30pm Mon to Sat, closed Thur. Access, Eurocard, Mastercard. Cheap, basic, household furniture. Divans from £49.95, three-drawer wooden chests £41, large wooden wardrobes £79 and round pine tables £55.

Wicker and Gear 177 New Cross Rd, SE14, tel 732 3433, and 74 Peckham High St, SE15, tel 732 8587. Open 9am–6pm Mon to Sat. Access, Visa. Bargains in household wares, wicker furniture, kitchen, garden and bedroom equipment. Plain white medium-sized plant pot £1.29, small wicker chair £10.99, big plain coloured bath towel £3.99, medium-sized stainless steel saucepan £4.99, coloured enamel plates 39p and five 60-watt light bulbs for £1.

Wickes Plough Lane, SW17, tel 947 9817. Open 8am–8pm Mon to Sat, and 8.30am–5pm Sun. Access, Amex, Visa. Efficiently run DIY supplier, particularly good on doors, windows and kits for bathrooms and kitchens. Paints, tools, etc; well-designed fully illustrated catalogue available.

FOOD

See also Street Markets

Arif Bakery 212 Walworth Rd, SE17, tel 708 2540. Open 8am–8pm daily. No credit cards. Wonderful Turkish bakery (who cook on the premises) which is as good for its British and Mediterranean breads as it is for its outstanding filo pastries.

Costa Coffee Shop 324 Vauxhall Bridge Rd, SW1, tel 828 5215. Open 7.45am–6.30pm Mon to Sat. Access, Visa. Freshly roasted and ground coffee; they offer a tasting facility but the bargain is a good, strong Continental at £3.60. Mail order service.

Tony's Delicatessen 39 South Lambeth Rd, SW8, tel 582 0766. Open 8am–6.30pm Mon to Fri, and 8am–5.30pm Sat. Terrific Italian delicatessen where most produce is directly imported and prices, as well as quality, rival nearby Sainsbury's. Especially good for salami, olive oil in various sized containers, pasta and pulses.

Use Your Loaf Bakers 9 Turpin Lane, SE10, tel 853 2018. Open 6am–8pm daily. Located in an alley behind the *Cutty Sark* in Greenwich, this bakery is a gem. They make many different styles of bread but their stuffed breads are so tasty and such good value, that bulk purchases for the freezer are common. With notice, they will make bread or a cake to any shape or size.

BOOZE

The Bitter Experience 129 Lee Rd, SE3, tel 852 8819. Open 11am–9.30pm Mon to Fri, 10am–9.30pm Sat, and noon–2pm Sun. Access, Amex, Visa. This is an exceptional shop specializing in beer (over 100 from all around the world) and with the unusual facility of offering a rotation of 26 beers on draught.

London Wine Chelsea Wharf, 15 Lots Rd, SW10, tel 351 6856. Open 9.30am–9pm Mon to Fri, and 10am–7pm Sat. Access, Amex, Visa. A small, pleasantly run wine warehouse with a testing facility and option of making up mixed cases. There is much for the pauper from France (country wines) and Bulgaria at under £3 a bottle. Free local delivery, glass loan and sale or return party service.

Oddbins 2 Denbigh St, SW1, tel 834 0991; 219 Brompton Rd, SW3, tel 589 7492; 167 Clapham High St, SW4, tel 622 1682; 98 Wandsworth Bridge Rd, SW6, tel 736 1302; 70 Gloucester Rd, SW7, tel 589 2080; 531 King's Rd, SW10, tel 351 1536 and 142 Fulham Rd, SW10, tel 373 5715. Open 10am–9pm daily. All credit cards. Part of a vast chain which is able to pass on great savings thanks to bulk purchases. Well chosen wines in all price brackets, but a very large part of their extensive stock is at the cheaper end of the market. Helpful, amusing tasting notes accompany their catalogue (illustrated by Ralph Steadman) and there are further reductions on case purchases and free local delivery.

Majestic Albion Wharf, Hester Rd, SW11, tel 223 2983. Open 10am–10pm daily; 9–13 Catford Hill, SE6, tel 690 3094; 12 Balham Hill, SW12, tel 675 6929; 421 New King's Rd, SW6, tel 736 0335; Arch 84, Goding St, SE11, tel 587 1830, all open 10am–8pm Mon to Sat, and until 6pm Sun. All major credit cards, including their own. Nation-wide wine warehouse chain that stocks over 1000 wines that are sold by the case. Free local delivery, tasting service and mix and match facility. Prices for all pockets, but plenty of bargains for paupers.

South of the Bordeaux 123 King's Rd, SW3, tel 352 2255. Open 10am–8pm Mon to Fri, 10am–7pm Sat. Access, Amex and their own gift vouchers. Chic, modern wine shop that is actually owned by the Victoria Wine Group, so it isn't what it seems. They keep a wide range of champagnes (in all sizes) and top vintages, but Victoria's buying policy means there are bargains too, especially at the more serious end of the market.

Two Brewers 97 Dartmouth Rd, SE23, tel 699 1326. Open 10.30am–10.30pm Sat. No credit cards. Absolutely everything, including helpful and willingly given advice, for the home brewer. They will even rent out their grape press!

Winecellars Wine Warehouse 153 Wandsworth High St, SW18, tel 871 2668. Open 10.30am–8.30pm Mon to Fri, 10am–8.30pm Sat, and 10am–6pm Sun. Access, Visa. Wines by the bottle or, with a discount, by the case. Well chosen list, with an eye to everyday drinking wines for paupers. Italian wines are a particular speciality. Free local delivery and glass hire.

WEST LONDON

Bayswater, Notting Hill, Shepherd's Bush and Hammersmith, High Street Kensington

Bayswater is a mecca for tourists on Sundays, when Hyde Park railings become an art market. Nearby Queensway, which leads down to Westbourne Grove, is a cosmopolitan area with its mini-Chinatown and ethnic food shops that is now dominated by the new-look shopping arcade-style Whiteleys store.

Notting Hill is famous for Portobello Road antiques market and its shopping identity is associated with antique shops. Many are located in Kensington Church Street, which links into Kensington High Street. Ken Hi Street, as Londoners call it, is now a mini-Oxford street with branches of all the multiple fashion and footwear shops, two department stores and several branches of Next. Kensington Market, a survivor of 60s Flower Power days, remains as popular as ever and is full of street-wise fashion.

Hammersmith, now in the throes of a major re-development which will include a giant shopping arcade, and Shepherd's Bush have no strong intrinsic shopping identity. There are junk and antique shops, evidence of new gentrification, but both have great street markets and several eccentric cut-price shops.

Portobello Market Portobello Rd, W11. Open 8am–5pm Mon to Wed, Fri and Sat, and until 1pm Thur for fruit and vegetables; 8am–3pm Fri, and until 5pm Sat for general household stuff; and 8am–5pm Sat for antiques and junk. Portobello is one of London's most famous antique and flea markets and is much frequented by dealers. A great many things change hands between stallholders in the early hours of the market and goods often reappear with a hefty mark-up at one of the many shops that line the street. The market is a major tourist attraction and is a real mixed bag of stalls, but antiques and junk predominate. At the junction with Elgin Crescent, the market turns into a food market with a mixture of English, West Indian and African stalls. Under the arches supporting the motorway above, the market changes again and is second-hand everything; most particularly clothes. It's colourful and lively and there are often live musicians, escapologists, men who'll perch a parrot or a monkey on your shoulder and take your photograph, hot chestnut and other food vendors. A great way to spend a few hours.

Hammersmith Market Hammersmith Grove, W6. Open 8.30am–5pm Mon to Sat, until 1pm Thur, but best on Sat. This is a great little food market in a slip road behind Hammersmith roundabout which leads into King Street, the area's main shopping drag. Most noteworthy are the cheese, shellfish and fish stalls and the health foods. Most of the fruit and veg stalls seem to be inter-related, sell the same stuff and prices rarely differ.

North End Road Market North End Rd, W14. Open 9am–5pm Mon to Sat. The entire road is packed with fruit and veg, plus cheap new clothes stalls and on Saturdays, when it's at its peak, it's jam-packed with people. Shop around for fruit and veg bargains and look out for the cheese stall and a great wet fish, smoked and shellfish stall. Cheap butchers and clothes shops complement the market. Also new and old Kelim rugs.

Shepherd's Bush Market Uxbridge and Goldhawk Rds, W12. Open 9am–5pm Mon to Sat, until 1pm Thur. Railway Approach (the market is under the Goldhawk Road railway arch) runs between the Uxbridge and Goldhawk Roads and is a terrific, small cosmopolitan food and general market backed up with lock-ups, shops and an arcade. There is everything here from broken biscuits to big sacks of rice, Afro hair gear, hand and electrical tools, pets and pet foods, luggage, shoes, foam chips, and numerous fruit and veg stalls. The arcade is good for bulk quantities of West Indian produce.

Wembley Sunday Market Stadium Way, Wembley, Middx. Open 9am–2pm Sun. Worth the excursion for cheap and cheerful homeware (most notably whole dinner services sold amid a lot of spectacle at knock-down prices), children's and adults' fashion clothes. Also record and tape dealers and a few fruit and veg stalls.

CLOTHES, FOOTWEAR AND ACCESSORIES

Almost New Menswear 203 Uxbridge Rd, W13, tel 579 5954. Open 9.30am–5.30pm Mon to Fri, and from 9am–5.30pm Sat. Old fashioned shop where the rails are crammed with cut-price menswear. Much is second-hand (including dinner suits), but there are also dirt cheap end of lines, samples and factory seconds in suits, jackets, trousers and shirts.

Artifice 16 Portobello Green, 281 Portobello Rd, W10, tel 960 8840. Open 10am–6pm Mon to Sat. Amex, Diners Club. Twenty-odd young jewellery designers sell their work through this gallery. Prices are low (there is much below £10), the work is original and interesting, and for both sexes. Much of the jewellery is made in non-precious metals, acrylics and unexpected materials.

Cage 181 Portobello Rd, W10, tel 229 3684. Open 10am–6pm Mon to Sat. No credit cards. Two hundred different T-shirts from £2 (seconds).

Dickie Dirts 58a Westbourne Grove, W2, tel 229 1466. Open 10am–6pm Mon to Sun, until 8pm Thur, until 9pm Fri. All credit cards. Nigel Wright opened this shop in 1977 and his policy of low profit margins and a large turnover led to huge success and the opening of several mega branches. Sadly, bad management and a boom in copy-cat shops took Nigel to the Debtors' Court but this shop, now under new management, escaped closure. Here you will find cheap shirts (Dickie Dirts is rhyming slang for shirts), sweat shirts and hundreds of different jeans from all the leading makers.

The Dresser 39–41 Sussex Pl, W2, tel 724 7212. Open 10am–5pm Mon, and 11am–6pm Tue to Sat. Access, Amex, Visa. Women's *haute couture*, second-hand clothes shop. All the leading designers at prices between £25 and £200. Somewhere worth checking out regularly.

Kensington Market 49–53 Kensington High St, W8, tel 937 1572. Open 10am–6pm Mon to Sat. A large building with three floors divided into various sized stalls. Fashion has always dominated the 25-year-old market and reflected street-wise as opposed to high street fashion. Currently the stalls reflect the continued interest in second-hand clothes of all periods (20s to 60s), but also American cowboy, young fogy and plenty of tat. Also jewellery.

Tie Rack 11 Kensington Shopping Mall, Kensington High St, W8, tel 937 5168. Open 8.30am–7pm Mon to Sat. All major credit cards. Cheap, stylish neckwear at keen prices. Also boxer shorts.

295 Portobello Rd 295 Portobello Rd, W10. Open 8.30am–5pm Fri and Sat. No credit cards. This market-style shop has been going for years and remains stuck in a 60s time-warp. Men's and women's clothes of all styles and in varying condition at prices far cheaper than similar sources listed in this book.

HOUSEHOLD, ELECTRICAL AND RECREATIONAL

Big Table Furniture Co 56 Gt Western Rd, W9, tel 221 5058. Open 10am–6pm Mon to Sat, and 2pm–5pm Sun. No credit cards. Basic design and low-priced pine beds, not tables, are sold here. The company is co-operatively run and they make all their beds in the basement of their huge warehouse premises. Double frame costs from £69 and double mattresses from £75.

Buyers and Sellers 120–22 Ladbroke Grove, W10, tel 229 1947. Open 9am–5pm Mon to Sat, 9.45am–11.45am Thur. Access, Visa. Cynthia Coyne reckons to undercut every other retailer of fridges and freezers by 20 per cent. She does this by selling 'soiled' showroom stock and end of lines, but everything is fully guaranteed. Her stock of white goods, as fridges, freezers, hobs and cookers are called in the trade, is crammed into her showroom. She knows all her goods inside out and will proffer advice as well as place special orders if she hasn't got what you need in stock. Fast, efficient and, usually, same-day delivery if required.

Colourway 112a Westbourne Grove (entrance Chepstow Rd), W2, tel 229 1432. Open 10am–6.30pm Mon to Fri, and 10am–6pm Sat. Visa. Cheap, natural yarns for home knitters. Also a range of knitting needles, patterns, buttons.

Cubestore 58 Pembroke Rd, W8, tel 602 2001. Open 10am–4pm Tue to Sat, until 7pm Thur, and 10am–5pm Sat. No credit cards. Basic storage system based on a cube that can either be hollow, with shelves or drawers or be purpose built to hold anything. Sold in kit form, and made in white and grey melamine or in unfinished chipboard (to be sealed before dyeing, painting or varnishing). Versatile, cheap and easy to construct. Catalogue available and mail order service.

Furniture Exchange 92 Shepherd's Bush Rd, W6, tel 602 7865. Open 9.30am–6pm Mon to Sat. No credit cards. There are several 'houses cleared' type second-hand furniture and domestic appliances shops in Shepherd's Bush Road; this is the biggest and the best. Go here to furnish your home on the cheap; beds, chairs, sofas and three-piece suites, TVs, fridges, tables, mirrors, etc. A place to have a good root around. They can deliver.

Hot and Cold Inc. 13 Golborne Rd, W10, tel 960 1300. Open 10am–6pm Mon to Sat. No credit cards. Similar to Buyers and Sellers (q.v.) but specializing in perfect end of line kitchen goods. Ovens, hobs, hoods, dishwashers, fridges and washing-up machines at cut-price rates.

Honest Jon's Records 278 Portobello Rd, W10, tel 969 9822. Open 10am–6pm Mon to Sat, and 11am–5pm Sun. Access, Amex, Visa. A famous record shop that specializes in jazz but which also has above average stocks of soul, reggae, Latin, and African artistes. Good prices too.

HSS Hire Shops 14 The Vale, Ealing, W3, tel 743 6300; 192

Campden Hill Rd, W8, tel 727 0897. Open 8am–5.30pm Mon to Fri and 8.30am–5pm Sat. Tool and equipment hire for home and car. *See* North London section for full details.

Junk Corner and **Great Expectations** 115–21 Shepherd's Bush Rd, W6, tel 603 2284. Open 10am–6pm Mon to Sat. No credit cards. Two shops selling better than average second-hand furniture and domestic household objects. Quality and age is variable; the best stuff is to be found in Junk Corner, while cheaper and less desirable pieces are sold at Great Expectations.

C. Kent (Fireplaces) 14 Greyhound Rd, W6, tel 385 1494. Open 10am–5pm Tue to Fri, and 9am–4pm Sat. Access, Visa. The cheapest source of new Victorian reproduction fireplaces and fireplace surrounds in West London. The cheapest work out at around £100 a piece, although Mr Kent keeps an extensive range, including elaborate antique versions.

Kitchen Tech 123 The Vale, W3, tel 749 7606. Open 9am–6pm Mon to Sat. Access, Visa. Reconditioned kitchen equipment (fridges, cookers, hobs and ovens, etc) with a three-month parts guarantee. Also cut-price new equipment. They offer an emergency repair service and can deliver.

Music and Video Exchange 56 Notting Hill Gate, W11, tel 727 0424. Open 10am–8pm daily. No credit cards. One of London's best sources of second-hand musical equipment. Guitars, amps, audio equipment and PA systems.

Necklace Maker Workshop 25 Portobello Green, 281 Portobello Rd, W10, tel 968 5599. Open 11am–5pm Mon to Fri, and 10am–6pm Sat. No credit cards. One of my prized possessions is a necklace made by the lady who owns this shop, bought many years ago when the idea of a shop was an unattainable dream. The speciality of the shop is the old and antique beads, but there are beads from Africa, Japan, India, Czechoslovakia, Italy and Turkey. The range and variety is a marvel; prices start at 1p.

FOOD

See also Markets and Restaurants

Adamou 124 Chiswick High Rd, W4, tel 994 0752. Open 8.30am–

6.30pm Mon to Sat, and 10am–1pm Sun. No credit cards. This, my local greengrocers, is run by a Cypriot family and they import a wide range of fruit and veg from their home country. They are particularly good for their range of potatoes, big bunches of Cyprus parsley, coriander and exotic tinned and dried produce. Their olives are excellent, so, too, is their Greek bread and the preserved sausages. It is wise to buy from the back of the store and to request alternatives (there is a big store room at the rear) if stuff looks a bit wilted. It's the sort of shop where it's necessary to strike a relationship with the family (very easy) to get the best results.

Athenian Grocers 16a Moscow Rd, W1, tel 229 6280. Open 8.30am–7pm Mon to Sat, and 9.30am–1pm Sun. No credit cards. One of many ethnic food shops in Bayswater (check out Westbourne Grove too), it stocks a good range of Greek, Lebanese, Syrian and Cypriot dried, tinned, packaged and fresh produce.

Matahari Impex 102 Westbourne Grove, W2, tel 221 7468. Open 10am–8pm daily. Matahari directly import foods from South East Asia and at this shop they specialize in Thai and Malaysian produce. There are weekly shipments of herbs and exotic fruit and veg, though not at especially bargain prices, but their noodles, beansprouts, groceries and ready-prepared dried meals work out very cheap.

Patisserie Française Maison Pechon, 127 Queensway, W2, tel 229 0746. Open 8am–7pm Mon to Sat, and 9am–6pm Sun. No credit cards. I was once shown round the kitchens of this third generation bakery and patisserie where they daily prepare a rotation of cakes and a wide range of English and French breads. Recipes are a strictly guarded secret and results are perfection. Croissants, brioche, pizza slices, fruit tarts, Danish pastries, cakes, *petits fours*, elaborate cakes and meringue-stuffed confections that are pure heaven. There is also a tea room that serves basic, everyday French-ish food that is cheap and sustaining, and they have another branch in Kensington Church Street.

Portobello Wholefoods 266 Portobello Rd, W10, tel 960 1840. Open 9.30am–6pm Mon to Sat, and until 5pm Thur. Visa. Originally related to the Neal's Yard Co-operative and now offering a similar health food stock with the emphasis on plain packaging and greater savings on bulk purchases. Muesli and other dried cereals, grains and pulses, dried fruit, nuts and herbs, organic yoghurts and vegetarian cheeses, etc.

BOOZE

Fuller Smith and Turner Griffin Brewery, Chiswick Lane South, W4, tel 994 3691. Open 9am–4.30pm Mon to Fri. No credit cards. Traditional, long established brewery (145 years as FS&T but the site has been a brewery for over 300 years) where they sell their famous ESB and London Pride beers in polypins (34 pints/20 litres) to the general public. Ideal for a party and cheaper than you'll find the equivalent anywhere.

Fuller's 372 King St, Hammersmith, W6, tel 748 2916. Open 9am–9pm Mon to Sat, and noon–3pm and 7pm–9pm Sun. Access, Visa. One of 50-odd retail outlets for the Fuller Smith and Turner brewery listed above. The five beers made by FS&T are sold in various sized containers (bottles to polypins) and a 10 per cent discount for CAMRA (Campaign For Real Ale) members. Also reasonable range of wines, etc.

Majestic Wine Warehouse 165–69 Goldhawk Rd, W12, tel 740 4641. Open 10am–8pm Mon to Sat, and until 6pm Sun. All credit cards, including their own. Nation-wide wine warehouse chain that stocks over 1000 wines that are sold by the case. Free local delivery, tasting service and mix and match facility. Prices for all pockets but plenty of bargains for paupers.

Oddbins 12 Westbourne Grove, W2, tel 727 4356; 178 Chiswick High Rd, W4, tel 994 0942; 223 Kensington High St, W8, tel 937 5143; 2 Stratford Rd, W8, tel 937 1858 and 141 Notting Hill Gate, W11, tel 229 4082. All credit cards. Pat of a vast chain which is able to pass on great savings thanks to bulk purchases. Well chosen wines in all price brackets but a very large part of their extensive stock is at the cheaper end of the market. Helpful, amusing, tasting notes accompany their catalogue (illustrated by Ralph Steadman) and there are further reductions on case purchases and free local delivery.

EATING OUT

People are very fond of saying how expensive it is to eat out in London. While that is true in general, this selection of restaurants, cafés, pubs and wine bars proves that Londoners are also well served with a varied diet of cheap, interesting and wholesome food with as much choice for vegetarians as there is for meat and fish lovers.

This selection is a personal, tried-and-tested one, built up over 25 years of living in London, 15 of which were spent being an authority on life on the cheap writing a weekly column for *Time Out* magazine in the days when value for money was its priority.

Over those 25 years eating out in London has changed dramatically. We've seen an onslaught of fast food burger and pizza chains, a boom in ethnic eating, the rise and demise of the bistro and, lately, a boom in restaurants offering set price meals.

In the mid-70s, the expected change in the licensing laws (this came on 1 May 1987) led to the metamorphosis of many pubs into pseudo-continental cafés. New names, that usually incorporated the word brasserie, were displayed in tubular lighting, espresso machines were given prominent positions on the bar and quasi-French menus were introduced in favour of pub grub. These places rarely represent value for money.

As a gross generalization, pub food now is fuel food and the microwave ('baked' potatoes, pizza, lasagne, etc) has taken over the kitchen. I am glad to say that there are still many pubs, usually Irish run, that provide good meat-and-two-veg-style lunches, but they tend to be away from the West End.

Although it's now legal for restaurants to stay open all afternoon and serve food with alcohol, very few have taken advantage of the law change.

A WORD ABOUT COVER AND SERVICE CHARGES

Although the government has issued guidelines designed to encourage restaurants to include all extraneous charges in the cost of the food advertised on a menu, it is customary in the restaurant business to charge what they call 'cover'. Many of the cheaper restaurants, and that means most of the places listed here, don't bother with cover anyway, which is a traditional levy to cover the cost of linen and flowers; 50p–£1.50 is standard.

The normal, minimum tip expected at restaurants offering a waitress service is 10 per cent. It is increasingly popular, however, for restaurants to add an automatic 12½ per cent to the bill. If you don't feel that the service warrants such a tip, you are within your rights to refuse payment, but you must explain your reasons to the manager.

A GUIDE TO THE GUIDES

The most comprehensive guide to London's restaurants is published by *Time Out* magazine. *Eating Out In London* costs £4.95, is magazine size and is published each autumn with an updated listing of about 1200 restaurants, cafés, pubs and wine bars. Some of it is pertinent to paupers, but the majority isn't. It is best used as an area guide; criticisms are not reliable. A filofax insert version is also available. The only other guide to specialize in London restaurants is published by Nicholsons. This is a handy, slim, pocket-size paperback called *Nicholson London Restaurant Guide*.

The London listing magazines *Time Out* and *City Limits* both publish a restaurant column each week, as does London's only evening paper, the *Evening Standard* (Tuesday edition). All of them occasionally feature cheap restaurants. Free information about restaurants can be had from **Restaurant Switchboard**, who operate between 9am and 8pm Mon to Sat on 888 8080; merely describe what you are after and they will check their computer for suggestions.

EATING OUT HIT LISTS

This is a quick reference to good, cheap places that stay open late at night, are within museums and galleries and in parts of town that are dense with rip-off cafés and restaurants. There is a greater selection of places to eat in the main restaurant section on p.105. All the restaurants included provide an adequate quantity of good food to satisfy a normal appetite for under £10 a head. Many places charge far less. Price guidelines are: £ = under £5, ££ = under £10.

AFTER MIDNIGHT

Canton 11 Newport St, Soho, WC2, tel 437 6220. Open 24 hours. Chinese café where barbecued pork with rice is the speciality. Licensed.

The Clifton 126 Brick Lane, E1, tel 247 2364. Open noon–12.30am daily. Cheap, easy-going Indian restaurant serving big portions of all your favourite dishes.

Harry's 19 Kingly St, W1, tel 434 0309. Open 10pm–9am Mon to Fri, and until 6am Sat. Fry-ups and breakfast any which way. Licensed.

IN MUSEUMS AND GALLERIES

Café within museums and galleries seem to operate on the principle that they have a captive audience and for the main part offer undistinguished, expensive, convenience food. There are gems, however, and these are run by outside caterers Leith's, Justin de Blank and Millburns. Use the main Eating Out listing for other nearby alternatives.

The Artist's Studio Café Leighton House Museum, 12 Holland Pk Rd, W10, tel 602 3316. Open 11.30am–4pm Tue to Sat. Top caterers Leith's prepare coffee (and newspapers) in the morning, cream teas in the afternoon, good sandwiches all day and interesting wholesome salads, soups and cold plates at lunch. Take your own wine. £–££.

British Museum Great Russell St, WC1, tel 636 1555. Open noon–

4.45pm Mon to Sat and 2.45pm–4.45pm Sun. Delicious, whole-some, fresh food from Justin de Blank served in new, modern café. Licensed. £–££

Museum of London 150 London Wall, EC2, tel 726 4446. Open 10am–5pm Mon to Sat, and until noon Sun. Catering to all needs, Millburns prepare all their food daily and kick off with good croissants, offer a buffet of sandwiches, cakes and pastries, hot savouries and several choices per course to make up a three-course meal. Licensed. £–££

National Gallery Trafalgar Sq, WC2, tel 930 5210. Open 10am–5pm Mon to Sat, and until 2pm Sun. Generous portions of wholesome food chosen from a blackboard menu: moussaka, interesting sub-stantial salads and desserts. Licensed. £–££

Victoria and Albert Museum Café, Cromwell Rd, SW7, tel 938 8366. Open 10am–5pm Mon to Sat, and until 2.30pm Sun. Millburns run this (and the Museum of London's) very good self-service restaurant with a buffet counter for snacks, salads and full hot meals. Plentiful portions of wholesome food; great cooked breakfasts. Licensed. From £

IN COVENT GARDEN

Diana's Diner 39 Endell St, tel 240 0272. Open 9am–7pm Mon to Sat. For big portions of fry-up and fuel food with an Italian bias and always a vegetarian dish. £–££

Rock and Sole Plaice 47 Endell St, tel 836 3785. Open 11.30am–10pm Mon to Sat. Great fish and chips, eat in or carry out. £

Porters 17 Henrietta St, tel 836 6466. Open noon–3pm and 5.30pm–11.30pm Mon to Fri, noon–11.30pm Sat and until 10.30pm Sun. 200-seater British pie restaurant, friendly to children and offering good value set lunch at the weekend. £–££

IN SOHO

Pollo 20 Old Compton St, tel 734 5917. Open noon–11.30pm Mon to Sat. Cheap, good Italian café.

Jimmy's 23 Frith St, tel 437 9521. Open 12.30pm–3pm and 5.30pm–

10.45pm Mon to Sat. Big portions of Greek food with chips. £–££

Amalfi 29 Old Compton St, tel 437 7284. Open noon–2.45pm and 6pm–11.15pm Mon to Sat, noon–10.30pm Sun. Old fashioned Italian café and patisserie; great value set lunch. £ set lunch, ££

Mildreds 58 Greek St, tel 494 1634. Open noon–10pm. Wholesome, cheap vegetarian café with a short menu of interesting food, plus home-made cakes. Busy at peak meal times. £–££

IN SOHO'S CHINATOWN

Kowloon 21 Gerrard St, tel 437 0148. Open noon–11.45pm daily. Chinese bakery whose window is piled with stuffed pastries that make delicious, cheap and surprisingly substantial snacks. £

New World 1 Gerrard Place, tel 734 0677. Open 11am–11.30pm daily. 600-seater Chinese restaurant serving good lunchtime *dim sum* and long menu of Cantonese food. £–££

Dragon Inn 12 Gerrard St, tel 494 0870. Open noon–midnight daily. The best *dim sum* in Chinatown; get there early. £–££

IN OXFORD STREET

Monte Bello 84 Great Titchfield St, tel 636 3772. Open noon–3.30pm and 5.30pm–11pm Mon to Sat. Italian café/restaurant with menu of good cheap and familiar dishes. £–££

IN THE CITY

Sweetings 39 Victoria St, tel 248 3062. Open 11.30am–3pm Mon to Fri. Go early to this old-fashioned pub-style fish bar and queue for great fish pie, and fine British fish dishes; don't miss the chips or puddings. ££

IN SMITHFIELD

The Cock Tavern 5 Dean's Court, tel 428 2918. Open 5.30am–noon Mon to Fri. The best breakfasts in London and between 6.30am–9.30am you can drink a pint with it!

THE SOUTH BANK

The Archduke Concert Hall Approach, off Belvedere Rd, SE1, tel
928 9370. Open 11am–3pm and 5.30pm–11pm Mon to Fri,
5.30pm–11pm Sat. Huge, hi-tech, multi-level wine bar under the
railway arches. All sorts of sausages – Cumberland, smoked Bav-
arian, Italian, game and good old British banger. Live jazz some
nights. Licensed. ££

HAYS GALLERIA

Café Pelican Du Sud Hays Galleria, Tooley St, SE1, tel 378 0096.
Open 10am–10pm Mon to Fri, until 6pm Sat and Sun. French
brasserie offering adaptable menu that encompasses baguette
sandwiches, croques, set lunches, patisseries, steak or sausage and
chips and wide ranging à la carte. From £

IN THE KING'S ROAD

Chelsea Kitchen 98 King's Rd, tel 589 1330. Open 8am–11.45pm
Mon to Sat, noon–11.30pm Sun. Fry-ups and continental staples
like spaghetti bolognese and goulash. ££

IN KNIGHTSBRIDGE

Pasta Prego 1a Beauchamp Place, tel 225 1064. Open noon–3pm and
6pm–11pm. Functional pasta bar. £–££
Chicago Rib Shack 1 Raphael St, Knightsbridge Green, tel 581
5595. Open noon to midnight daily. At lunchtime pig on as many
chicken wings as you can eat for under £.

IN KENSINGTON HIGH STREET

The Muffin Man 12 Wright's Lane, tel 937 6652. Open 8.15am–
6.30pm Mon to Sat. Genteel coffee and tea rooms where they
serve utterly wonderful cooked breakfasts, home-made British
savouries and high tea.

The Phoenicia 11 Abingdon Rd, tel 937 0120. Open noon–2.30pm Mon to Fri. Terrific eat-as-much-as-you-like buffet of hot and cold Lebanese food for £–££

IN BRIXTON

Pizzeria Franco Electric Lane end of Brixton Market Row, SW9. Open 11.30am–4pm Mon to Sat, closed Wed. Excellent, cheap pizzas, pizza sandwiches, filled rolls and great coffee. £

THE RESTAURANT SELECTION
THE WEST END
FAST, FUEL AND TAKEAWAY

It would be virtually impossible to spend more than £5 a head on food at these places; £3 is more realistic.

Barocco 13 Moor St, Soho, W1, tel 437 2324. Open noon–10.45pm Mon to Sat. Not licensed. No credit cards. Popular Italian café/coffee bar serving big portions of cheap, familiar food. Home-made minestrone, spaghetti bolognese, pasta bakes, etc.

Diana's Diner 39 Endell St, Covent Garden, WC2, tel 240 0272. Open 9am–7pm Mon to Sat. Not licensed. No credit cards. Bistroesque café where they serve big portions of cosmopolitan, Italian-biased food. Casseroles, fish and chips, meat pies, etc, plus a vegetarian dish.

The Granary 39 Albemarle St, W1, tel 493 2978. Open 11.00am–8.00pm Mon–Fri and 11.00am–2.30pm Sat. Licensed. No credit cards. Modest, yet pleasant, self-service basement restaurant where the short blackboard menu changes daily. Large portions of interesting, fresh, international food and always plenty of salads and pasta. Children are welcome and in the summer there are several pavement tables.

Harry's 19 Kingly St, W1, tel 734 8708. Open 10pm–9am Mon to Fri, 10pm–6am Sat. Licensed. No credit cards. Caters to London's clubbers and offers a fry-up breakfast menu of black pudding, fried bread, baked beans, scrambled eggs, etc and even smoked salmon or pancakes with maple syrup and whipped cream.

Lorelei 21 Bateman St, Soho, W1, tel 734 0954. Open noon–midnight Mon to Sat. Not licensed. No credit cards. Ignore the rest of the menu and choose one of the pizzas; they are terrific, made to order and great value. Lorelei is tiny, so you often have to wait for a table but it's worth it.

Pollo 20 Old Compton St, W1, tel 734 5917. Open noon–11.30pm Mon to Sat. No credit cards. Long established Italian café/coffee bar now adopted by the young Soho set. Food remains cheap and well prepared.

Rock and Sole Plaice 47 Endell St, Covent Garden, WC2, tel 836 3785. Open 11.30am–10pm Mon to Sat. Not licensed. No credit cards. No-nonsense fish and chip bar with tiny, cramped dining room where a fast turnover is encouraged. Fish is battered and cooked to order and chips are the real thing. Takeaway.

EXOTIC

Some of the best and best-value meals in London are to be found at ethnic restaurants, most particularly at Indian, Chinese, Korean (for lunch), South East Asian, Middle East and Eastern Mediterranean and East European places. I have used an approximate price guideline, which refers to a decent meal for one including service but not cover or drink: £ = under £5; ££ under £10.

A greater selection of ethnic restaurants, with a full explanation of what to expect of each cuisine, can be found in *A Guide to London's Ethnic Restaurants*, Pan, £4.99.

Agra 135 Whitfield St, W1, tel 387 4828. Open noon–3pm and 6pm–midnight daily. Licensed. All credit cards. One of London's first Indian restaurants and still run by the same family. All your favourite curries and *tandoori*. £–££

Ajimura 51 Shelton St, WC2, tel 240 9424. Open noon–3pm Mon to Fri and 6pm–11pm Mon to Sat, until 10.30pm Sun. Licensed. All credit cards. Relaxed and informal Japanese restaurant where the staff are young and friendly and the menu explicit. There are various set meals but always a special of the day and great value set lunch which doesn't leave you hungry; always the problem with Japanese food. ££

Anwar's 64 Grafton Way, W1, tel 387 6664. Open 10am–10pm daily. Not licensed. No credit cards. Indian sweetmeat shop and café which is very popular for its cheap food. Terrific breads for mopping up one of the specials of the day. Turnover is fast and most customers are regulars. £

Arirang 31 Poland St, Soho, W1, tel 437 9662. Open noon–3pm and 6pm–11pm Mon to Sat. Reckoned to be London's oldest Korean restaurant and with a helpful, explicit menu. Korean cooking is a cross between Chinese and Japanese. Their set lunch is very good value £–££

The Calabash at the Africa Centre, 38 King St, Covent Garden, WC2, tel 836 1976. Open 6pm–11pm daily, and until 12.30am Mon to Sat during the summer months. Licensed. Amex, Visa, Diners Club. Basement restaurant that offers dishes from all over Africa. Most are casserole-style; as an accompaniment, don't miss the fried plantain. The restaurant is informal and relaxed. Great rum cocktails. ££

Canton 11 Newport St, Soho, WC2, tel 437 6220. Open 24 hours daily. Licensed. Amex, Diners Club, Visa. Fast, functional Cantonese café where the speciality is barbecued pork (*char sui*) and roast duck (*char gnap*). Each with plain boiled rice. £

Cho Won 27 Romilly St, W1, tel 437 2262. Open noon–3pm and 6pm–11pm Mon to Sat., 5pm–10pm Sun. Licensed. All credit cards. Korean restaurant offering one of the cheapest set lunches in town. £

Curri-Express 17 Swallow St, W1, tel 434 3959. Open 11am–6pm Mon to Sat. Not licensed. No credit cards. Tiny, tacky little café and carry out where the food is served on disposable plates and dining means perching on a high stool at a shelf. Set lunch is great value and very generous. £

Cypriana 11 Rathbone St, W1, tel 636 1057. Open noon–2.15pm Mon to Fri and 6pm–11.15pm Mon to Sat. Licensed. No credit cards. This part of town (particularly around the corner in Charlotte St) is thick with Greek restaurants. This is one of the best and offers big portions of nicely cooked Greek food. £–££

Dragon Inn 12 Gerrard St, Soho, W1, tel 494 0870. Open noon–midnight daily. Licensed. All credit cards. The best *dim sum* (served between noon and 4.45pm) in London. Also terrific rice-based and very cheap congee soup. Three floors, but always busy, so get there early for lunch. £ *dim sum*; otherwise £–££. Other recommended Chinatown restaurants serving *dim sum*: **Chuen Cheng Ku** 17 Wardour St, W1, tel 437 1398; **Jade Garden** 15 Wardour St, W1, tel 437 5056; **Ley-Ons** 56 Wardour St, W1, tel 437 6465; **Man Fu Kung** 29 Leicester Sq, WC2, tel 839 4146, and **New World** 1 Gerrard Pl, W1, tel 434 2508.

Ikkyu 67 Tottenham Court Rd, W1, tel 636 9280. Open 12.30pm–2.30pm and 6pm–10.15pm Mon to Fri, and 7pm–10pm Sun. Licensed. Access, Amex, Diners Club, Visa. Japanese restaurant where they specialize in country-style cooking which, roughly translated, means big portions of hearty cooking. Everything is terrific value for money but their set meals are outstanding. £–££

India Club 143 Strand, WC2, tel 836 0650. Open noon–2.30pm daily and 6pm–10pm Mon to Sat, until 8pm Sun. Not licensed. No credit cards. Eccentric, canteen-style restaurant located up two flights of stairs. Terrific food and a very varied choice that includes *tandoori*, egg curry, *masala dosai*, vegetable curries, *dal*, rice and *chapatis*. £

Indian YMCA 41 Fitzroy Sq, W1, tel 387 0411. Open 8am–9am Mon to Sat and 8.30am–9.30am Sun; 12.30pm–1.45pm Mon to Sat, 12.45pm–1.30pm Sun and 7pm–8pm daily. Not licensed. The (self-service) canteen for the YMCA, but open to the general public. There is a choice between two meat and two main course vegetable dishes, plus, rice, breads and *dal*. Best value are the set meals. £

Jimmy's 23 Frith St, Soho, W1, tel 437 9521. Open 12.30pm–3pm and 5.30pm–10.45pm Mon to Sat. Licensed. No credit cards. A Soho landmark where Jimmy's son and wife now run the quasi Greek café/restaurant. Chips with everything and big portions of *kleftiko*, *stifado*, moussaka and kebabs, plus a welcome that makes you feel like a regular. £–££

Kowloon 21 Gerrard St, Soho, W1, tel 437 0148. Open noon–

11.45pm daily. Licensed. Access, Amex, Diners Club, Visa. Soho's oldest Chinese bakery whose freshly baked meat-stuffed buns are the best in Chinatown. £

Malaysian Hall Dining Hall 46 Bryanston Sq, W1, tel 723 9484. Open noon–2.30pm and 5pm–9pm daily. Not licensed. No credit cards. Despite its role as a canteen for the students who live in Malaysia Hall, the basement restaurant is open to anyone and is *the* place for cheap, authentic Malaysian fuel food. Daily changing menu. £

Melati 31 Peter St, Soho, W1, tel 437 2011. Open noon–2.30pm and 6pm–11.30pm Mon to Sat; also 21 Great Windmill St, Soho, W1, tel 437 2745. Open noon–11.30pm Mon to Thur and Sun, noon–12.30am Fri and Sat. Licensed. All credit cards. Indonesian/Malaysian café/restaurant where the spicy, tasty food with a bias towards fish is served in generous portions. Terrific noodle and rice one-dish composite meals.

The Olive Tree 11 Wardour St, Soho, W1, tel 734 0808. Open 11.30am–11.30pm Mon to Sat, until 10.30pm Sun. Licensed. Access, Visa. Functional yet pleasant dining room with the novel idea of serving a vegetarian and Middle Eastern menu. Great soups, *hummus* and other dips served with pitta bread and salad, charcoal-grills with rice, salad or chips and a great mixture of English (apple pie) and Middle Eastern (*baklava*-style) puddings. Cheap set lunch. £

Pho 2 Lisle St, Soho, W1, tel 437 8265. Open noon–11pm daily. Not licensed. No credit cards. One of an increasing number of Vietnamese cafés, this one specializes in *pho*, the traditional, noodle-based soup that gives the café its name. The set meals are good value; *cha gio* (spring roll) followed by *pho*. £

Poons 4 Leicester St, Soho, WC2, tel 437 1528. Open noon–11.30pm Mon to Sat. Licensed. No credit cards. The speciality of this very popular branch of a small chain is wind-dried meats. Choose from pork, duck, sausage or offal and eat with rice and a dish of noodles and beansprouts. £

Sav's 53 Cleveland St, W1, tel 580 7608. Open noon–3pm and 6pm–10.30pm Mon to Fri. Licensed. All credit cards. Family-run

Greek Cypriot restaurant where the *meze* is a snip and there is always a good value dish of the day. £–££

Shan Restaurant 200 Shaftesbury Ave, Covent Garden, WC2, tel 240 3348. Open noon–9.30pm Mon to Sat. Not licensed. No credit cards. Small and tatty Indian vegetarian café where the food is both exceptionally good and exceptionally cheap. Terrific value set meals. £

Wong Kei 41 Wardour St, Soho, W1, tel 437 8408. Open noon–11.30pm daily. Licensed. No credit cards. Reckoned to be the cheapest restaurant in Chinatown. They can seat over 500 and service is fast and sometimes slapdash, but they do great one-dish meals. £

SOMEWHERE YOU CAN TAKE THE WIFE TO

This is a round-up of restaurants where paupers can dine in style knowing that the bill won't break the bank. They are chosen for their value for money and because they are ideal for special occasion meals.

The average price per head for a two- or three-course meal (including cover but not service or drinks) is £10 a head. Many offer set meals, which are mentioned at the end.

Amalfi 29 Old Compton St, Soho, W1, tel 437 7284. Open noon–2.45pm and 6pm–11.15pm Mon to Sat, noon–10.30pm Sun. Licensed. All credit cards. Bustling, old-fashioned and long established Italian café, patisserie and trattoria. Everything is cheap and recommended, but the special deal of a pasta dish with garlic bread and a salad is great value.

Le Bistingo 57–59 Old Compton St, W1, tel 437 0784. Open noon–2.30pm and 6pm–11.30pm Mon to Sat. One of a small chain of French bistros that offer a menu of familiar French food. Informal, relaxed and cosy; best value is the two-course set meal that falls well within the £10 a head limit.

Café Pasta 184 Shaftesbury Ave, W1, tel 379 0198. Open 9.30am–11.30pm Mon to Sat, until 11pm Sun. Branch of a small, well conceived chain where the decor is neat, comfortable and tasteful and the menu short and centred on pasta. Good salads.

Covent Garden Pasta Bar 30 Henrietta St, Covent Garden, WC2,

tel 836 8396. Open noon–3pm and 5.30pm–11pm Mon to Sat,
12.30pm–10.30pm Sun. Licensed. Access. Most of the action
takes place downstairs at this pasta bar that often suffers from
being too busy. However, if you can get a table (queuing is
normal), the food is good. *See* South London section for details of
the Fulham Road branch.

Ed's Easy Diner 12 Moor St, Soho, W1, tel 439 1955. Open
11.30am–midnight Mon to Thur, until 1am Fri and Sat, and until
11pm Sun. No credit cards. Licensed. Trendy American diner
that serves excellent and surprisingly cheap US grub. Burgers,
fries with a chilli dip, full range of US sandwiches and beers.

Fields St Martin in the Fields Church, Duncannon St, WC2, tel 839
4342. Open 10am–8.45pm Mon to Sat, noon–7.30pm Sun.
Licensed. Access, Visa. 180-seater restaurant in the crypt of St
Martin in the Fields church. Good value home cooking with a
menu that changes daily to include three meat and one vegetarian
main dishes, all of which are priced to include vegetables. Carrot
and cumin soup; veal escalope stuffed with spinach and served
with a white wine sauce and salmon Wellington are typical.
Home-made breads, cakes and pastries are served in the morning
and at tea time.

Mildreds 58 Greek St, Soho, W1, tel 494 1634. Open noon–10pm.
Not licensed. No credit cards. Small, functional and very busy
vegetarian café/restaurant opened by a group of women because
they couldn't find anywhere serving healthy, interesting and cheap
vegetarian food in the West End. The menu changes daily, they
make their own breads (the garlic and olive stuffed one is very
good), cakes and puddings, and stir-fry is the mainstay of the main
course menu.

Milli Pini 33 Boswell St, WC1, tel 242 2434. Open noon–3pm Mon
to Fri, 6pm–11pm Mon to Sat. Licensed. Access, Visa. Long
established and very popular Italian café serving generous portions
of homely fare. Spaghetti bolognese, spaghetti with veal escalope,
lasagne and other pasta dishes. Family-run and offering terrific
value.

Mon Plaisir 21 Monmouth St, Covent Garden, WC2, tel 836 7243.
Open noon–2.15pm Mon to Fri, 6pm–11.15pm Mon to Sat.

Licensed. Access, Visa. Atmospheric French bistro that's been going strong for 20-odd years and sticks to a menu of classic French cooking. *Coq au vin, entrecôte béarnaise*, steak and *frites*, etc. Paupers need to take care to keep within the price range, but there's an excellent value three-course set lunch and pre-theatre dinner (with wine).

Monte Bello 84 Great Titchfield St, W1, tel 636 3772. Open noon–3.30pm and 5.30pm–11pm Mon to Sat. Licensed. No credit cards. In the heart of the rag trade and a stroll from Oxford Circus, this Italian café/restaurant offers value for money in its short menu of familiar Italian food. Big portions of unfussy grub; best value are the pasta bakes and spaghetti with various sauces.

North Sea Fish Restaurant 7–8 Leigh St, WC1, tel 387 5892. Open 5.30pm–10.30pm Mon to Sat. Licensed. All credit cards. Brightly lit, neat and clean fish and chip bar/restaurant. Huge portions of fresh fish in delicious batter made with egg and matzo meal. Very popular with cabbies.

Pizza Express 30 Coptic St, WC1, tel 636 3232. Open noon–midnight daily. Licensed. All credit cards. Now 25 years old and rivalling the Dean Street branch and Kettners as my favourite Pizza Express. Great Italian pizzas cooked to order with a choice of 20 toppings. In the evening there is sometimes live music, often a quartet.

Porters 17 Henrietta St, WC2, tel 836 6466. Open noon–3pm and 5.30pm–11.30pm Mon to Fri, noon–11.30pm Sat and until 10.30pm Sun. Licensed. Two hundred-seater restaurant owned by the Earl of Bradford and run on informal brasserie lines. British pies and puddings are the speciality, but there are big salads and British stalwarts such as liver, onion and bacon, plus homely puddings such as rhubarb crumble and treacle tart to finish. They are friendly to children and offer them a cut-price menu. Excellent value set lunch on Sat and Sun.

Spaghetti House 15–17 Goodge St, W1, tel 636 6582. Open noon–11pm Mon to Thur, until 11.30pm Fri and Sat, 5.30pm–10.30pm Sun. No credit cards. Licensed. Opened in the mid 50s and now the flagship of a chain of cheap, Italian cafés. Stick to the pasta and you can't go wrong; cannelloni, spaghetti bolognese and lasagne are particularly recommended. It's noisy, cheerful and unpretentious and offers a lot better value than many of the trendy, new pasta places.

Stockpot 40 Panton St, SW1, tel 839 5142. Open 8am–11.30pm Mon to Sat, noon–10pm Sun. Licensed. No credit cards. The best and best value restaurant for miles, it is frequented by the *commis* chefs from Le Caprice, one of London's top restaurants which is just round the corner. Choose from a menu of familiar cosmopolitan favourites such as spaghetti bolognese, cannelloni, casseroles or kidneys in red wine.

NORTH LONDON

FAST, FUEL AND TAKEAWAY

It would be virtually impossible to spend more than £5 a head on food at these places; £3 is more realistic.

Alfredo's 4 & 6 Essex Rd, Islington, N1, tel 226 3496. Open 7am–2.30pm Mon to Sat, and until noon Sun. Behind a beautiful art deco frontage is a great working-man's café. Terrific fry-up breakfasts and home-made fruit pies. Very popular with stall-holders from the nearby Camden Passage antiques market.

The Basement Café at **Earth Exchange** 213 Archway Rd, N6, tel 340 6407. Open noon–10pm Mon and Thur, noon–10pm Fri to Sun; 6pm–10pm Mon. Licensed. No credit cards and no Barclays Bank cheques. Co-operatively run refectory-style vegetarian and vegan café that is part of a centre for alternative interests. Food is wholesome and at pains to be interesting, with combinations such as tofu, seaweed, potato and banana in their vegan bake. Organic wines and home-made cakes and breads.

Charlotte Restaurant 221 West End Lane, NW6, tel 794 6476. Open 7.30am–10.30pm Mon to Sat (breakfast is served until 10.30am). Licensed. The dining room of a small guest house that is open to the public for wonderful home-made English breakfasts (eggs, bacon, sausage, tomato etc), and the rest of the time they serve great English savouries like toasted sandwiches and Welsh rarebit.

Copenhagen Patisserie 196 Haverstock Hill, Belsize Park, NW3, tel 435 7711. Open 8am–8pm daily. Not licensed. No credit cards. Danish bakery, patisserie and café serving delicious open sandwiches, great pastries and marvellous coffee. Good for breakfast; in the summer you can sit outside.

Fallen Angel 65 Graham St, Islington, N1, tel 253 3996. Open 12.30pm–midnight Mon to Fri, 1pm–midnight Sat, and 1pm–11.30pm Sun. Licensed. Once a pub and now a café-bar offering outstanding vegetarian food and memorable desserts. Cheap, wholesome and tasty food, with a relaxed informal atmosphere and, frequently, live music. Popular gay hang-out.

Huffs Foodstuff 55 South End Green, NW3, tel 794 8145. Open 10am–5pm daily. Not licensed. Once a butcher's shop and now a pleasant, friendly and informal wholefood café. Terrific salads, bakes, baked potatoes with various stuffings and hot dishes of the day, also a range of home-made cakes and desserts laid out at the bar. £1 corkage if you take your own wine, although most people settle for the fresh orange juice, mineral water, tea or coffee. Very pleasant after a walk on the Heath or for breakfast.

Nosh Bar 134 Finchley Rd, NW3, tel 794 3434. Open 10am–11pm Tue to Fri and Sun, and until 1.30am Sat. Licensed. All credit cards. Modelled on a New York deli and offering a take-out service. Perch at the bar or grab a table for great Jewish deli grub – pastrami on rye, salt beef, potato *latkes*, cheesecake and great coffee.

Primrose Patisserie 136 Regent's Park Rd, Primrose Hill, NW1, tel 722 7848. Open 8am–9pm Mon to Sat, and 9am–9pm Sun. Delightful, pretty little bakery/patisserie that offers a welcome refuge after a walk on Primrose Hill. Filled croissants, Polish fruit fritters, wonderful sandwiches (made with freshly baked breads), salads and savoury pastries. Tea and coffee. The place is small, very popular and gets busy mid-morning, at teatime and in the early evening.

Ristorante Trevi 16–18 Highbury Corner, N5, tel 607 3976. Open 7.30am–7.30pm Mon to Sat. Family-run Italian café which offers low-priced portions of freshly prepared and cooked food. Wonderful breakfasts are served throughout the day and there are daily specials such as roast pork with apple sauce and two veg or braised steak and two veg for around £3. Also a short menu of substantial pasta dishes such as cannelloni, lasagne and spaghetti bolognese, plus grills and fruit tarts with custard for pudding. Very friendly, pleasant place. Good coffee and sandwiches.

Victoria Plum 30 Duncan St, Islington N1, tel 278 7515. Open 9am–6pm Mon to Sat, 9am–4pm Sun. Bakery/patisserie that sells marvellous French-style vegetable flans (onion, *ratatouille*, etc), pies, pastries, croissants and wonderfully indulgent cakes. Functional, and not a place to linger, but pleasant for breakfast; good coffee.

EXOTIC

Some of the best and best-value meals in London are to be found at ethnic restaurants, most particularly at Indian, Chinese, Korean (for lunch), South East Asian, Middle East and Eastern Mediterranean and East European places. I have used an approximate price guideline, which refers to a decent meal for one including service but not cover or drink: £ = under £5; ££ = under £10.

A greater selection of ethnic restaurants, with a full explanation of what to expect of each cuisine, can be found in *A Guide to London's Ethnic Restaurants*, Pan, £4.99.

Afric-Carib 1 Stroud Green Rd, Finsbury Park, N4, tel 263 7440. Open 11.30am–midnight daily. Licensed. All major credit cards. The relaxed and easy-going atmosphere here makes a meal out at the Afric-Carib a happy experience. The Nigerian and Caribbean food consists of spicy, tasty casserole-style dishes and the menu is thoroughly explained. Try an African wine. ££

Anglo-Asian Tandoori Restaurant 60 Stoke Newington Church St, N16, tel 254 9298. Open noon–2.30pm and 6pm–midnight daily. Licensed. All credit cards. Very busy, dimly-lit, long narrow restaurant where the food is a cut above the average. Outstanding *nan* bread, good *tandoori*, especially the chicken *tikka masala*, eaten with rice and the spicy potato dish Bombay *aloo*. Drink beer. Exceptionally friendly service. £–££

Bengwan Solo 45 Kilburn High Rd, NW6, tel 624 7477. Open noon–3pm Sat and Sun, 6pm–11.30pm Mon to Fri. Weekend booking advisable. Licensed. All major credit cards. Friendly Indonesian restaurant with a helpful, explicit menu that specializes in fish. Terrific value noodle dishes, unusual prawn *sate* and exceptionally cheap (£) three-course lunch with coffee. £–££

Beewees 96 Stroud Green Rd, N4, tel 263 4004. Open noon–3pm and 6pm–11pm Mon to Sat, and 5pm–10pm Sun. Licensed. No credit cards. This cheap and cheerful place is the oldest Caribbean restaurant in the area. Terrific stuffed *rotis* (a bread similar to Indian *paratha*), saltfish and ackee, beef stew with dumplings, rice and peas, fried plantains and sweet potatoes. ££

Bintang 93 Kentish Town Rd, NW1, tel 284 1640. Open 6pm–11.45pm Mon to Sat. Licensed. Access and Visa. Small, family-run restaurant specializing in Indonesian, Malaysian and Singaporean cooking. Especially recommended is Bintang's *sate, lumpia* (a variation on spring roll), *bayam tumis* (spinach cooked with chilli and garlic), seafood and coconut soup/stew *laksa* and spicy beef *rendang*. ££

Cosmo 4–6 Northways Parade, Swiss Cottage, NW3, tel 722 1398. Open noon–11pm daily. Licensed. All credit cards. Cosy, comfortable, old fashioned coffee bar/restaurant serving a menu of Central and Eastern European food such as meatloaf with red cabbage and sauté potatoes (*zwiebel hackbraten*), *bratwurst* with *sauerkraut* and sweet and sour braised beef with dumplings and red cabbage (*rheinischer sauerbraten*). Puddings are equally substantial. Excellent value weekday set lunch. £–££

Dalat 11 Willesden Lane, Kilburn, NW6, tel 624 8521. Open 6pm–10.45pm daily. Licensed. Access, Diners Club. Unpretentious Vietnamese café run by boat people which serves large portions of cheap, authentic food. I especially recommend their spring rolls, DIY rice paper stuffed pancakes (a Vietnamese speciality), and chicken cooked with beansprouts. The menu is long but quite helpful and there are set meals for two, three or four. £–££

Daphne 83 Bayham St, Camden Town, NW1, tel 267 7322. Open noon–2.30pm and 6pm–11.30pm Mon to Sat. Licensed. Access. Welcoming and efficiently run Greek restaurant with the usual *tara-hummus-kebab-moussaka* menu, but here it's all especially good and generous in portion. In the summer there are tables on the roof and pavement. ££

Their second restaurant, **Lemonia**, 154 Regent's Park Rd, Primrose Hill, NW1, tel 586 7454, is more atmospheric and trendy, and has a more interesting menu but is less good value for money.

Falafel House 95 Haverstock Hill, Belsize Park, NW3, tel 722 6187. Open 6pm–11.30pm daily. Licensed. Visa. Go here for generous portions of cheap Middle Eastern food. The speciality is *falafel*, a surprisingly delicious deep fried ball of roughly ground chick peas, but I'd also recommend their *boreks* (pastries stuffed with feta cheese, egg and parsley, then deep fried) and various kebabs. A good place for parties of both vegetarians and meat eaters. Booking is advisable at the weekend. £–££

Geeta 57–59 Willesden Lane, Kilburn, NW6, tel 624 1713. Open noon–2.30pm Mon to Sat, 6pm–10.45pm Mon to Thur, until 11.45pm Fri and Sat and noon–11.45pm Sun. Licensed. The speciality at this long established and consistently good Indian restaurant is their Southern Indian food. Try their *masala dosai*, a ground rice pancake stuffed with spiced potato, and their rice pancakes with hot spicy lentil curry, which is called *iddly sambar*. Also wonderful are their stuffed *paratha* breads and the range of home-made Indian desserts. £–££

Hodja Nasreddin 53 Newington Green Rd, N1, tel 226 7757. Open noon–1.30am Mon to Thur, noon–3.30am Fri to Sun. Licensed. Amex, Access, Visa. In the heart of London's greatest concentration of Turkish restaurants, Hodja serves homely Turkish cooking. Turkish food is similar to Greek food, and the mainstay of the menu is *mezze* (small dishes of dips, stuffed vegetables, salads, etc), plus kebabs served with a spicy tomato sauce. Useful for meals at irregular hours, although it is often very busy. Try to get an upstairs table.

Indian Veg 92 Chapel Market, Islington, N1, tel 837 4607. Open noon–3pm and 6pm–11pm daily. Booking essential. All major credit cards. Pleasant, functional and easy-going Indian vegetarian restaurant that specializes in *bhel poori* (snacks). Especially good *thali* (set meal), *aloo papri chat* (chick peas with potatoes) and *masala* and *paper dosai* (stuffed rice flour pancakes). Great buffet lunch on Sundays. £–££

Laurent 428 Finchley Rd, NW2, tel 794 3603. Open noon–2pm daily, 6pm–11pm Mon to Sat. Licensed. Access, Visa. Modest neighbourhood café run by a Tunisian family who make a speciality of *cous cous*, their national dish. Start with *brik à l'oeuf*, a filo pastry envelope stuffed with an egg, chopped parsley and onion and deep fried, and follow with the *cous cous complet* (when the steamed semolina is piled with vegetables, lamb and spicy sausages) or royal (also with lamb chops and kebab). Both are served with gravy and chilli hot *harissa* sauce. £–££

Ming Court 5 New College Parade, Finchley Rd, NW3, tel 722 9552. Open noon–11.30pm daily; *dim sum* served until 5pm daily. Licensed. No credit cards. One of the few restaurants in North London to serve the Cantonese snacks called *dim sum*. Order these steamed and deep fried dumplings, buns and sweetmeats from an explicit menu and drink Chinese tea. £

   Dim sum is also served at **Local Friends** 28 North End Rd, Golders Green, NW11, tel 455 9258. £

Penang Satay House 9 Turnpike Lane, N8, tel 340 8707. Open 6pm–11pm Mon to Thur, 6pm–midnight Fri and Sat. Licensed. No credit cards. Run by a Malaysian family who've created an evocative atmosphere in their bamboo-decorated restaurant. The helpful menu takes the strain out of ordering, but I recommend their *laksa* as a main dish (vermicelli, prawns, fish cake, chicken and beansprouts in a coconut broth); their *sate* and chicken dish, *nasi goreng*. Distinctive flavours and generous portions. Good value set dinners. £–££

Le Petit Prince 5 Holmes Rd, Kentish Town, NW5, tel 267 0752. Open 12.30pm–2.30pm Tue to Fri, 7pm–11.30pm Mon to Fri; 7pm–11.45pm Sat and until 11.15pm Sun. Licensed. No credit cards. Atmospheric, relaxed and popular Algerian café/restaurant where the speciality is *cous cous* (*see* Laurent entry), but also steak and chips and kebabs. They also serve a daily special. There is often live music and a party mood. ££

Roxy Café Cantina 297 Upper St, Islington, N1, tel 226 5746. Open noon–11.30pm Mon to Sat, 12.30pm–10.45pm Sun. Licensed.

Access, Visa. Mexican food hasn't really taken off in London, but this is one of the best exponents of this chilli-hot cuisine. Big portions of *tortillas* and *burritos* stuffed with chicken, beef or vegetables and piled high with re-fried beans, salad, cheese and spicy sauce. Lively, bright and busy. Great Mexican beers and cocktails. ££

Sabras 263 High Rd, NW10, tel 459 0340. Open 12.30pm–9.30pm Tue to Sun. Not licensed. Open in 1973, this was one of the first restaurants to popularize authentic Indian vegetarian food. The menu embraces Southern Indian, Gujarati and Bombay cuisines and is one of the most enticing I know. Paupers will love their *thali* (set meal) and buffet lunch. £–££

Singapore Garden 83 Fairfax Rd, NW6, tel 328 5314. Open noon–2.45pm and 6pm–10.45pm Mon to Sat. Licensed. All major credit cards. Head straight for the footnote menu that specializes in Singaporean dishes. Do try their *kway pie tee* (little top hats of batter literally brimming over with prawns, bean shoots and chicken), the coconut broth fish soup *laksa*, followed by the deliciously sweet *gula malaka* (a sort of rice pudding) to finish. Paupers must take care to keep within ££.

Standard Tandoori Restaurant 87 Holloway Rd, Islington, N7, tel 607 1637. Open noon–3pm and 6pm–midnight daily. Licensed. All credit cards. The best Indian restaurant in the Holloway Road (and that's saying a lot!); great *dals*, vegetable curries and freshly cooked *tandoori*. £–££

Suruchi 18 Theberton St, Islington, N1, tel 359 8033. Open noon–2.30pm and 6pm–10.30pm. Not licensed, no corkage. Access, Visa. Related to **Diwana** (*see* West London section), this is a clean, comfortable and very pleasant vegetarian Indian restaurant. The menu is essentially *bhel poori* (snacks) and you eat as much or as little as you like. My favourites are the *sev dahi*, a crispy, deep, hollow pancake stuffed with potato, onions and doused in a sweet/sour sauce, and *dosai*, a wafer-thin rice flour pancake stuffed with spicy potato and onion, or the set meal *thali*. £–££

Tuk Tuk 330 Upper St, Islington, N1, tel 226 0837. Open noon–3pm and 6pm–11pm Mon to Sat. Licensed. Access, Amex, Visa. Booking is advisable before and after Screen On The Green performances (the cinema opposite). Tuk Tuk refers to the three-wheel taxis of Bangkok. The menu is short and concentrates on Thai fast food such as deep-fried snacks, rice and noodle-based dishes and clay-pot stews. £–££

Vijay 49 Willesden Lane, NW6, tel 328 1087. Open noon–2.45pm and 6pm–11.45pm daily. Licensed. All major credit cards. Outstanding and consistently good Southern Indian restaurant that has two menus; one devoted to vegetable, pulse and steamed grain dishes (which are the cheapest and the best) and the other to meat curries. £–££

You Me House 510a Hornsey Rd, N19, tel 272 6208. Open noon–3pm and 6pm–11pm daily. Not licensed, minimal corkage charge. Also larger branch at 33 Pratt St, Camden Town, NW1, which is licensed. No credit cards. Delightful little Korean restaurant run by a husband and wife team. There is plenty of advice about the food (a cross between Chinese and Japanese with Thai overtones) and everything is recommended. Especially good are their *pa jurn* (a sort of pizza) and the national dish called *bulgogi*, which comprises soy-marinated beef that is barbecued at the table and eaten with relishes and rolled in lettuce.

Zamoyski 85 Fleet Rd, NW3, tel 794 4792. Open noon–3pm and 5.30pm–11pm Mon to Sat (wine bar); 6.30pm–10pm Mon to Sat (restaurant). Atmospheric Polish wine bar and restaurant that is always busy and often has live music. Big servings of hearty grub such as beef strudel and stuffed cabbage in the restaurant; international bakes and snacks in the wine bar. £–££

SOMEWHERE YOU CAN TAKE THE WIFE TO

This is a round-up of restaurants where paupers can dine in style knowing that the bill won't break the bank. They are chosen for their value for money and because they are ideal for special occasion meals.

The average price per head for a two- or three-course meal (including cover but not service or drinks) is £10 a head. Many offer set meals, which are mentioned at the end.

Billboard Café 222 Kilburn High Rd, NW6, tel 328 1374. Open noon–3.45pm Sat and Sun, 7pm–11.45pm Mon to Sat, and until

11.45pm Sun. Licensed. All credit cards. Informal, lively restaurant with an Italian-biased menu of simple, wholesome food (pasta, salads, charcoal grilled meats and fish). Most evenings there is live jazz.

La Bougie 7 Murray St, Camden Town, NW1, tel 485 6400. Open noon–2pm Tue to Fri and Sun, and 7pm–10.30pm Tue to Sun. Licensed. No credit cards. Informal and easy-going French/continental bistro where the menu changes seasonally. All starters and desserts cost under £2, and all main courses (with vegetables) under £4. A classical guitarist plays on Sunday nights.

Café Flo 205 Haverstock Hill, Belsize Park, NW3, tel 435 6744. Open noon–3pm daily and 6pm–11.30pm Mon to Fri, 6.30pm–11.30pm Sat and 6.45pm–11pm Sun. Licensed. Access, Visa. Functional French café complete with tabac-style French beer posters on the walls and a hissing espresso machine on the bar. Great menu of regional French dishes with a daily speciality plus their utterly excellent *L'Idée Flo* – a three-course set meal of soup or salad, steak and *frites* or a vegetarian dish for £5. Note, however, that *L'Idée Flo* is served at lunch, before 7pm and after 10.30pm.

Camden Brasserie 216 Camden High St, Camden Town, NW1, tel 482 2114. Open noon–3pm daily, and 6.30pm–11.30pm Mon to Sat, 6pm–11.30pm Sun. Licensed. No credit cards. Justifiably one of the most popular restaurants in the area, offering a short menu of classic, simple French food in a relaxed, comfortable bistroesque room. Char-grilled dishes are the speciality and their *pommes frites* come highly recommended. In the summer they fold back the window/doors; in the winter they light the fire. Do book.

Chez Liline 101 Stroud Green Rd, Finsbury Park, N4, tel 263 6550. Open noon–2.30pm and 6.30pm–11pm Mon to Sat. Licensed. No credit cards. More like a café than a restaurant, Chez Liline is owned by French Mauritians and their menu specializes in native fish dishes. Everything is cooked to order (so don't expect a quick meal), is delicious and served in huge portions. Daily changing menu, which is dependent on what's in the market. Do book.

The Lantern 23 Malvern Rd, Kilburn, NW6, tel 624 1796. Open noon–3pm and 7pm–midnight daily. Licensed. All major credit cards. Also **La Cloche** 304 Kilburn High Rd, N6, tel 328 0302.

Yugoslav Peter Ilic hit the spot with this, the 1980s equivalent of the bistro, when he opened it six years ago. The menu is chalked on a board, all starters and desserts are priced at £1.95 and all the main courses at £4.65. It's candlelit, fun and lively. The food comes in big portions and is tasty and Frenchified. Booking is advisable.

Maxwells of Ealing 177 Haverstock Hill, Belsize Park, NW3, tel 586 9277. Open noon–2.30pm and 5pm–10pm Mon to Sat. Not licensed. No credit cards. The best fish and chip shop/restaurant for miles. Fish is cooked in a deliciously thin batter and the chips are big and crisp.

Nautilus 27–29 Fortune Green Rd, NW6, tel 435 2532. Open 11.30am–2.30pm, and 4.30pm–11.30pm Mon to Sat. No credit cards. Kosher fish and chip shop/restaurant where they offer the choice of a matzo meal, egg and matzo meal or regular batter (all thin, crisp and quite delicious). Great chips and very big portions of fish.

Pasta Underground 214 Camden High St, Camden Town, NW1, tel 482 0010. Open noon–3pm Mon to Sat, 6pm–11pm Mon to Thur, and until 11.30pm Fri and Sat. Licensed. No credit cards. Fresh pasta served with various sauces at a flat rate below £5. Located in a cellar, it is often busy and weekend booking is advisable.

Perfect Pizza 1 South End Rd, Belsize Park, NW3, tel 794 2864. Open 11.30am–midnight daily. Licensed. No credit cards. American-owned pizza parlour offering choice of six fillings served on either a thin and crispy Italian-style pizza or a deep-pan US-style base. Local delivery service.

Solopasta 27 Liverpool Rd, Islington, N1, tel 359 7648. Open 5.30pm–10.30pm Tue to Sat. No credit cards. Licensed. Useful to know about if you're visiting Camden Passage antique market, although it's tiny and very popular. All the pasta is home-made and their sauces are authentic Italian stalwarts. Bag one of the cramped tables or take away and warm it up at home.

Tiny Tim 7 Plender St, Camden Town, NW1, tel 388 0402. Open noon–2pm Mon to Fri, until 4pm Sun, and 6.30pm–11pm Mon to Sat. Licensed. No credit cards. Run by a Frenchman in the style of a real French bistro with a short menu and stunningly good value set lunches, Tiny Tim just creeps within the £10 a head price range. Good homely, everyday French food, but do book, as it's small and very popular.

EAST LONDON

FAST, FUEL AND TAKEAWAY

It would be virtually impossible to spend more than £5 a head on food at these places; £3 is more realistic.

AA Restaurant 5 Dean's Court, EC4, tel 248 5487. Open 7am–2.30pm (breakfast until 11.30am) Mon to Sat. Not licensed. Huge café which serves fry-up breakfasts with chips, and these are recommended in preference to the rest of the menu, which consists of international fillers such as lasagne. Great jam roly-poly and fruit tarts with custard.

The Cock Tavern Poultry Ave, Central Markets, EC1, tel 248 2918. Open 5.30am–noon Mon to Fri. Licensed 6.30am–9.30am. Like most of the pubs in the vicinity of Smithfield (the wholesale meat market, *see* p.70) the Cock is licensed first thing in the morning. Many of these pubs serve outstandingly good and very cheap breakfasts and I think the Cock is the best. Choose what you like and avert your eyes from the blood-soaked overalls.

Hatchetts 5 Clerkenwell Rd, Barbican, EC1, tel 251 2587. Open 11.30am–4.30pm Mon to Fri, 11.30am–3.30pm Sun; sandwich bar 7am–5.30pm Mon to Fri, and 8am–4pm Sun. Licensed. Kosher and non-kosher Jewish sandwich bar and café/restaurant. Generous portions of fry-up grub but it's the salt beef sandwiches that are the great attraction here.

E. F. Kelly 284 Bethnal Green Rd, E3, tel 739 8676. Open 10am–3pm Mon to Thur, until 6.30pm Fri, and 3.30pm Sat. Pie and mash shops date back to Victorian days and food is still made to original recipes. Service is swift and no-nonsense and the idea is to eat up quick and be on your way. Food is washed down with tea. As is traditional, everything is made fresh on the premises every day. Queue for a plate of jellied eels, stewed eels served with

123

liquor (parsley sauce) or a meat pie with mashed potatoes and grab a place at one of the large communal tables. This shop is marginally more modern than many (it's only 50 years old); all of them offer a takeway service.

Other recommended East End pie and mash shops: **F. Cooke** 9 Broadway Market, E8, tel 254 6548. Open 10am–6pm Mon to Thur, until 8.30pm Fri and Sat; **F. Cooke and Sons** 41 Kingsland High St, E8, tel 254 2878. Open 10am–8pm Mon and Thur, until 6pm Tue and Wed, and until 10pm Fri and Sat; and **G. F. Kelly** 526 Roman Rd, E3, tel 980 3165. Open 10am–2.30pm Mon to Thur, until 6.30pm Fri, and 5.30pm Sat.

The Kosher Luncheon Club Morris Kasler Hall, Greatorex St, E1, tel 247 0039. Open noon–2.45pm Mon to Fri. Kosher house wine. Aimed at the local Jewish community, but busy with a mixed clientele because they offer such value for money. Great homemade barley and chicken soup, haddock or plaice with chips and apple strudel or pie or *lokshen* (vermicelli) pudding to follow. Takeaway available.

The Nosherie 12–13 Greville St, Hatton Garden, EC1, tel 242 1591. Open 8am–5pm Mon to Fri. Licensed. In the heart of London's jewellery area, this is a kosher and non-kosher Jewish café that dishes out huge portions of chopped liver, meat balls, chicken soup, viennas, *wursts* and *lokshen* (vermicelli) pudding.

Oasis 113 Lower Clapton Rd, E5, tel 985 2675. Open noon–3pm, 5pm–11pm Mon to Fri and Sun, and noon–2pm, 7pm–10.30pm Sun. Licensed. Popular wine bar with an exotic interior decor that includes a fake palm tree. The menu is international in the real sense of the word and offers good value for money. Stunningly good value set lunch.

Paloma 10 Gt Eastern St, EC2, tel 247 9064. Open 7am–5pm Mon to Fri and until 2pm Sat and Sun. Colourful café offering a staple diet of fry-ups (egg, bacon, sausage, etc) and big portions of international everyday grub.

Peris 10 The Broadway, Stratford, E15, tel 519 3894. Open 11am–8pm Mon to Sat. Licensed. Pleasant pizza bar for eat in or takeaway, also cheap pasta and extra cheap children's menu.

EXOTIC

Some of the best and best-value meals in London are to be found at ethnic restaurants, most particularly at Indian, Chinese, Korean (for lunch), South East Asian, Middle East and Eastern Mediterranean and Eastern European places. I have used an approximate price guideline, which refers to a decent meal for one including service but not cover or drink: £ = under £5; ££ = under £10.

A greater selection of ethnic restaurants, with a full explanation of what to expect of each cuisine, can be found in *A Guide to London's Ethnic Restaurants*, Pan, £4.99.

Aladin 132 Brick Lane, E1, tel 247 8210. Open 9.30am–10pm daily. No credit cards. Indian café serving generous portions of snacks and curries throughout the day. Takeaway service. £

Blue Gardenia 136 Barking Rd, E6, tel 471 6685. Open 6.30pm–10.30pm Mon and Tue, until 11.30pm Wed and Thur, and until 12.30pm Fri and Sat. Access, Amex, Visa. Licensed. With a bit of ducking and diving paupers can eat well at this friendly, up-tempo Caribbean restaurant. ££

The Clifton 126 Brick Lane, E1, tel 247 2364. Open noon–12.30am daily. Licensed. All credit cards. Famous, 25-year-old Indian restaurant that serves big portions of all your favourite Indian food. Cheap and good fun. £–££

Lahore Kebab House 2 Umberston St, E1, tel 488 2551. Open 12.30am–11pm daily. Not licensed. No credit cards. Can be very busy at lunchtime because they are famous around Brick Lane for their big portions of *tandoori*, kebabs and curried quails eaten with a pile of *chapatis*. Takeaway available. £

Lahore Restaurant 218 Commercial Rd, E1, tel 791 0112. Open noon–11pm daily. Not licensed. No credit cards. They do a roaring takeaway trade in microwaved *samosas* at this pristine Pakistani café, but you can also eat in at one of the nine formica-topped tables and enjoy a freshly cooked, well spiced and ungreasy curry or Indian kebab. £

Mumtaz Tandoori 102 Station Rd, E4, tel 529 2620. Open noon–3pm and 6pm–midnight daily. Licensed. All credit cards. The best Indian restaurant in the area and particularly rated for its *tandoori* mix which, when eaten with rice and *nan*, is enough for two. £–££.

New Friends 53 West India Dock Rd, E14, tel 987 1139. Open noon–11pm daily. Licensed. Access, AmEx, Visa. This area, known as Limehouse, was London's first Chinatown and New Friends was one of its first *chop suey* houses. It remains little changed and though much of the food is bastardized, their *char siu* (barbecued pork), duck and noodle dishes are excellent. £–££

Paradise Cottage 477 Bethnal Green Rd, E2, tel 729 6119. Open noon–midnight daily. Licensed. Access, Visa. A real find in an area where there are few decent places to eat. Comfortable, clean, pleasant little restaurant serving excellent cheap and generous Turkish food. Great *boreks* (little pastries filled with cheese and deep fried), various kebabs served with yoghurt and spicy tomato sauce, rice and salad. Freshly made sugar-water drenched pastries, Turkish delight and murky, sweet coffee to finish. £–££

Ronak 317 Romford Rd, E7, tel 534 2944. Open 11am–10pm Tue to Sun. Licensed. Exceptional Southern Indian vegetarian café/restaurant where the food is unbelievably cheap, the staff pleasant and the place run with efficiency. The emphasis is on filling fuel food and I can vouch for their special of potato chips with apple and coconut chutney and yam chips with a tamarind sauce. Also recommended is their *masala dosai* (potato-stuffed rice flour pancake) and *samosas*. £

Young Friends 11 Pennyfields, E14, tel 987 4276. Open noon–11.30pm daily. Licensed. Access, Amex, Visa. Tiny Cantonese café/restaurant that has remained popular throughout its 25-year life. Big portions of all your favourite dishes; spring rolls, sesame prawn toasts, beef in oyster bean sauce, crispy or braised duck and chicken in black bean sauce. £–££

SOMEWHERE YOU CAN TAKE THE WIFE TO

This is a round-up of restaurants where paupers can dine in style knowing that the bill won't break the bank. They are chosen for their value for money and because they are ideal for special occasion meals.

The average price per head for a two- or three-course meal

(including cover but not service or drinks) is £10 a head. Many offer set meals, which are mentioned at the end.

Café Pelican Du Sud Hays Galleria, Tooley St, E14, tel 378 0096. Open 8am–10.30pm Mon to Fri, 10am–6pm Sat and Sun. Licensed. The most useful and reliable place to eat within the stylish, riverside Hays Galleria shopping complex. Modelled on its parent branch in St Martin's Lane, it is versatile in providing French snacks (baguette sandwiches and croques), steak or sausage and chips, as well as a lengthy menu of ambitious French brasserie food that moves out of our price bracket.

The Cherry Orchard 241 Globe Rd, Bethnal Green, E2, tel 980 6678. Open noon–3pm and 6pm–10.30pm Mon to Sat. Not licensed, corkage charge. Access, Visa. Vegetarian café/restaurant run by a Buddhist co-operative, but not as alarming as that might sound. Friendly, relaxed, quite cosy, yet functional place with interesting, wholesome vegetarian food.

East/West 188 Old St, EC1, tel 608 0300. Open 11am–10pm Mon to Fri, 11am–3pm Sat and Sun. Licensed. Access, Visa. Refectory-style dining room within an alternative health community centre. Interesting vegetarian and macrobiotic cooking with Japanese influences. Delicious sugar-free desserts and cakes; organic wines and bottled beers.

Grapes Ale House 76 Narrow St, E14, tel 987 4396. Open noon–2pm Mon to Fri, and 7pm–9.30pm Tue to Sat. Licensed. Access. Superb, spankingly fresh fish and shellfish pub restaurant with views across the river (specify when booking). Jellied eels, potted shrimps, oysters, all fish and shellfish in season and great chips. Paupers have to watch, however, to keep within the £10 a head price bracket.

Mustards Smithfield Brasserie 60 Long Lane, EC1, tel 796 4920. Open for a pre-theatre menu between 5pm–7pm Mon to Sat. All major credit cards. Licensed. Left Bank-style wine bar and restaurant that offers an exceptionally good value pre-theatre two-course meal that is likely to include grilled steak and *frites*.

Pizza One, Pancakes Too! 464 Bethnal Green Rd, E2, tel 729 0233. Open noon–11pm daily. All major credit cards. Licensed. Slightly mad and definitely eccentric (one look at the menu and you'll know what I mean!), but offering terrific value food. Generously topped pizzas available with a very wide choice of toppings and sweet and savoury-stuffed French *crêpe*-style pancakes. Set lunch £–££; Sunday lunch, student discounts, children welcomed and party room available.

Sweetings 39 Victoria St, EC4, tel 248 3062. Open 11.30am–3pm Mon to Fri. No credit cards. Licensed. More like a pub than a restaurant and originally opened as an oyster bar. Customers drink or queue for a seat at one of the four bars or try for a table in the tiny, cramped adjoining dining room. Fabulous fishy menu that encompasses fish pie, great chips, smoked haddock with poached eggs and roes on toast. Delicious English nursery puddings like rice pudding and treacle tart. Get there either early or late, as it's a popular City haunt.

Venus Steak House 366–68 Bethnal Green Rd, E2, tel 739 2650. Open noon–2.30pm Mon to Fri, 6pm–1am Mon to Thur, and until 2am Fri and Sat. Access, Amex, Visa. Licensed. Great value steak house; sticking at two courses, it's possible to feast on their mammoth mixed grill and get change from £10.

SOUTH LONDON
FAST, FUEL AND TAKEAWAY

It would be virtually impossible to spend more than £5 a head on food at these places; £3 is more realistic.

Maggie Brown 179 Battersea High St, SW11, tel 228 0559. Open 7am–3pm and 5.30pm–11pm Mon to Sat. 'The cheapest food in London' used to be the claim of Maggie of her 70-year-old pie and mash shop. Queue at the counter and choose between the daily made meat pies with or without mash (mashed potato) and stewed or jellied eels and liquor (parsley sauce). As is traditional, the decor of the shop is plain and functional with high-backed wooden benches, marble-topped tables and engraved mirrors on the walls. Turnover is brisk and dished out with plenty of tongue pie. Tea is served by the mug.

Other recommended South London pie and mash shops:

W. J. Arment 7 & 9 Westmoreland Rd, SE17, tel 703 4974. Open 10.30am–5pm Tue to Fri, until 4pm Thur, and 6pm Sat.

B. J. Atkins 140 Wandsworth Bridge Rd, SW6, tel 731 1232. Open 11.45am–6pm Tue and Wed, 12.45pm–8pm Thur and Fri, and 11.45am–5pm Sat.

Burroughs 426 Coldharbour Lane, Brixton, SW9, tel 274 1492. Open 10.30am–3.30pm Mon to Sat, and until 1.30pm Wed.

Cookes 84 The Cut, Waterloo, SE1, tel 928 5931. Open 10.30am–2pm Mon to Thur, and until 3.30pm Fri and Sat.

Manze's 87 Tower Bridge Rd, SE1, tel 407 2985. Open 11am–2pm Mon to Thur, until 2.30pm Fri and Sat.

Peter's 59 Pimlico Rd, SW1, tel 730 5991. Open 7am–10pm Mon to Sat, and 8am–4pm Sun. Not licensed. No credit cards. This is a popular cabbie haunt, which is a great compliment to the food. Aside from a complete fry-up repertoire (eggs, bacon, sausages, tomatoes, etc), there is a range of home-made homely fare such as soups, pasta bakes, liver and onions, chicken escalopes and fruit crumble with custard. Girls on their own need to develop a thick skin.

Pizzeria Franco Electric Lane end of Brixton Market Row, SW9. No phone. Open 9am, but food on sale from 11.30am–4pm Mon to Sat, closed Wed. Not licensed. Informal pizzeria and coffee bar that is packed at all times because of its extremely good, cheap pizzas. Also pizza sandwiches (*calzone*), filled rolls, salads and wicked coffee.

EXOTIC

Some of the best and best-value meals in London are to be found at ethnic restaurants, most particularly at Indian, Chinese, Korean (for lunch), South East Asian, Middle East and Eastern Mediterranean and East European places. I have used an approximate price guideline, which refers to a decent meal for one including service but not cover or drink: £ = under £5; ££ = under £10.

A greater selection of ethnic restaurants, with a full explanation of what to expect of each cuisine, can be found in *A Guide to London's Ethnic Restaurants*, Pan, £4.99.

Anarkali 229 Streatham High Rd, SW16, tel 769 3012. Open noon–2.45pm daily, and 6pm–11.50pm Mon to Sat, 7pm–11.50pm Sun. Licensed. Access, Visa. The best Indian restaurant in the area and far cheaper too. Everything is recommended, but they do particularly good onion *bhajis*, chicken *tikka* or *korma* and vegetable *biryani*. Weekend booking is advisable.

Café On The Hill 91 Brixton Hill, SW2, tel 671 6012. Open 6.30am–4pm Mon to Fri, 6.30am–1pm Sat, and 6pm–10pm Tue to Sat. Not licensed. No credit cards. Like the Bedlington and Norma's Café (q.v.) in West London, this is a greasy spoon café by day (with one Thai special of the day) but in the evening it turns into a modest, cheap Thai restaurant. Short menu and helpful, cheerful, friendly staff. £

Daquise 20 Thurloe St, South Kensington, SW7, tel 589 6117. Open 10am–11pm daily. Licensed. No credit cards. Homely Polish café/restaurant, busy in the morning and afternoon for tea and coffee with pastries, and at lunch and dinner for its huge servings of East European dishes. Cheapest of all is the set lunch. Very handy for the Victoria and Albert, Science and Natural History Museums. £

Inde's Jamaican Grub 183 New Kent Rd, SE1, tel 403 7897. Open noon–2.30pm and 6pm–10.30pm Mon to Sat, and 7pm–10pm Sun. Not licensed. No credit cards. Jamaican home cooking presented on a menu that is chilli-coded! Try avocado stuffed with saltfish and ackee, fried pickled fish (*escovitch*), *callaloo* (a spinach-like vegetable) and sweet potato pie. ££

Lam 12a Station Way, Rye Lane, Peckham, SE13, tel 639 6814. Open 11am–11.30pm Mon to Sat. Licensed. No credit cards. There is a flourishing Vietnamese community in Peckham and this restaurant, and **Viet Hing**, 18 Peckham High St, SE13, tel 639 1888, is run by boat people. Their English is faltering, but there is explanation on the short menu; I'd recommend the traditional, substantial soup called *pho*, their tasty, coriander flavoured spring rolls called *cha gio* and any of the specials of the day. Vietnamese food is similar to Thai cuisine. £–££

Nancy Lam's Enak Enak 56 Lavender Hill, SW11, tel 934 3148. Open 7pm–10.45pm Mon to Sat. Licensed. Access, Visa. Everything is cooked to order using fresh ingredients at this homespun little South East Asian restaurant. Do book, and be prepared for a long session; *sate, gado-gado,* beef *rendang* and coconut flavoured stuffed pancakes are especially recommended, but there is plenty of advice on hand. ££

Ognisko Polskie 55 Prince's Gate, Exhibition Rd, South Kensington, SW7, tel 589 4635. Open 12.30pm–3pm and 6.30pm–11pm daily. Licensed. All credit cards. While this is a club for London's Polish community, its restaurant is English speaking, friendly and open to the general public. Each day there is a marvellous multi-choice three-course set meal of delicious, robust Eastern European food. To drink there is vodka and Pils lager. The club is set in a large terrace opposite Imperial College and the dining room is quiet and elegant, decorated in pale lemon, and hung with oil paintings. £–££

Satay Satay 112 St John's Hill, Clapham, SW11, tel 585 1802. Open 12.30pm–11.30pm Mon to Sat, 12.30pm–10.30pm Sun. Licensed. Amex, Visa. Feast on hot pitta stuffed with six skewers of *sate* (prawn, chicken, pork or beef) with salad and peanut dip. Otherwise there's a great value set lunch. £

Sree Krishna 192 Tooting High St, SW17, tel 672 4250. Open noon–2.45pm daily, 6pm–10pm Mon to Thur, and 6pm–11.45pm Sun. Licensed. Access, Visa. Southern Indian vegetarian restaurant with a reputation for delicate spicing and fresh ingredients. *Masala dosai,* the crisp potato-stuffed pancake or *uppama,* a dish of lightly fried semolina cooked with onions and spices, are delicious centre pieces. ££

SOMEWHERE YOU CAN TAKE THE WIFE TO

This is a round-up of restaurants where paupers can dine in style knowing that the bill won't break the bank. They are chosen for their value for money and because they are ideal for special occasion meals.

The average price per head for a two- or three-course meal (including cover but not service or drinks) is £10 a head. Many offer set meals, which are mentioned at the end.

The Archduke Wine Bar Concert Hall Approach, South Bank, SE1, tel 928 9370. Open 11am–3pm, 5.30pm–11pm Mon to Fri, and 5.30pm–11pm Sat. Licensed. Located under the arches of Hungerford Railway Bridge which links Waterloo with Charing Cross Station. Hi-tech, but comfortable, and with a buzzy atmosphere. The menu is short and concentrates on sausages – bangers and mash, *bratwurst*, game sausages, etc.

Battersea Arts' Café Battersea Arts Centre, Old Town Hall, Lavender Hill, SW11, tel 223 6557. Open 11am–10pm daily. Licensed. No credit cards. Although inside the Arts Centre, the café is open to the general public. The short menu of wholesome, home-made food encompasses a roast on Sunday, substantial soups, imaginative vegetable curries and bakes, and unusual puddings. Nice atmosphere.

Bistro Vino 303 Brompton Rd, SW3, tel 589 7898. Open noon–3pm, 6pm–11.45pm daily. Licensed. Access, Visa. Pleasant, comfortable, 30-year-old bistro that provides large portions of consistently good international, cosmopolitan food. Chicken Kiev, spaghetti bolognese, steaks, etc, with a choice of rice, fries, boiled or croquette potatoes. Similarly, puddings range over chocolate mousse, crème caramel and apple pie.

Brandons 25 Tower Bridge Rd, SE1, tel 403 6697. Open noon–3pm Mon to Fri, and 7pm–10pm Thur to Sat. Licensed. Visa. There is a no minimum charge policy and there are discounts of 10 per cent on parties of ten. The food relies on what's available in the market, but is best described as international with plenty of French influences. At lunch the menu is severely reduced (usually to four dishes) and the food is much cheaper. Hence you might get sirloin steak with vegetables for £4.95, pan-fried fish cooked with thyme and finished with cream, or Japanese-style charcoal grilled chicken served with rice and vegetables for 3.50.

Bridge 74 Battersea Bridge Rd, SW11, tel 738 0198. Open 8am–11pm daily. Access, Visa. Licensed. A pub conversion by Peter Ilic, who is mentioned elsewhere in this book for his nine-strong chain of bistroesque restaurants where all starters and desserts cost £1.95 and main dishes £4.65. International, Frenchified food, such as *moules marinière*, cheeseburgers, stuffed pancakes, etc.

Chelsea Bun Diner corner Limerston St and King's Rd, World's End, SW10, tel 352 3635. Open 7am–11.30pm. Not licensed. No credit cards. This used to be a famous World's End greasy spoon but has prettied itself up and changed its menu. Now the food is more health-conscious, but the Diner retains its predecessor's reputation for large portions. Omelettes are a speciality and are made with four eggs and a choice of fillings.

Chelsea Kitchen 98 King's Rd, SW3, tel 589 1330. Open 8am–11.45pm Mon to Sat, and noon–11.30pm Sun. Licensed. No credit cards. A Chelsea landmark that has survived the Swinging 60s, when it was an 'in-spot'. Related to the Stockpot chain (q.v.), the menu is a mixture of fry-ups and continental staples like spaghetti bolognese, curried eggs, goulash, pasta and omelettes. Pleasant, easy atmosphere.

Chelsea Pot 356 King's Rd, SW3, tel 351 3605. Open noon–11.30pm daily. Licensed. No credit cards. Long-term favourite of visitors to the King's Rd; big portions of comforting international food such as kidneys in red wine, chicken à la king, omelettes, grills and spaghetti bolognese.

The Pot 5a Hogarth Place, Earls Court, SW5, tel 370 4371 and **New Hot Pot** 314 Earl's Court Rd, SW5, tel 370 3101. Open noon–midnight daily. Access. When I first came to live in London, I lived a short stroll from Earls Court. Whenever I could afford it I used to eat at one of several Pots in the area; my favourite is long gone, and although they have always denied it, I am sure they have a central kitchen. The menu never changes and neither do the tastes. My favourite meal was egg mayonnaise followed by kidneys in wine (with rice and sometimes chips too) and dutch apple with ice cream. Others swore by their minestrone soup, beef casserole, chicken à la king and crème caramel. Not a smart place, but pleasant, warm and friendly.

Jack's Place 12 York Rd, Battersea, SW11, tel 228 8519. Open noon–3pm Tue to Sun, and 6pm–11pm Tue to Sat. Licensed. Access, Visa. Jack King is a justifiably proud host and runs an informal, friendly restaurant decorated with memorabilia of all sorts. He serves excessively generous portions of plain, well cooked British fare such as home-made vegetable soup, gammon, steaks, Dover sole and vegetables. There is a no minimum charge policy and no obligation to eat more than one course. Outstanding set lunches.

Leek's Fish Bar 23 Lavender Hill, Clapham, SW11, tel 228 9460. Licensed. No credit cards. Open 5.30pm–10.45pm Mon to Sat. This is how I imagine a French fish and chip bar might look. Frying is done at the street end of a long bar, while steaming is done on the bar, the 20-odd tables are covered with waxed cloths and the walls are hung with fishy pictures. The fish is prepared at the back of the restaurant and brought freshly filleted into the restaurant. The batter for the deep-fried fish is light and crisp and the home-made fish cakes with tomato sauce are outstanding. There is a limited range of tasty, thoroughly British, puddings (a steamed pudding of the day; home-made ice cream and trifle). Cheap wines too.

Parsons 311 Fulham Rd, SW10, tel 352 0651. Open noon–12.30am Mon to Sat, and noon–midnight Sun. Licensed. Access, Amex, Diners Club, Visa. The attraction of this noisy, lively, dinner-style restaurant is its spaghetti. There is a choice of pesto, tomato or bolognese sauce, the dish is served with garlic bread and there are free second helpings. Otherwise, burgers, Tex-Mex specialities and US sandwiches.

Pizza On The Park 11–13 Knightsbridge, SW1, tel 235 5273. Open 8.30am–midnight daily (breakfast until 11.30am). Licensed. All credit cards. Together with Kettners and the Dean Street branch of Pizza Express (for both *see* The West End) these are my favourite branches of the successful and excellent chain. At all three branches, live jazz is an additional feature, and here, and at Kettners, the menu is more varied and more expensive. It remains good value, however, and their pizzas, available with a wide range of toppings (for vegetarians too), are excellent.

Pizzeria Castello 20 Walworth Rd, Elephant and Castle, SE1, tel 703 2556. Open noon–11pm Mon to Fri, and 5pm–11pm Sat. Licensed. Access, Visa. Word is out about the fabulously good pizzas made here and it is wise to book a table in advance. Standard range of Italian toppings, but generous and good quality ingredients. There is a guitarist most nights and waiting can be done in the downstairs wine bar.

Rebato's 169 South Lambeth Rd, SW8, tel 735 6388. Open noon–2.30pm Mon to Fri, 6pm–11.15pm Mon to Sat. Licensed. All credit cards. This is arguably the most authentic *tapas* bar in London and it gets very, very busy. At the rear is a restaurant (excellent value Spanish set meal) but the *tapas* – little spicy snacks such as *tortilla*, meat balls, sausage, stews and calamares served in terracotta dishes and costing around £2 each – are enjoyed either at the long bar or squeezed on to one of the few tables. It's noisy, and a great party place. Drink Spanish beer, wines and sherries.

South Kensington Pasta Bar 60 Old Brompton Rd, SW7, tel 584 4028; **Chelsea Pasta Bar** 330 Fulham Rd, SW10, tel 352 6912. Open noon–midnight daily. Licensed. Access. Two branches of a small chain offering a short menu that features several different types of pasta with a choice of tasty, home-made sauces. It's informal and relaxed with a no-bookings policy.

Stockpot 40 Panton St, Piccadilly Circus, SW1, tel 839 5142. Open 8am–11.30pm Mon to Sat, and noon–10pm Sun; 6 Basil St, Knightsbridge, SW3, tel 589 8627. Open 8am–10.45pm Mon to Sat, and noon–9.45pm Sun; 273 Kings Road, SW3, tel 823 3175. Open for breakfast 8am–11pm Mon to Sat and 11.30am–11.45pm daily. Licensed. No credit cards. For years, the Stockpot has been providing Londoners with outstanding value for money. The menu never changes and consists of international filler favourites such as spaghetti bolognese, lasagne, cannelloni, liver casserole, beef stroganoff, and cottage pie.

WEST LONDON

FAST, FUEL AND TAKEAWAY

It would be virtually impossible to spend more than £5 a head on food at these places; £3 is more realistic.

Acton Grill 17 High St, Acton, W3, tel 992 9139. Open 10am–9pm Mon to Sat. Licensed. No credit cards. Very popular café/grill where the set lunches are stunning value in the meat with two veg mode, but note that there is always a hot dish for vegetarians. Homely British puds to follow.

Blue Sky 106 Westbourne Grove, W2, tel 229 0777. Open 7.30am–10pm Mon to Sat. Licensed. No credit cards. Large café that is good on fry-ups, though the menu also encompasses international grills, pasta and bakes.

A. H. Cooke 48 Goldhawk Rd, W12, tel 743 7630. Open 11am–4pm Tue, Wed and Sat, until 2pm Thur, and until 5pm Fri. Hard by Shepherd's Bush market, Cooke's is the only pie and mash shop in the area. Queue at the bar and place your order for a meat pie, liquor (parsley sauce) and mash or perhaps jellied or stewed eels. As with all pie and mash shops, service is swift; you eat up and push off.

Costas Fish Restaurant 18 Hillgate St, W8, tel 727 4310. Open noon–2.30pm and 5.30pm–10.30pm Tue to Sat. Licensed. No credit cards. Small waiting lobby with a fryer and surprisingly large rear dining room. Eat in or carry out battered and deep-fried fish that is cooked to order, good fish roes and chunky chips. Rather good pineapple fritters or fresh *baklava* to finish.

The Galleon 35 Pembridge Rd, Notting Hill Gate, W11, tel 727 9620. Open 11.30am–10pm Mon to Fri, and until 8.30pm Sat. Not licensed, no corkage. No credit cards. Old fashioned dining rooms that have been going strong for 40-odd years. Huge portions of international stodge that is unbelievably cheap. The set lunch might include spaghetti bolognese, Vienna steak, a curry, or steak and kidney pie all served with a pile of vegetables. Stalwart British puds to follow.

Hearth Café at Earthworks 132 King St, Hammersmith, W6, tel 846 9357. Open 9.30am–6pm Mon to Wed, and 9.30am–10pm Thur to Sat. Not licensed, no corkage. No credit cards. Shambolic country-kitchen style vegetarian café at the rear of the excellent co-operatively run warehouse-style Earthworks health food shop. Unusual and interesting wholesome food and occasionally special evenings when the menu is devoted to a different country's vegetarian food. In the evening the mood is softened with candles.

Maids of Honour 288 Kew Rd, Richmond, tel 940 2752. Open 9.30am–1pm Mon, 10pm–5.30pm Tue to Fri, and 9am–5.30pm Sat. Licensed. No credit cards. Country-cottage style tea room that is also a bakery and cake shop and serves excellent meat and two veg style set lunches. Wonderful cream tea.

The Muffin Man 12 Wright's Lane, Kensington High St, W8, tel 937 6652. Open 8.15am–6.30pm Mon to Sat. Not licensed. No credit cards. If I lived or worked near here, I reckon I would be a regular. It's a tea-shoppe style place where they make all their sandwiches, cakes, savouries and snacks to order. They use top quality produce, maintain high standards and, not surprisingly, are very busy. Great for country-style breakfasts, light lunches and high tea.

Pizzaland 142 Kensington High St, W8, no phone. Open noon–11.30pm daily. Licensed. All credit cards. Quick and cheap lunches of a pizza slice, a dish of coleslaw, a jacket potato and garlic bread for £2.55.

Pizza Place 5 Lanark Place, W9, tel 289 4353. Open 11.30am–11pm daily. Licensed. Access, Visa. Good quality deep-pan pizzas made in sizes to suit lone diners and up to four people. Takeaway and local home delivery service.

Ravenscourt Park Teahouse Ravenscourt Park, W6, tel 748 9513. Open 10am–5pm Mon to Fri, and until 5.30pm Sat and Sun. Not licensed, no corkage. No credit cards. Delightful little teahouse located next to the bowling green and with views to the 'river'. Breakfast is served until 11am and there is a wholefood vegetarian menu with the occasional meat dish. Pre-baked dishes such as lasagne, moussaka and savoury flans are popular, but there are also unusual salads, fruit crumbles and cakes. Popular with young mums, especially at tea time.

EXOTIC

Some of the best and best-value meals in London are to be found at ethnic restaurants, most particularly at Indian, Chinese, Korean (for lunch), South East Asian, Middle East and Eastern Mediterranean and East European places. I have used an approximate price guideline, which refers to a decent meal for one including service but not cover or drink: £ = under £5; ££ = under £10.

A great selection of ethnic restaurants, with a full explanation of what to expect of each cuisine, can be found in *A Guide to London's Ethnic Restaurants*, Pan, £4.99.

Ajanta 12 Goldhawk Rd, W12, tel 743 5191. Open noon–2.30pm and 6pm–11.45pm daily. Licensed. All credit cards. One of the best neighbourhood Indian restaurants in West London and very popular with the (nearby) BBC. Terrific onion *bhajis*, good, freshly made *tandoori* and exceptional *Moghlai korma* dishes. Nice staff but queuing normal, even if you've booked a table. £–££

Baba Bhel Poori House 29 Porchester Rd, W2, tel 221 7502. Open noon–3pm and 6pm–10.45pm Tue to Sun. Licensed. Pretty little restaurant that serves excellent Indian vegetarian food. The house speciality is *thali*, the set meal, but their potato-stuffed pancake (*masala dosai*) is also recommended. £

Bedlington Café 24 Fauconberg Rd, W4, tel 994 1965. Open 6.45pm–10.30pm Mon to Sat. Not licensed. No credit cards. Small café run by a Thai family who serve exceptional and very cheap authentic spicy Thai food. Great *sate*, prawn and beef salad and fish curry; I can recommend everything, but the menu is getting longer and longer! Very friendly, informal and cheap. £–££

Dragon Inn 63 Westbourne Grove, W11, tel 792 9185. Open noon–11.30pm Mon to Sat, and until 11.15pm Sun. Licensed. All credit cards. Branch of the excellent Dragon Inn in Soho and serving the same superior *dim sum* and long menu of Cantonese food. Outstanding *congee*, the cheap and sustaining rice soup.

Elgin Lokanta 239 Elgin Ave, W9, tel 328 6400. Open noon–midnight daily. Licensed. All credit cards. Reliable Turkish kebab house serving generous portions of fresh and nicely prepared food. For a change from the kebabs, try their *sis baste*, a dish of marinated lamb served on a mound of rice with salad. ££

Ethiopia 2000 (formerly Blue Nile) 341a Harrow Rd, W9, tel 286 5129. Open 7pm–11.30pm daily. Licensed. Access, Visa. Delightful and very welcoming Ethiopian café/restaurant. Much of the food is vegetarian, cassorole-like and spicy, and is eaten either with the fingers or scooped up with a steamed millet pancake called *ingera*, although spoons and forks are provided. There are set menus for two. £–££

Hung Toa 54 Queensway, W2, tel 727 6017. Open noon–11pm daily.

Licensed. Access. Always packed because Hung Toa is famous for its barbecued pork and roast duck. Otherwise, it's a regular Cantonese restaurant, although it also serves notable noodle composite dishes. £–££

(New) Kam Tong 59 Queensway, W2, tel 229 6065. Open noon–11.15pm daily. Licensed. Amex. Comfortable but functional large Cantonese restaurant that rivals the Dragon Inn as the best place in the area for *dim sum* (served until 5.45pm). £

Khan's 13–15 Westbourne Grove, W2, tel 727 5420. Open noon–3pm and 6pm–midnight daily. Licensed. All credit cards. Huge, spartan Indian restaurant with a fast turnover and ludicrously low prices. Their *tandoori* chicken costs £1.80 for half a chicken, which must be the cheapest in London. £–££

Lowiczanka First floor, 238 King St, Hammersmith, W6, tel 741 3225. Open noon–3pm daily and 6pm–10.30pm Mon to Sat but closed Tue. Huge restaurant within a Polish cultural centre. Waitresses wear national dress and most customers are Polish. Ignore the bulk of the continental-style menu and choose from the Polish specialities such as superb potato dumplings, the hunter's stew called *bigos*, and pancakes stuffed with cream cheese for pudding. Watch out for the flavoured vodkas. The set lunch is a real bargain and within £; otherwise ££.

Manzala 24 Pembridge Rd, Notting Hill Gate, W11, tel 727 3062. Open 6.30am–11.30pm Mon to Fri, and 11.30am–11.30pm Sat and Sun. Highly recommended Turkish restaurant that serves a generous *mezze*. Of their main dishes, I particularly like *incik*, a huge knuckle of lamb cooked with rosemary and served with rice and vegetables, and *choban kavurama*, lamb stewed with onions, tomatoes and oregano. *Imam bayildi*, cold grilled aubergine stuffed with stewed onion, green peppers, tomatoes, parsley and garlic is a delicious appetiser. ££

Meson Dona Ana 37 Kensington Park Rd, W11, tel 243 0666. Open noon–3pm and 5.30pm–11pm Mon to Sat. Licensed. Access, Visa. Two-floor *tapas* bar offering a choice of over 40 different dishes. Great place to go in a group; the more of you there are, the more difficult it is to go outside our price limit. £–££

Micro-Kalamaras 66 Inverness Mews, W2, tel 727 5082. Open

7pm–11.30pm Mon to Sat. Not licensed. All credit cards. London's most authentic Greek restaurant with daily specials and a menu in Greek that must be explained. I particularly recommend the garlic and lemon-flavoured aubergine dip *melitzanosalata* and the deep fried pastries stuffed with feta cheese, oregano and mint called *tyropites* to start. Main dish choices are more difficult; everything is recommended! ££

Norma's Café 183 Acton Lane, W4, tel 994 1093. Open 6pm–10pm Mon to Sat. Not licensed. No credit cards. By day a greasy spoon café and by night a terrific Thai restaurant. Short menu and helpful family who explain the intricacies of their delicious, spicy food. £–££

Penang 41 Hereford Rd, W2, tel 229 2982. Open 6pm–11pm Mon to Sat, and 6pm–10.30pm Sun. Scruffy basement Malaysian restaurant where the food is delicious, generous and good value for money. Try their *sate*, shrimp omelette, lipstick chicken and the deep fried dumplings with a chilli dip. £–££

Phoenicia 11 Abingdon Rd, W8, tel 937 0120. Open noon–midnight daily. Licensed. All credit cards. Family-run Lebanese restaurant that provides a hot and cold buffet at lunch time (finished by 2.30pm) which is both excellent and excellent value – the perfect way to experiment with this spicy and exotic cuisine. The buffet changes daily, but is likely to include *hummus*, chicken wings and livers marinated in lemon and garlic and barbecued, spicy sausages, and a chopped salad with parsley and tomato called *tabbouleh*. Desserts are sugar water drenched pastries or pancakes stuffed with cream cheese and chopped pistachios. £–££ buffet lunch only

Raj Doot 291 King St, Hammersmith, W6, tel 748 7345. Open noon–2.30pm and 6pm–11.45pm daily. Licensed. All credit cards. In a part of King Street that is packed with Indian restaurants, this is the best. Utterly reliable (apparently the chef is the owner) and everything is recommended; my favourite dishes include onion *bhajis*, prawn *bhoona* with *puri*, Bombay *aloo*, *tarka dal*, chicken *tikka masala* and *pilau* rice. They also make an exceptional *kulfi* (carrot ice cream). Raj Doot is large, but frequently full. £–££

Saavas' Kebab House 7 Ladbroke Rd, W11, tel 727 9720. Open noon–2.45pm and 6pm–10.45pm Mon to Sat. Licensed. Visa. Welcoming, family-run, 30-year-old kebab house. The best meal is garlicky *hummus* with *pitta* bread followed by barbecued lamb with a salad. Huge portions and wonderful smells as the bar-becuing is done in the restaurant. Outside tables on a deep pavement in the summer. ££

Tsiakkos 5a Marylands Rd, W9, tel 286 7896. Open 5.30pm–11pm Mon to Sat. Licensed. No credit cards. Wonderful, home-style Greek Cypriot restaurant where the family make everyone feel welcome. Atmospheric and candlelit, it's the perfect location to share a generous *mezze*. Alternatively settle for their superb *kleftico* (lamb baked until it virtually falls off the bone) served with beans, cucumber and potato stew. £–££

Unity Unit 45, Thorpe Close, W10, tel 969 3603. Open noon–11pm Mon to Sat. Licensed. Access, Visa. Unity is a co-operative started by a self-help black project, Unity Association. They cook daily specials but most of the food is popular Guyanese and Jamaican dishes such as saltfish and ackee, *roti*, *callaloo* soup, as well as takeaway snacks and cakes. £–££

SOMEWHERE YOU CAN TAKE THE WIFE TO

This is a round-up of restaurants where paupers can dine in style knowing that the bill won't break the bank. They are chosen for their value for money and because they are ideal for special occasions.

The average price per head for a two- or three-course meal (including cover but not service or drinks) is £10 a head. Many offer set meals, which are mentioned at the end.

Geales 2 Farmer St, Notting Hil Gate, W8, tel 727 7969. Open noon–3pm and 6pm–midnight Tue to Sat. Licensed. Access. Ninety-five people can be seated at this tea-shoppe style fish restaurant that has been consistently popular since it opened in 1919. Short blackboard menu that features the day's fish, which are available in two sizes. My favourite meal is haddock or skate with their great chips, a slice of bread and butter and ketchup.

Pizza Express 137 Notting Hill Gate, W11, tel 229 6000; 26 Porchester Gardens, W2, tel 229 7784; and 252 Chiswick High Rd, W4, tel 747 0193. Open noon–midnight daily. Licensed. All credit cards. Smart, simple decors with black and white tiled floors, marble-topped tables, bentwood chairs and fast order pizzas cooked in big ovens within the restaurants. Always atmospheric, busy and good value. The best high street pizza chain that is rigorously policed to maintain standards.

Reginette 16 Garway Rd, W2, tel 229 0457. Open noon–3pm and 6.30pm–11.30pm daily. Licensed. Access. Visa. Inspired by Peter Ilic's restaurants The Lantern and Bridges (q.v.), the food is Frenchified international bistro fare and prices are fixed with all starters at one price (£1.95) and likewise for all mains (£4.65) and desserts. Interesting and sometimes wacky food combinations, but there's a good atmosphere and it's nice to know exactly what the bill will be.

ENTERTAINMENT

CULTURE

London's cultural scene is rich and varied and offers something for everyone. The London listing magazines *Time Out* and *City Limits* provide the most comprehensive guide to what's on, but borough information offices (*see* Accommodation, Which Part of Town, p.3) all publish broadsheets about cultural activities within their locality.

Also invaluable is **Artsline**, tel 388 2227, who give out information about clubs, cabaret, events and exhibitions between 10am and 5.30pm Monday to Friday. They will also give information over the phone that is helpful to disabled people (whether there are steps, easy-access loos and whether an escort is necessary). A free magazine called *Disability Arts in London* is available monthly to individuals from Greater London Arts, 5 Crowndale Rd, NW1; companies are charged £10 a year. The magazine is also a vehicle for airing grievances and for articles about all aspects of entertainment facilities for the disabled.

ARTS CENTRES, CULTURAL CENTRES AND INSTITUTES

These places offer a variety of cultural facilities and activities, many of which are free, and are open to anyone.

Barbican Centre Silk St, EC2, tel 638 4141, 24-hour recorded
  information 628 2295, cheap tickets 638 8891. Open 9am–11pm
  Mon to Sat, and noon–11pm Sun. The Barbican consists of eight
  levels devoted to culture and it is home to the Royal Shakespeare
  Company (RSC), who perform in the Barbican Theatre and Pit,
  and the London Symphony Orchestra (LSO), who perform in the
  Barbican Hall. There is also a cinema (*see* Cinema, p.163, for
  membership details), free foyer exhibitions and music, a lending,

music and children's library, a bookshop, gallery, sculpture court and, in summer, events beside the 'lake' on level 8. There are also various bars and restaurants. Guided tours set off at 12.15pm and 5.15pm Monday to Saturday.

Battersea Arts Centre 176 Lavender Hill, SW11, tel 223 6557 or 5063, box office 223 8423. Open 10am–6pm Mon and Tue, and (generally) 10am–10pm Wed to Sun; 6pm–11pm (café and bar); 10am–8pm Tue to Sun (bookshop). Membership for one year costs £10, concessionary membership £5, joint membership £15, which entitles members to half-price tickets, priority invitation to shows and 10 per cent discount in the bookshop. Associate membership costs £1 for six months and gives limited access to discounts available to full members. Regularly changing (usually free) exhibitions, theatre, cinema and adult education institute.

Camden Arts Centre Arkwright Rd, NW3, tel 435 2643. Open 10.30am–5.30pm Mon to Fri, and noon–6pm Sat and Sun (galleries); 9.30am–7.15pm during term time, and 9.30am–5.30pm daily (bookshop and art shop). Monthly changing, free exhibitions of contemporary, ethnic and right-on painting and photography, plus events and art courses. There's also a bookshop, art shop and café. Programme of events available.

Commonwealth Institute Kensington High St, W8, tel 603 4535. Open 10am–5pm Mon to Sat, and 2pm–5pm Sun. Free access to permanent exhibition that gives an insight into each of the Commonwealth countries. Also events, art and cultural exhibitions from artists all over the Commonwealth, plays by visiting theatre groups, films about life in Commonwealth countries, etc. Most events are free, but there are always concessionary rates for children and OAPs if they do charge. Café, book and crafts shop. Lavish what's on calendar of events available on request.

French Institute Queensberry Place, South Kensington, SW7, tel 589 6211. Open 9am–1pm Sept to June daily. Membership costs £25 a year, and £15 for students which gives reduced prices for events and free use of (essentially French written word) library. French courses, but also film club, theatre productions, exhibitions, concerts, library, video club, café and access to their noticeboard.

Goethe Institute (incorporating the **German Cultural Institute**) 50 Prince's Gate, SW7, tel 581 3344. Open 10am–6pm Mon to Thur (summer), and 10am–8pm Mon to Thur, noon–6pm, and 10am–6pm Sat (the rest of the year). Set up to promote German culture abroad, the Institute runs German language courses, has the largest comprehensive German library in London (25,000 books in the lending section on all aspects of German life and culture; reference, records and tapes, plus video cassettes with viewing facility), and also holds regularly changing free exhibitions of work by German artists and photographers, shows films and acts as an information point about German culture on show or in performance throughout London and the rest of the country. A leaflet of events is available on request. Film tickets (which have to be booked by post or in person) usually cost £1.

Institute of Contemporary Arts (ICA) The Mall, SW1, tel 930 3647. Open noon–8pm daily (galleries), noon–11pm (bar), and noon–9pm (restaurant). Day pass £1, annual membership £15, which gives access for two people. Concessions to children (free with an adult) OAPs and students (half price memberships). Very little is free at the ICA, a centre for lively contemporary exhibitions, talks, seminars, one-man shows, contemporary performing arts and cinema. A programme of events with prices is available to members. Bookshop also selling posters and postcards. *See also* Cinema, p.163.

The Italian Cultural Institute 39 Belgrave Sq, SW1, tel 235 1461. Open 9.30am–5pm during academic year. Membership £15 per year or £7 to students and teachers. Italian language courses, superb library, occasional artistic exhibitions and literary meetings. Everything is free and available to the general public but special events require membership.

Polish Cultural Institute 34 Portland Place, W1, tel 636 6032. Open 8.30am–4.30pm Mon to Fri. Free entrance to concerts, lectures, video showings and exhibitions. Catalogue of events available on request.

Riverside Studios Crisp Rd, W6, tel 748 3354. Open 10am–11pm daily; 1pm–8pm (gallery); 1pm–8pm (bookshop); 11am–8pm (café). Membership: Friends Scheme £8 for individuals and £12 for two, which gives concessionary rates for some events. Free exhibitions, lively theatre venue, cinema, bookshop, café and bar. Saturday morning events for children. *See also* Dance, p.162.

South Bank Centre Belvedere Rd, Waterloo, SE1, tel 928 3002, student standby and cheap ticket enquiries 633 0932. Open 10am–10pm daily. The biggest arts centre in Western Europe which incorporates, in one building, the Royal Festival Hall, Queen Elizabeth Hall, Purcell Room and Haywood Gallery. Leaflets of what's going on can be picked up at the South Bank but 12 advance monthly diaries are available at £4 (from Mailing List Dept, RFH, SE1 8XX). Various bars and food bars (none particularly recommended).

The Foyer of the RFH has its own range of activities which includes exhibitions, a poetry library, a Sherratt & Hughes bookshop (open 11am–10pm daily), and the Festival Records and Festival Music shop (open 11am–10.30pm). Every day between 12.30pm and 2pm there is a live musical performance (free; programme available) and between 5.15pm and 6.45pm on Fridays there is a jazz session. Guided tours of the RFH, which include a visit backstage, begin at 12.45pm and 5.30pm daily and cost £1.

The Centre also incorporates the **National Film Theatre (NFT)** South Bank, SE1, tel 928 3232. Various levels of membership: weekly 90p, students £7.50, full £10.25 and £25, when it includes bi-annual *Sight and Sound* magazine. Tickets £3.25, £3 for standby and £2 for OAPs, UB40s and registered disabled. Over 2000 films a year are shown in two cinemas. The programme is available on request, but automatic to members. Film bookshop, café and bar. *See also* Cinema, p.163.

The National Theatre (NT), South Bank, SE1, tel 633 0880; 24-hour recorded booking information 928 8126 and cheap tickets 240 7200. The Olivier, Lyttelton and Cottesloe theatres all have several productions running concurrently in repertory.

Spanish Institute 102 Eaton Sq, SW1, tel 235 1484. Open 10am–1pm, 2.30pm–6pm Mon to Thur, and 9.30am–1pm, 2.30pm–5.30pm during academic year. Membership £12 a year, which entitles members to free entry to films, exhibitions and lectures. The library is open to the general public.

Watermans Arts Centre 40 High St, Brentford, tel 847 5651. Open 11am–9pm daily (bar and restaurant), box office noon–7pm Mon to Sat and 2pm–7pm Sun. Very detailed programme of events is published three weeks in advance and is free on request. Membership £11, joint £16, life £50, OAPs, UB40 holders and students free. Membership entitles you to £1 off theatre and cinema tickets (Mon to Thur), a monthly programme and newsletter, invitations to opening nights in the gallery, and reciprocal membership with selected UK arts centres. Overlooking the Thames at Kew, this is a lively, friendly and locally-orientated arts centre for cinema, visual and performing arts, music, parties, children's activities and irregular one-off festivals and events. There is also a bar and restaurant.

LIBRARIES

Access to any library's reading room for study or looking at their books is available to anyone. They are a good place to find out about local facilities and cultural attractions, as well as local events and information about local history. They also keep local and daily papers.

To join a library and borrow books (often tapes, records and videos too) it is necessary to be resident in that borough or to produce a membership card from another borough. All local libraries are listed together in the telephone directory under libraries and membership is free. The following specialized reference libraries (no books can be removed) are also free. *See also* Museums.

The British Library (within The British Museum) Great Russell St, WC1, tel 636 1555; recorded information 580 1788. Open 10am–5pm Mon to Sat, and 2.30pm–6pm Sun. £1 donation admission requested. A new home for this library that keeps microfilmed copies of every magazine and book published (thus adding an average two miles of new books each year) is currently being built in King's Cross. This, the ultimate reference library, has two of the four Magna Cartas, Shakespeare's first folio, the Chinese Diamond Sutra dated AD 868 and the first recorded example of printing. Well researched exhibitions (also free) are a regular feature.

Chelsea Library King's Rd, SW3, tel 352 6056. Open 10am–5pm Mon to Sat, and until 1pm Wed. Particularly impressive collection of botanical books and bookplates, local history (bohemian and artistic) and costume and fashion.

Guildhall Reference Library Aldermanbury, EC2, tel 606 3030. Open 9.30am–5pm Mon to Sat. This is the main reference library for London, its history and cartography. The ground floor is devoted to books, the first floor to maps and a stunning collection of prints and manuscripts.

Holborn and Camden Reference Library 32–38 Theobald's Rd, WC1, tel 405 2706. Open 9.30am–8pm Mon and Thur, 9.30am–6pm Tue, and 9.30am–5pm Fri and Sat. In the heart of London's legal land, this is particularly good for books on law and business.

The Local History Library Central Library, Borough of Tower Hamlets, Bancroft Rd, E1, tel 980 4366. Open 9am–8pm Mon, Tue, Thur and Fri, and 9am–5pm Wed and Sat. This reference library (upstairs) is a good source of information about Cockney London, immigrants from Huguenots to Bengalis, and gives special attention to the rejuvenation of Docklands. Maps and photographs augment the extensive collection of books and manuscripts.

The London Library 14 St James's Square, SW1, tel 930 7705. Open 9.30am–5.30pm Mon to Sat, and until 7.30pm Sat. It costs £75 a year for full membership to this delightful library and elegant, club-style reading room. £10 a month gives access to the reference material, which, in my book, is worth every penny. The library was founded in 1841 by the Scottish historian Thomas Carlyle who was apparently fed up with the slow service at The British Museum. It is particularly good on London and has over a million old and new books. It also subscribes to countless specialist magazines.

Westminster Central Reference Library St Martin's St, WC2, tel 798 2034. Open 10am–7pm Mon to Fri, and 10am–5pm Sat. Excellent arts library, but most notable for its collection of telephone directories from most countries.

FESTIVALS

Annual Dance Umbrella Festival for contemporary dance is run by Riverside Studios. Full details from Crisp Rd, W6, tel 741 4040. Takes place during October and November.

Annual Festival of Street Entertainers Golden Sq, Soho, W1, tel 287 0907. Takes place in Golden Square and Carnaby Street throughout the day and evening during the third or fourth weekend in July. Music, dance, comedy, theatre, magicians, acrobats and performing artists from all over the world culminating in awards for the best within each category.

Camden Festival including **Jazz Week**. Celebration of the arts which takes place at venues throughout Camden (that includes Covent Garden) during March and April. Full information from 278 4444.

Chinese New Year This falls somewhere between 21 Jan and 19 Feb and is generally celebrated throughout Soho's Chinatown on the first Sunday of February. Lion dance and procession, fireworks and special feasts served at the restaurants.

City of London Festival Non-stop events throughout the City, during July, often in City livery halls and other buildings not normally open to the public. Full details from the City of London Information Centre, tel 606 3030, or the City Arts Trust, tel 377 0540.

Clerkenwell Festival Street entertainment, exhibitions, concerts and events in various venues throughout historic Clerkenwell for ten days during July. Details from the Festival Organizer, tel 354 7127.

East End Festival Celebration of locally-bred talent from mid-March for three weeks: music, dance, theatre and more. Details from Arts Offices, tel 790 1818.

London Film Festival Hosted by the NFT (*see* p.146) during 10–26 November. Programme and ticket information 928 3232.

London International Festival of Theatre (LIFT) Takes place every other year during July and August at various venues throughout London. Performances from companies from all around the world. Full details from LIFT, 44 Earlham St, WC2, tel 836 7433.

London International Mime Festival Performances at arts centres and fringe theatre venues around town featuring mime artists from all over the world. Takes place during January. Full details published in *Time Out* and *City Limits*, but also available from London Tourist Board Information Centres (*see* Help and Advice, p.5).

Notting Hill Carnival Caribbean carnival with steel bands, floats, processions, food stalls, dancing and, hopefully, no violence, centred around Portobello Road and throughout Notting Hill Gate. Takes place over the three days of the August Bank Holiday weekend. Full details from Carnival and Arts Committee, tel 960 5266.

Summer in the City Family-orientated festival organized by The Barbican Centre. Takes place during the first week of August. Full details from The Barbican Centre, tel 638 8891.

MUSIC

CONCERTS

Paupers do rather well when it comes to free concerts. There's a lunchtime concert that's different every day in the Foyer of the Royal Festival Hall (*see* Arts Centres, p.146, for full details), lunchtime concerts at St James's Church, Piccadilly (donation appreciated) and also at many City churches (listed below), plus, in the two weeks before Christmas, there are carol singers in Trafalgar Square and Christmas Oratorios in many churches. By booking in advance it is also possible to attend a concert being performed for a radio recording (see below).

Numerous societies exist to encourage enthusiasts; **The National Federation of Music Societies**, Francis House, Francis St, SW1, tel 828 7320, keep a catalogue of 200 of them, but **The Society for the Promotion of New Music**, 10 Stratford Pl, W1, tel 491 8111, is the source of all information about new classical music. They also publish a London events programme.

Also consult Festivals, p.149, which gives contact numbers for information about many free events throughout the year.

CHURCH VENUES

Events in the City of London lists many concerts and is available free from London Tourist Offices and from the City of London Information Centre, St Paul's Churchyard, EC4, tel 606 3030. For other locations contact the various borough information offices listed on p.3.

St Anne and St Agnes Church Gresham St, EC2, tel 606 4986.
St Bartholomew-the-Great West Smithfield, EC1, tel 606 5171.
St Clement Danes Strand, WC2, tel 242 8282.
St James's Church Piccadilly, W1, tel 734 4511.
St John's Smith Square, SW1, tel 222 1061.
St Giles Cripplegate Fore St, Barbican, EC2.
St Martin-in-the-Fields Trafalgar Sq, WC2, tel 839 1930.
St Martin-within-Ludgate 40a Ludgate Hill, EC4.
St Michael's Cornhill EC4, tel 626 8841.
St Paul's Cathedral, Ludgate Hill, EC2, tel 248 2705.

RECORDED CONCERTS

Apply for tickets for concerts being recorded for broadcast on Radio 3, the station devoted to classical music. Ticket Unit, BBC Broadcasting House, Portland Place, W1, tel 580 4468.

RESTAURANTS WITH LIVE CLASSICAL MUSIC

Chelsea Classic Brasserie 500 King's Rd, SW3, tel 352 5901. Live and recorded classical music and a menu of French brasserie fare. £10–£15.
Crotchets Chamber Music Club 157 Denmark Hill, SE5, tel 737 4361. Run by a musical family who provide a set dinner followed by a recital performed by a group of young musicians. Takes place once a month September to May. Advance booking is essential. £15–£18 inclusive.
Terrazza Est 109 Fleet St, EC4, tel 353 2680. Dine on spaghetti (stick to set meals for best value) to the accompaniment of opera. £10–£15.

MUSIC COLLEGES

All the London music colleges hold concerts of classical music and opera during term time; full details from the colleges.

Guildhall School of Music and Drama at the Barbican, tel 628 2571.

Lewisham Academy of Music 77 Watson St, Deptford, SE8, tel 691 0307.

The London College of Music 47 Gt Marlborough St, W1, tel 437 6120.

Queen Alexandra's House Bremner Rd, SW7, tel 589 4053.

Royal Academy of Music Marylebone Rd, NW1, tel 935 5461.

Royal College of Music Prince Consort Rd, SW7, tel 589 3643.

HISTORIC HOUSES

Concerts set inside or, in the summer, in the gardens of London's historic houses are memorable occasions and ticket prices are modest. Details of forthcoming events on request, but advance booking is essential.

Kenwood House Hampstead Lane, NW3, tel 379 4444.

Lauderdale House 12 Holland Park Rd, W14, tel 602 2316.

Waterlow Park Highgate Hill, N6, tel enquiries to Camden Arts 278 4444.

JAZZ

London's jazz scene is dominated by Ronnie Scott's Club (47 Frith St, Soho, W1, tel 439 0747), which is run by a jazz musician for jazz enthusiasts. It is not for paupers (tickets from £10) and only students get concessionary rates.

Peter Boizot, the founder of the 25-year-old Pizza Express chain, is also a jazz enthusiast and top artists appear at Pizza on the Park (*see below* under restaurants), less famous musicians at the Dean St branch of Pizza Express and at Kettners. Boizot also publishes *Jazz Express*, which includes an extensive what's on guide to his and all main London venues, plus reviews of performances, records and gossip.

Theoretically the magazine costs £1, but I've only ever seen it lying around at Kettners (29 Romilly St, W1, tel 437 6437). The most comprehensive listing of jazz events is in *City Limits*.

Free jazz can be heard between 5.15pm and 6.45pm in the Foyer of the South Bank Centre (Commuter Jazz) and jazz musicians often feature on the daily list of live turns at lunchtime (12.30pm–2pm). There is often live jazz performed in the Piazza, Covent Garden.

Jazz Restaurants, Pubs, Clubs and Wine Bars

Restaurants make good locations for jazz and many of the places here double-up as clubs with separate jazz rooms. In most cases there is an admission charge.

Top venues

Bass Clef 35 Coronet St, EC1, tel 729 2476. Music from 8.45pm Tue to Fri and Sun, and from 9.30pm Sat. Admission from £4, but free on Tue. Top jazz venue for famous as well as aspiring musicians. Large venue that spills into adjoining bar. The restaurant is separate and serves okay bistro-style cosmopolitan fare between 8pm and midnight for about £10 a head.

Jazz Café 56 Newington Green, N16, tel 359 4936. Music from 9pm Mon to Sat, and from 8.30pm Sun. Admission (after 7pm) £1–£3, but half price for students and UB40 holders. Vegetarian food (about £8 a head) served at tables ranged back from the stage (they can be booked).

Bull's Head 373 Lonsdale Rd, Barnes, SW13, tel 876 5241. 8.30am–11pm Mon to Sat. London's top jazz pub with performances from a wide range of established and aspiring artistes.

Pizza Express 10 Dean St, W1, tel 437 9595. Open for music 8.30pm–1am Tue to Sun. Admission £4–£7 to jazz cellar, which is only accessible to people who eat their (great) pizzas.

Pizza on the Park 11 Knightbridge, Hyde Park Corner, SW1, tel 235 5550. Open 7.30pm–2am daily; music from 9.15pm Tue to Sat. Admission £4–£10 for huge downstairs jazz room with its own (Pizza Express) pizza restaurant.

Others

Archduke Wine Bar Concert Hall Approach, South Bank, SE1, tel 928 9370. Open 11am–11pm Mon to Sat. Menu of sausages every which way and live jazz combo Monday to Saturday.

HQ West Yard, Camden Lock, Camden High St, NW1, tel 485 6044. What's on catalogue on request but jazz from 8.30am Thursday to Saturday and from noon Sunday. Ambitious menu of pricey French food; from £15 a head.

Pizza Express 94 Golders Green Rd, NW11, tel 455 9556. Open noon–midnight daily. Modern jazz, free to diners on Tuesday nights.

La Salle à Manger 153 Battersea Park Rd, SW8, tel 720 4457. Dine on French food (around £15 a head) and get free jazz Tuesday to Saturday.

606 Club 90 Lots Rd, SW10, tel 352 5953. Music 9.30pm–2.30am Mon to Sat, 8.30pm–midnight Sun. Long established musicians' club in a tiny basement. Two sessions a night and regular jamming from the audience. Food is cheap and filling; around £4 for shepherd's pie.

Vortex Jazz Bar 139 Stoke Newington Church St, N16, tel 254 6516. Great venue, good jazz every night.

FOLK

Cecil Sharp House is the obvious starting point for anyone interested in folk music. Apart from holding events and concerts throughout the week, it's staffed and attended by enthusiasts. Traditionally, folk music is informal, pub entertainment. *Time Out* and *City Limits* both list week-by-week events, but the following pubs and clubs (many of which are in pubs) are regular venues.

Clubs and Venues

Events at the following venues are intermittent, details of forthcoming performances are available on request.

Cecil Sharp House 2 Regent's Park Rd, NW1, tel 485 2206. Open 9.30am–5.30pm Mon to Wed and Fri, and 9.30am–5.30pm,

7.30pm–11pm Sat. Music from 7.30pm Sat. Admission from £2–£3.50.

Battersea Folk Club at The Plough, St John's Hill, SW11, tel 874 6637.

Beckenham and Croydon Folk Club Perth Rd, Beckenham, tel 304 0398.

Brent Irish Cultural Club 72 Salisbury Rd, NW6, tel 625 9585.

Clapham Folk and Blues Club Railway Tavern, 18 Clapham High St, SW4, tel 737 0107.

Dartford Folk Club Railway Hotel, Dartford, tel 854 2400.

Islington Folk Club The George, 57 Liverpool Rd, N1, tel 607 0710.

Pubs

Bull and Gate 389 Kentish Town Rd, NW5, tel 485 5358.

Dublin Castle 94 Parkway, NW1, tel 485 1773.

Half Moon 93 Lower Richmond Rd, Putney, SW15, tel 788 2387.

Mean Fiddler 24 Harlesden High St, NW10, tel 961 5490.

Hare and Hounds 181 Upper St, N1, tel 226 2992.

Power Haus (previously the Pied Bull) 1 Liverpool Rd, N1, tel 837 3218.

Sir George Robey 240 Seven Sisters Rd, N4, tel 263 4581.

Spotted Dog 35 High Rd, Willesden, NW10, tel 459 2220.

ROCK

Over 800 bands play live in London every week in a variety of venues that are as diverse as outside at Covent Garden's Piazza, in pubs or private clubs and, in concert-style, at various-sized arenas and stadia. Performers are equally diverse and most venues are associated with particular types of artistes, be they young-hopefuls, established international stars or rarified specialist bands. The *Independent* and *Guardian* give good selective listings of what's up and coming, but the hippest, most objective and comprehensive rock, reggae, blues and soul listing is in *Time Out*.

Also worth checking out is Madame Tussaud's **Rock Circus**, at the London Pavilion, Piccadilly Circus, W1, which is an extraordinary show that celebrates the history of rock 'n' roll. Admission is a pricey

£4.20 for adults, £3.15 for children; the cheapest deal is for two adults and two children at £11.60 and pays for a video show with lots of film footage and waxworks and then a stunning audio, moving robotic 'live' show from some of rock's legends. Incidentally, each figure (including a great Janis Joplin, Bowie and Dylan, etc) cost £100,000 to make.

For a 'behind-the-scenes' view of London's music scene, join the **Rock Tour of London** (Rock Tours Ltd, 40 Dean St, W1, tel 734 0227 for concessionary group bookings). Tours operate from a special bus stop in Regent Street opposite the Café Royal and leave at 10.45am and 2.15pm Tuesday to Sunday and take approximately two hours. Aided by a commentary and video, the tour traces the history of rock 'n' roll in terms of studios, etc, around London. £7.50 per person.

Some of the Best Venues

See also Where To Boogie (p.173), Festivals (p.149) and Jazz (p.152).

Academy Brixton 211 Stockwell Rd, SW9, tel 326 1022. Open 7pm–11pm daily, club night until 3am every other Sat. Admission from £6. Around 4,000 people can be accommodated at this top venue, which is particularly known for promoting top reggae names as well as top international stars.

Africa Centre 38 King St, Covent Garden, WC2, tel 836 1973. Open 9pm–2am Thur, and 9pm–3am Fri. African cultural centre with various large rooms for events. Top bands and plenty of space for dancing.

Astoria 157 Charing Cross Rd, WC2, tel 434 0403. Open 7.30am–3.30pm Mon to Thur, and 10pm–3.30am Fri and Sat. Admission from £4. Large theatre with a big dance floor and upstairs seating; good on R and B but also on the circuit for top African bands.

Dingwalls Camden Lock, NW1, tel 267 4967. Open 8pm–2am Mon to Wed, 10pm–3am Thur and Fri, 12.30pm–4pm and 10pm–3am Sat, and 12.30pm–5pm and 8pm–11.30pm Sun. Admission from £1.50 depending on artiste.

Gossips 69 Dean St, W1, tel 434 4480. Open 10pm–3.30am Mon to Sat, music from 12.30am Mon and Thur. Admission £5. Steamy basement club that's a top spot for new hot acts. Note the opening hours.

100 Club 100 Oxford St, W1, tel 636 0933. Open 7.45pm–1am Mon to Sat, and 7.45pm–11.30pm Sun. Admission from £3 depending on artiste. One of London's most famous and enduring clubs. There's generally a queue, and it's always hot, sweaty and difficult to see the stage.

London Arena 4 Lime Harbour, E14, tel 538 1212. Open from 7.30pm. Admission from £10. New venue with a 12,000 seating capacity that is geared to attract top acts.

Marquee 105 Charing Cross Rd, WC2, tel 437 6603. Open 7pm–11pm daily. Legendary, 30-year-old live music club that still attracts top names.

Mean Fiddler 24 Harlesden High St, NW10, tel 961 5490. Open 8pm–2am Mon to Sat, and noon–3pm and 8pm–1am Sun. Admission from £3. Originally a folk venue, it now leans towards blues and rock bands, though C&W acts still perform in the smaller Acoustic Room.

Rock Garden 6–7 The Piazza/James St, Covent Garden, WC2, tel 240 3961. Open 7.30pm–3am Mon to Sat, and 8pm–midnight Sun, music from 8pm daily; meals served noon–midnight Mon to Thur, and noon–1am Fri and Sat. Admission from £4. A mecca for tourists because of its location and always busy.

Town and Country Club 9–17 Highgate Rd, Kentish Town, NW5, tel 284 0303. Open 7pm–11pm Mon to Thur and Sat, and until 2am Fri. Admission from £6. North London's top venue and increasingly the most popular club in town for big bands of all types. It's a vast place with plenty of room for dancing, mooching around and drinking. Seating is on a tier system, so there are good views for everyone.

THEATRE

London's theatrical scene divides between the West End, the companies who are government subsidized (Royal Court, National Theatre at the South Bank and Royal Shakespeare Company at the Barbican), and the fringe.

The cheapest way to get tickets for West End theatres is to attend matinées or previews, which run for a week before the show officially opens. It is also worth checking with individual theatres for standby discount tickets on seats not sold. **The Society of West End Theatres (SWET)** Bedford Chambers, Covent Garden, WC2, tel 836 0971 will send a list of theatres on their standby system. They also run a ticket booth in Leicester Square, where, between noon and 2.30pm, they sell same-day matinée tickets at a nominal £1 (or slightly more) and, from 2.30pm to 6.30pm, tickets for that evening.

The cheapest West End theatre seats are £5 ('in the gods') but, with advance warning, it's possible to get discounted seats if you're a student, UB40 holder, OAP or in a large group. SWET also publish the fortnightly *London Theatre Guide*, which is available free from London Tourist Board centres (*see* p.5), in theatres and libraries and on subscription from SWET.

Another useful organization is the **Theatre Advice Bureau (TAB)**, 10a The Avenue, Hatch End, Middx, tel 421 2470. They will send enquirers a detailed questionnaire about their theatrical interests and then make up a special, personal TAB pack.

To find out more about the history of London's theatres, join a **London Theatre Walk**, starting from the Theatre Museum, Russell St, WC2, tel 839 2498. Various walks start out at 10.30am on Wednesdays and 2pm on Sundays. Similarly, **Stage by Stage**, 156 Shaftesbury Ave, WC1, tel 359 5822, organize tours around various West End theatres which start at 11am, last around an hour, and cost £5.

FRINGE

Alternative theatre, which blossomed in the mid-60s, has become an important outlet for new talent and performances often transfer to the West End. Known as Fringe Theatre, it has its own circuit of theatres and theatre clubs (*see also* Arts Centres, p.143) but many performances take place in small, uncomfortable venues ('theatre upstairs'), which often lack a stage, so the actors can be perilously close to the audience. Ticket prices start at around £3.50.

If you're interested in this kind of theatre, you should contact **The Fringe Theatre Box Office**, Duke of York's Theatre, St Martin's Lane, WC2, tel 379 6002, open 10am–6pm Mon to Sat, who will advise on shows and book tickets (they charge 50p per booking), and the **Pub Theatre Network**, 168 Battersea Park Rd, SW11, tel 622 4553, who advise on what's on where.

TOP VENUES

Almeida Theatre Almeida St, N1, tel 359 4404. Membership £3 per year.

Boulevard Theatre Walkers Court, off Peter St, W1, tel 437 2661.

Bush Theatre upstairs at The Bush pub, Shepherd's Bush Green, W12, tel 743 3388. Membership 50p per year.

Canal Café Theatre The Bridge House, Delamere Ter, Little Venice, W2, tel 289 6054.

Corner Theatre at Hen and Chickens pub, Highbury Corner, N1, tel 226 3724.

Donmar Warehouse 41 Earlham St, Covent Garden, WC2, tel 240 8230.

Drill Hall Chenies St, WC1, tel 637 8270.

Finborough upstairs at Finborough Arms, Finborough Rd, SW10, tel 373 3842.

Gate Theatre upstairs at Prince Albert pub, 11 Pembridge Rd, W11, tel 229 0706. Membership £1 per year.

Hackney Empire 291 Mare St, E8, tel 985 2424.

Half Moon Theatre 213 Mile End Rd, E1, tel 790 4000.

Hampstead Theatre Club Swiss Cottage Centre, Avenue Rd, NW3, tel 722 9301. Membership £2.50 per year.

ICA Theatre The Mall, SW1, tel 930 3647. Membership 75p per day, £15 per year, students £7.50.

King's Head 115 Upper St, N1, tel 226 1916. Membership 50p per year.

Latchmere Theatre 503 Battersea Park, SW11, tel 228 2620.

Lilian Baylis Sadler's Wells, Arlington Way, off Rosebery Ave, EC1, tel 278 8916.

London Bubble Central Park, High Street South, E6, tel 237 4434.

Oval House 54 Kennington Oval, SE11, tel 582 7680.

Riverside Studios Crisp Rd, W6, tel 748 3354.

Tabard 2 Bath Rd, Turnham Green, W4, tel 995 6035.

Theatre Royal Stratford East Gerry Raffles Sq, E15, tel 534 0310.

Tricycle Theatre 269 Kilburn High Rd, NW6, tel 328 1000.
Young Vic 66 The Cut, SE1, tel 928 6363.

STREET THEATRE

Street theatre thrives in the summer and there are performances every day by buskers, clowns, jugglers and magicians, as well as by theatre groups in Covent Garden's Piazza. Another popular venue is the Courtyard of St Martin-in-the-Fields, off Trafalgar Square, WC2, tel 278 0907. Details of events taking place throughout London during the summer are available from **The Soho Street Theatre**, Carnaby St, W1, tel 278 0907.

COMEDY AND REVIEW

Alternative comedy and review, which has been popularized by Ben Elton, Alexei Sayle, Dawn French, Joan Collins Fan Club and others is the hottest ticket in town. While there are set venues that attract a hard core of regular performers, most shows go on a circuit and appear at different venues under a corporate name such as The Chuckle Club, Jongleurs and Mousetrap Cabaret. The price of entrance depends on the venue, but few places charge more than £3 for a show that usually starts at 8pm and lasts a couple of hours.

The Stir Fry Club, who have a show designed to promote new acts, give free performances which alternate once a fortnight between **Chats Palace**, 42 Brooksby's Walk, E9, tel 986 6714, and **The Trolley Shop**, 28 Stamford Rd, N1, tel 241 0581.

Tickets are available (free) on the door, and in advance by post, for recordings of BBC radio comedy shows at the **Paris Studio**, Lower Regent St, SW1.

TOP VENUES

The Bedford Bedford Hill, SW12, tel 673 8904.
Canal Café Theatre The Bridge House, Delamere Ter, W2, tel 289 6054.

The Chair Theatre Kensington Park pub, 139 Ladbroke Grove, W11, tel 727 6798.
Comedy Store 28a Leicester Sq, WC2, tel 839 6665.
Corner Theatre Hen and Chickens, Highbury Corner, N1, tel 226 3724.
The Coronet 49 Lavender Gdns, SW11, tel 780 1151.
De Hems Macclesfield St, W1, tel 326 0953.
Donmar Warehouse Theatre 41 Earlham St, Covent Garden, WC2, tel 240 8230.
Gate Theatre Club Prince Albert, 11 Pembridge Rd, W11, tel 229 0706.
Horse and Groom 128 Gt Portland St, W1, tel 580 4726.
King's Head 2 Crouch End Hill, corner The Broadway, N8, tel 340 1028.
The Market Tavern 2 Essex Rd, N1, tel 800 2236.
Pembury Tavern 90 Amhurst Rd, E8, tel 624 5361.
The Plough 196 Clapham High St, SW4, tel 738 8763.
The Red Rose Club 129 Seven Sisters Rd, N7, tel 263 7265.
The Rose and Crown 199 Stoke Newington Church St, N1, tel 254 7497.
The Stag 15 Bressenden Place, SW1, tel 476 1672.
The Wheatsheaf 25 Rathbone Place, W1, tel 986 6861.
The White Hart 264 High St, W3, tel 673 8904.

DANCE

In London you can watch ballet, plus the finest contemporary and most outrageous experimental dance. Visiting foreign companies tend to perform at our leading venues: The London Coliseum, St Martin's Lane, WC2, tel 836 3161; Royal Opera House, Bow St, WC2, tel 240 1066; Sadler's Wells, Rosebery Ave, EC1, tel 278 8916; The South Bank Centre, SE1, tel 928 3191; and The Dominion Theatre, Tottenham Court Rd, W1, tel 580 9562. Advance booking is almost always essential at these places and cheapest tickets start at £4 ('in the gods'); occasionally, it is possible to get preview tickets. All publish calendars of performances.

The London Contemporary Dance School give performances during the summer at **The Place**, 17 Duke's Rd, WC1, tel 387 0031, while **Riverside Studios**, Crisp Rd, W6, tel 741 4040, co-ordinate the Annual Dance Umbrella Festival, which takes place during October and November and is a time to see some of the finest contemporary dance troupes.

There is little to choose between the coverage of all types of dance in the listings magazines *City Limits* and *Time Out* – both are good for advance warning of visiting troupes, for dance courses and odd one-off events. The following are good places for paupers to enjoy contemporary dance. (*See also* Arts Centres, p.143)

Ballet Rambert School Gordon House, 300 St Margaret's Rd, Twickenham, Middx, tel 891 0121.

The Bhavan Centre 4a Castletown Rd, W14, tel 381 3086.

Chisenhale Dance Space 64 Chisenhale Rd, E3, tel 981 6617.

Cockpit Theatre Gateforth St, NW8, tel 402 5081.

Interchange Studios Dalby St, Prince of Wales Rd, NW5, tel 267 9421.

Rosemary Branch Theatre Club 2 Shepperton Rd, N1, tel 359 3204.

CINEMA

On average, 200 films are shown every week in London cinemas. The blockbusters are first shown at the multi-screen West End Odeons, Empires and Cannons before going on general release. Despite the monopoly of the movie giants, London is peppered with independent cinemas and cinema clubs that show non-mainstream films at much cheaper ticket prices. Free films are shown at many of the cultural institutes (*see* p.143), main art galleries (*see* p.169) and at many museums (*see* p.164). Comprehensive listings of cinemas throughout London are published in *Time Out* and *City Limits*; they both do a useful Film A–Z, which is a quick way to find out if a particular film is on near you.

FILM CLUBS

Barbican Cinema Level 1, Barbican Centre, Silk St, EC2, tel 638 8891. Membership £2 per year, tickets £2. Specializes in French and Russian classics. What's On available.

Everyman Hollybush Vale, NW3, tel 435 1525. Membership 50p per year, tickets £3 and season ticket £25 (for ten tickets) available. Children's club. Premières, revivals and foreign language films.

ICA Cinema/ICA Cinématheque Nash House, The Mall, SW1, tel 930 3647. Membership £15 per year, £1 per day, tickets from £2.50. Children's Club. Ambitious policy to show the best of world cinema. Cinématheque, in a smaller cinema, shows animation, avant-garde films and organizes seasons of political films.

London Film-makers' Co-op 42 Gloucester Ave, NW1, tel 586 8516. Membership £2.50 per year, 30p per day. Tickets £2.50. The most avant-garde movie theatre in town, which specializes in underground, low-budget, rare and classic art movies.

National Film Theatre South Bank, SE1, tel 928 3232. Membership £10.25 per year, 40p a day, tickets £3.25. Run by the British Film Institute, they organize the London Film Festival, which takes place in November. The NFT show 2000 films every year. Subject, age and nationality of films is wide ranging and includes Hollywood musicals, old and new foreign classics, special previews of West End films and silent movies.

Ritzy Brixton Oval, Coldharbour Lane, SW2, tel 737 2121. Membership 50p per year, tickets £3. Well chosen mixture of films that includes new releases, documentaries, new British films, golden oldies and the best of European art movies.

Scala 275 Pentonville Rd, W1, tel 278 0051. Membership 50p per year, tickets £3. Daily changing programme that seems to favour horror, sci-fi, classics and obscure.

INDEPENDENT CINEMAS

Camden Plaza 211 Camden High St, NW1, tel 485 2443.
Chelsea Cinema King's Rd, SW3, tel 351 3742.
Gate Cinema Notting Hill Gate, W11, tel 727 4043.

Lumière St Martin's Lane, WC2, tel 836 0691.
Metro Rupert St, W1, tel 437 0757.
Minema 45 Knightsbridge, SW1, tel 235 4225.
Museum of London London Wall, EC2, tel 600 3699.
Phoenix High Rd, East Finchley, N2, tel 883 2233.
Renoir Brunswick Sq, WC1, tel 837 8404.
Rio Kingsland High St, Hackney, E8, tel 254 6677.
Screen On Baker Street 96 Baker St, NW1, tel 935 2772.
Screen On The Green Islington Green, Upper St, N1, tel 226 3520.
Screen On The Hill 230 Haverstock Hill, NW3, tel 435 3366.

MUSEUMS

There are hundreds of museums in London with collections of anything and everything. I found no exhaustive guide but London Tourist Board information centres (*see* p.5) publish various selective museum guides. Local borough information offices (*see* Accommodation: Which Part of Town, p.3) will supply details of museums in their locality.

THE BIG ONES

British Museum Gt Russell St, WC1, tel 636 1555. Open 10am–5pm Mon to Sat, and 2.30pm–6pm Sun. Admission free, but £1 donation requested. Special exhibitions are usually £2, with concessions to children, OAPs and UB40 holders. Enormous museum, founded in 1753, with fabulous collections of Western Asiatic, Egyptian, Greek and Roman antiquities; one of the best known being the Elgin Marbles.

Adjacent to the British Museum is the **British Library** (soon to be rehoused in Euston) where two of the four Magna Cartas (AD 1215) can be seen, also Shakespeare's first folio and the first dated example of the printed word.

Geological Museum Exhibition Rd, South Kensington, SW7, tel 938 8765. Open 10am–6pm Mon to Sat, and 1pm–6pm Sun. Admission £2 adults (joint entry with Natural History Museum) and concessions for children, OAPs and UB40 holders. Permanent

exhibitions include 'Britain Before Man', which provides an introduction to the geology of Britain, and 'The Story of the Earth', the
largest display of fundamental earth science in the world, which
relates the 5,000 million-year history of the planet from its cosmic
origins to the present-day world. Also extensive collections of gem
stones, fossils, a vibrating Earthquake Room, and an Apollo
moon-rock sample. Along with the Natural History Museum, it's
the museum most children (of all ages) never tire of visiting.

Imperial War Museum Lambeth Rd, SE1, tel 735 8922. Open
10am–6pm daily. Admission £2.50 adults, concessions for children, OAPs, students and UB40 holders, and free on Fri. Recently
redesigned and now incorporating very sophisticated techniques
that give visitors a total experience of what it was like during the
Blitz, in the trenches and during the Battle of the Atlantic. Stunning displays of tanks, fighter planes, submarines and guns, and an
impressive gallery of war artists as well as exhibits that will turn
your blood cold. There is great emphasis on educative information
and various themed packs are available. Archive films and lectures, well stocked shop and research facilities.

Museum of London 150 London Wall, EC2, tel 600 3699. Open
10am–6pm Tue to Sat, and 2pm–6pm Sun. Admission free.
Fascinating museum that charts London from pre-history to the
present day. There are lavish reconstructions of period pieces
such as a Victorian grocer's shop, a Roman room, as well as a
recreation of the horror of the Great Fire (1666) that devastated
the City.

National Maritime Museum Romney Rd, SE10, tel 858 4422.
Open 10am–6pm Mon to Sat, and 2pm–6pm Sun (Mar to Oct);
10am–5pm Mon to Sat and 2pm–5pm Sun (Nov to Feb). Admission £3, half price for all the usual concessionaries. The world's
largest collection of marine artefacts, including rooms full of
barges, models of famous ships, weapons, paintings and uniforms.
Admission also entitles visitors to walk up the hill to **The Royal
Observatory** (designed by Sir Christopher Wren) where you can
straddle the time zone.

Natural History Museum Cromwell Rd, SW7, tel 938 9123. Open
10am–6pm Mon to Sat, and 1pm–6pm Sun. Admission £2, half

price for usual concessionaries, family reductions and free between 4.30pm–6pm Mon to Fri, 5pm–6pm Sat and Sun, and all day on Bank Holidays. A fabulous exploration of evolution, including the famous tyrannosaurus rex dinosaur, but also wildlife, fish and fowl and a gallery of ecosystems which shows how they are being destroyed and why we should be concerned about their destruction.

Science Museum Exhibition Rd, SW7, tel 938 8111, recorded info 938 8123. Open 10am–6pm Mon to Sat, and 11am–6pm Sun. Admission £2 adults, half price for usual concessionaries. Very much a hands-on museum where you can measure your heartbeat, shake hands with yourself, work various exhibits and even star in your own video. Every aspect of science and technology is explained; a new addition is a nutrition gallery called Food For Thought.

Victoria and Albert Museum Cromwell Rd, SW7, tel 938 8411/8349 (exhibitions) and 938 8500 (recorded info). Open 10am–5.30pm Mon to Sat, and 2.30pm–5.50pm Sun. Admission free, but £2 donation requested. The V&A rivals the British Museum as my favourite place to while away a day. It covers over seven miles and houses famous collections of fine and applied art that illustrate artistic achievement (all around the world) from the 12th century. There's also a gallery devoted to fakes and a celebration of fashion called the Dress Collection.

SOME OF THE REST

Black Cultural Archives Museum 378 Coldharbour Lane, Brixton, SW9, tel 733 3044. Open 9.30am–3.30pm Mon to Fri. Admission free. Brand new museum devoted to exploring the connections and history of the Afro-Caribbean people with Britain, starting in the 15th century and going right up to the present day. Changing exhibitions include the work of contemporary artists, writers, composers and dancers.

Bethnal Green Museum of Childhood Cambridge Heath Rd, E2, tel 980 2415. Open 10am–6pm Mon to Thur and Sat, and 2.30pm–6pm Sun. Part of the V&A, which moved here in 1872.

Delightful, enchanting museum that houses a wondrous collection of dolls and dolls' houses, children's costumes, puppets, games and books and one of the most important collections of toys in Britain. Also 19th- and 20th-century wedding dresses and 19th-century European decorative arts.

Design Museum Butlers Wharf, SE1, tel 403 6933, 407 6261 for recorded info. Open 11.30am–6.30pm Tue to Sun. Admission £2, half price students, children under 15, OAPs and UB40 holders. A celebration of contemporary design classics, such as the Anglepoise lamp, the Sony Walkman, the Zippo lighter, Bauhaus chairs and Le Corbusier kettles. The **Boilerhouse**, a separate exhibition area, is home to temporary exhibitions. Conceived, designed and master-minded by Terence Conran, who founded Habitat and whose flagship is now the Conran Shop, situated within the stunningly restored Michelin Building on the Fulham Road, South Kensington.

Dickens House Museum 48 Doughty St, WC1, tel 405 2127. Open 10am–5pm Mon to Sat. Admission £1.50, students and OAPs £1, children 75p, family rate £3. The early home of Charles Dickens where he finished *Pickwick Papers* and wrote *Oliver Twist* and *Nicholas Nickleby*. See Dickens' pictures, furniture, personal relics, manuscripts and letters.

Freud Museum 20 Maresfield Gardens, NW3, tel 435 2002. Open noon–5pm Wed to Sun. Admission £2, concessions £1. Sigmund Freud's London home and working environment; exhibitions and videos show the life and work of Freud and his daughter Anna.

Geffrye Museum Kingsland Rd, E2, tel 739 8368. Open 10am–5pm Tue to Sat, and 2pm–5pm Sun. Admission free. Housed in a row of 18th-century almshouses, the Geffrye celebrates changes in domestic styles with a series of rooms reflecting different periods from the 1600s to the late 1930s. Also trade catalogues and interior design books of the periods, which make fascinating reading.

HMS Belfast Access to ship via Morgan's Lane, off Tooley St, SE1, tel 407 6434. Open 10am–6pm daily. Admission £3, children, students and OAPs £1.50. London's famous floating naval museum is moored in the Thames, opposite the Tower of London. Explore above and below deck and visit the gun turrets, bridge, galley, punishment cell, mess decks (where you can see the cat's hammock!), boiler and engine room.

Horniman Museum London Rd, SE23, tel 699 2339. Open 10.30am–6pm Mon to Sat, and 2pm–6pm Sun. Admission free. Founded by a 19th-century tea merchant who commissioned this beautiful art nouveau building to house his diverse collection of objects picked up on his world-wide travels. There is a natural history section, a celebration of life under canvas, thousands of tribal masks and objects as obscure as a Burmese Buddha, a Spanish Inquisition torture chair and an Egyptian mummy. There is also a nature trail in an adjacent park.

Museum of the Moving Image (MOMI) South Bank, SE1, tel 928 3232. Open 10am–8pm Mon to Sat, and 10am–6pm Sun. Admission £3.50 adults; £2.50 children, OAPs, students and UB40 holders; £10 family ticket. MOMI charts the story of film and television in 50 exhibition areas with working environments, film clips, posters, a mock-up foyer and numerous working exhibits. Allow plenty of time to get your money's worth.

Museum of Mankind 6 Burlington Gardens, W1, tel 437 2224. Open 10am–5pm Mon to Sat, and 2.30pm–6pm Sun. Admission free, £1 donation requested. The ethnographic department of the British Museum with such a hoard of exhibits that exhibitions are continually changing. Permanent exhibits include the stunningly beautiful Aztec turquoise mosaics and their famous exploration of the history and contemporary lifestyle of the Northern Canadian Indians.

National Postage Museum King Edward Building, King Edward St, EC1, tel 239 5420. Open 9.30am–4.30pm Mon to Thur, and 9.30am–4pm Fri. Admission free. One hundred and fifty years of postage stamp history from the Penny Black to the present day. Also Commonwealth and foreign stamps.

William Morris Gallery Lloyd Park, Forest Rd, E17, tel 527 5544. Open 10am–1pm and 2pm–5pm Tue to Sat, and 10am–noon and 2pm–5pm the first Sun of the month. Admission free. Textiles, wallpapers, ceramics, stained glass, carpets and furniture that traces the development of the great designer (painter, poet and social reformer) William Morris. Also work by fellow Pre-Raphaelites and followers of the Arts and Crafts Movement.

GALLERIES

There are 600-odd art galleries in London. They fall into four major groups; those that are funded through the Arts Council, those that are funded through local and government grants, or commercial sponsorship, or are privately owned collections. The top commercial galleries are centred around Cork Street, Mayfair, whereas the newer, fringe studio galleries, often run by artists, are dotted all over the place – anywhere, in fact, where there are large spaces with low rents, with the Portobello Road area of Notting Hill Gate, Smithfield and Clerkenwell and the East End being favourite.

With very few exceptions, admission is free, but there is usually a £2–£4 charge for visiting exhibitions. Some people find it intimidating to visit the commercial galleries. Don't be, just remember that they take at least 50 per cent of the price of every picture hanging on their walls.

Every Sunday, amateur artists hang their work on the railings of Hyde Park, Bayswater Road. This is not necessarily the source of bargain works by undiscovered artists, but it is an amusing way of spending a few hours and, who knows, you could pick up something special.

A comprehensive information service about London art galleries is provided by **Artsline**, 625 5666, and an excellent, clear and well designed map with a listing of new exhibitions of contemporary art is published bi-monthly by **NECA** (New Exhibitions of Contemporary Art), 152 Narrow St, E14, which can be picked up at all galleries.

MAJOR COLLECTIONS AND PUBLIC GALLERIES

Barbican Art Gallery Level 8, Silk St, EC2, tel 638 4141. Open 11am–7pm Fri and Sat, noon–6pm Sun and Bank Holidays. Two floors devoted to visiting exhibitions of thematic and international contemporary and historical paintings, often linked to other activities on at the Barbican. For example, notable recent shows include the work of Gwen John and 100 Years of Russian and Soviet Art.

Courtauld Institute Galleries Woburn Sq, WC1, tel 580 1015. Open 10am–5pm Mon to Sat, and 2pm–5pm Sun. Admission £1.50, under 16s, students and OAPs 50p. The whole collection is due to move to **Somerset House**, The Strand, WC2, tel 873 2782 some time this year, so you should ring before visiting. The collection was amassed by textile baron Samuel Courtauld and is famous for its stunning collection of French post-Impressionists (Gauguin, Van Gogh, Cézanne and others) but also Old Masters and baroque furniture.

Hayward Gallery South Bank, SE1, tel 928 3144. Open 10am–8pm Mon to Wed, 10am–6pm Thur to Sat, and noon–6pm Sun. Admission £4, but £1.50 all day Mon and 6pm–8pm Tue and Wed, £2 students, OAPs and UB40 holders. Large gallery within the concrete jungle of the South Bank. Popular venue for retrospectives (Lucian Freud, Andy Warhol) but also for large-scale exhibitions of contemporary art.

The Iveagh Bequest Kenwood House, Hampstead Lane, NW3, tel 348 1286. Open 10am–6pm daily (April to Sept); 10am–5pm daily (Feb, March and Oct); and 10am–4pm daily (Nov to Jan). Admission free. Fine collection of Old Masters.

Leighton House 12 Holland Park Rd, W14, tel 602 3316. Open 11am–5pm Mon to Sat. Admission free. The home of the celebrated Victorian artist Lord Leighton is hung with a permanent collection of his own and other Victorian and Pre-Raphaelite paintings. Also, monthly exhibitions by young, contemporary artists.

National Gallery Trafalgar Sq, WC2, tel 839 3321. Open 10am–6pm Mon to Sat, and 2pm–6pm Sun. Admission free. There are guided tours, talks, lectures and audio-visual shows to help you get a grip on the stunningly extensive and diverse collection of paintings housed here. All the leading European schools of art from the 13th to the 20th century are grouped in halls that lead off each other. A viewing strategy is essential. Also visiting exhibitions which are advertised nationally.

National Portrait Gallery St Martin's Place, WC2, tel 930 1552. Open 10am–5pm Mon to Fri, 10am–6pm Sat, and 2pm–6pm Sun. Admission free. Permanent exhibition of portraits, sculptures and photographs of the famous in British history, from the Tudors to today. Also regular exhibitions on some aspect of portraiture.

Queen's Gallery Buckingham Palace, Buckingham Palace Rd, SW1, tel 930 4832. Open 10.30am–5pm Tue to Sat, and 2pm–5pm Sun. Admission £1.20, under 16s, OAPs and UB40 holders 60p. Tacked on to the side of Buckingham Palace, this houses a rotating exhibition of the Royal Collection. Essentially Old Masters.

Royal Academy of Arts Burlington House, Piccadilly, W1, tel 439 7438. Open 10am–6pm daily. Admission varies. Founded in 1768 by George II with Sir Joshua Reynolds as president, the RAA has always shown the finest of British art. The Summer Exhibition, chosen from work submitted by living British artists, is legendary, but there are important historical loan and thematic exhibitions throughout the year.

Saatchi Collection 98a Boundary Rd, NW8, tel 624 8299. Open noon–6pm Fri and Sat. Admission free. Advertising supremo Charles Saatchi and his wife Doris have indulged their love of contemporary British art to create one of the finest collections in Britain. Exhibits change every few months.

Serpentine Gallery Kensington Gardens, W2, tel 402 6075. Open 10am–6pm Mon to Fri, until 7pm Sat and Sun (summer), and 10am–4pm daily (winter). An innovative programme of contemporary art exhibitions, in a delightful gallery overlooking Hyde Park.

The Tate Gallery and **Clore Gallery** Millbank, SW1, tel 821 1313. Open 10am–5.30pm Mon to Sat, and 2pm–5pm Sun. Admission free. Created by Sir Henry Tate (of the sugar family) in 1897, it is home to the national collection of British paintings dating from the 16th century to the present day. There is almost always a visiting exhibition.

The recently built Clore Gallery, which adjoins the Tate, is home to the extensive work of Turner's paintings and watercolours.

Wallace Collection Hertford House, Manchester Sq, W1, tel 935 0687. Open 10am–5pm Mon to Sat, and 2pm–5pm Sun. Admission free, but donation box. Fabulous collection of works of art bequeathed to the nation by Lady Wallace in 1897. Important works by artists from all the European schools, including Rubens,

Van Dyck, Rembrandt, Gainsborough, Delacroix and Titian. Also, unrivalled collection of 18th-century French art and a stunning collection of European and Oriental armour.

Whitechapel Gallery Whitechapel High St, E1, tel 377 0107. Open 11am–5pm Tue and Thur to Sun and 11am–8pm Wed. Admission free. Pioneering gallery that was founded with the express aim of hunting out and showing undiscovered young British artists. Great place to see the work of the best of contemporary British art. Regularly changing exhibitions.

FRINGE

Air Gallery 6 & 8 Rosebery Ave, EC1, tel 278 7751. Open 11am–6pm Tue to Fri, and 2pm–6pm Sat and Sun.

Anthony Reynolds Gallery 37 Cowper St, EC2, tel 608 1516. Open 11am–6pm Tue to Sun.

The Arthouse at Majestic Wine Warehouses Albion Wharf, Hester Rd, SW11, tel 223 2983. Open 10am–10pm daily.

Chisenhale Gallery 64 Chisenhale Rd, E3, tel 981 4518. Open 1pm–6pm Wed to Sat.

Francis Graham-Dixon Gallery 17 Great Sutton St, EC1, tel 250 1962. Open 11am–6pm Tue to Sun.

Matt's Gallery 10 Martello St, E8, tel 249 3799. Open noon–6pm.

Outsider Archive 213 South Lambeth Rd, SW8, tel 735 2192. Ring for an appointment.

Showroom 44 Bonner Rd, E2, tel 980 6636. Open 1pm–6pm Wed to Sun.

Slaughterhouse Gallery 63 Charterhouse St, EC1, tel 490 0847. Intermittent exhibitions, ring for details.

Smith's Galleries 54 Earlham St, Covent Garden, WC2, tel 836 6253. Open 11am–7pm Mon to Sat.

Vortex Galleries 139 Stoke Newington Church St, N16, tel 254 6416. Open 9.30am–6pm Mon to Sat, and 1pm–6pm Sun.

Young Unknowns Gallery 82 The Cut, SE1, tel 928 3415. Open noon–7.30pm Mon to Fri, and 10am–3pm Sat.

Camerawork 121 Roman Rd, E2, tel 980 6256. Open 1pm–6pm Tue to Fri, and 11am–3pm Sat.

Portofolio 345 Portobello Rd, W10, tel 969 0453. Open 9.30am–5.30pm Mon to Sat.

Photographers' Gallery 5 & 8 Gt Newport St, WC2, tel 831 1772. Open 11am–7pm Tue to Sat.

Special Photographers Company Kensington Park Rd, W11, tel 221 3489. Open 10am–6.30pm Mon to Fri, and 11am–5pm Sat.

NIGHTLIFE
CLUBS AND SOMEWHERE TO BOOGIE

London's club scene is in a constant state of flux and what's 'in' one week is likely to go out of fashion overnight. But, for some time, the name of the game has been for DJs to move round the circuit preparing shows for a particular club on a particular night. Admission charges vary from £1 to £15, depending on the club and the gig; some all-day or all-night events require tickets to be booked in advance. As the real action doesn't start until after 11pm, it is quite common practice for clubs to give free entry, particularly to girls, before 10pm. Also some clubs have concessionary nights when anyone gets in free; the first ten couples carrying a copy of *Time Out* or *City Limits* (who both provide a detailed, almost comprehensive day-by-day guide) or admission is slashed to £2.

All clubs have a door policy which means 'dress code' and entrance is monitored by a bouncer. Jeans and trainers are sometimes not acceptable, but then neither is looking too smart. As a guiding rule, the more outrageous you look, the greater chance you have of getting in, but it is wise to check with each club.

I don't recommend joining the queue for The Hippodrome, where 2,000 people go through the doors on a Friday night to see 'the world's greatest laser show' and dance on their space-age dance floor.

CLUBS WITH REGULAR FREE NIGHTS

Bill Stickers 18 Greek St, Soho, W1, tel 437 0582. Open every night until 3am; free before 10pm.

Sunday Night At Freud's Freud's, 198 Shaftesbury Ave, WC2, tel 240 9933. Open 7.30pm–10.30pm. Free evening of jazz and blues.

The Sanctuary Hungerford Lane, off Craven St, WC2, no phone. Open 10.30pm–3.30am. First ten people carrying a copy of *Time Out* get in free on Wed night.

The Cask and Glass Orchard St, W1, no phone. Free admission to first ten people carrying a copy of *Time Out*.

Prohibition 9 Hanover St, W1, tel 493 0689. Free admission on Mon, Tue and Wed; free before 9pm on Thur and Fri.

Ivory's 12 Sutton Row, W1, off Charing Cross Rd, WC1, tel 439 4655. Free admission before 9pm on Mon.

CLUB HIT LIST

Arena 6 Salisbury Prom, Green Lanes/St Anne's Rd, N8, tel 809 1460.

Astoria 157 Charing Cross Rd, WC2, tel 434 0403.

Bass Clef Club 35 Coronet St, off Hoxton St, N1, tel 729 2476.

Bill Stickers 18 Greek St, W1, tel 437 0582.

The Brain 11 Wardour St, W1, tel 437 7301.

Busby's 157 Charing Cross Rd, WC2, tel 734 6963.

Café de Paris 3 Coventry St, WC1, tel 437 2036.

Crazy Larry's 533 King's Rd, SW10, tel 376 5555.

Cricketers Kennington Oval, SE11, tel 735 3059.

Dingwalls Camden Lock, Chalk Farm Rd, NW1, tel 267 4967.

Dublin Castle 94 Parkway, NW1, tel 485 1773.

Electric Ballroom 184 Camden High St, NW1, tel 485 9006.

Fridge Town Hall Parade, Brixton Hill, SW2, tel 326 5100.

Gossips 69 Dean St, W1, tel 434 4480.

Gullivers 15 Ganton St, W1, tel 499 0760.

Heaven under the arches, Craven St, WC2, tel 437 4311.

100 Club 100 Oxford St, W1, tel 636 0933.

Legends 29 Old Burlington St, W1, tel 437 9933.
Le Scandale 53 Berwick St, W1, tel 437 6830.
Limelight 136 Shaftesbury Ave, WC2, tel 434 0572.
Loughborough Hotel corner Loughborough and Evandale Rds, Brixton, SW9.
Mean Fiddler 24 High St, Harlesden, NW10, tel 961 5490.
Moonlighting 16 Greek St, W1, tel 734 6308.
New Pegasus 109 Green Lanes, N5, tel 226 5930.
Notre Dame Hall 6 Leicester Sq, WC2, tel 437 5571.
The Park 38 Kensington High St, W8, tel 938 1078.
Prohibition 9 Hanover St, W1, tel 493 0689.
Town and Country Club 9–17 Highgate Rd, NW5, tel 284 0303.
Wag Club 35 Wardour St, W1, tel 437 5534.

IN THE OPEN AIR
ORGANIZED WALKS

Guiding people around London is very big business and there are specialist organizations dealing with virtually every aspect of London's history, its parks and gardens, its shops, graveyards, cultural life (*see* Theatres, p.157) and even tin pan alley (*see* Rock, p.155). Most walking guided tours are run by amateur enthusiasts, cost very little and average two hours. They rarely need to be booked.

A very comprehensive range of walking tours is organized by the **Museum of London**, 150 London Wall, EC2, tel 600 3699, who also publish a DIY walk around the original line of the City Wall with explanations to the 21 sites they highlight.

The London Tourist Board monitor this thriving walking industry and run their own **Blue Badge Guide** organization. Leaders must pass a stringent exam that requires a very detailed knowledge of their particular aspect of London. A list of Blue Guides, with all their special interests, can be had from **The Guild of Guide Lecturers**, 2 Bridge St, SW1, tel 839 7438. The guides can be booked direct on 839 2498.

Louise Nicholson's *London: The Definitive Guide* (Bodley Head,

£9.95) contains a very well researched section called 'exploring the centre on foot', which makes a splendid introduction and guide (if you xerox the appropriate section; the book would be a dead weight to carry around) to finding your own way around. Another good book is *London Walks*, by Anton Powell (Robson Books), which is written with infectious enthusiasm.

Citisights of London 102a Albion Rd, N16, tel 241 1323. Season of walks led by historians and archaeologists that centre on historical London and areas of London. Programme available on request.

City Walks of London 9–11 Kensington High St, W8, tel 937 4281. Extensive range of walks, including A Medieval Pub Walk; The Secret City – A Walk Back In Time; Beatles London; Political London and Ghost Walks. Send for their brochure.

Inland Waterways Association 14 Regent's Park Rd, NW1, tel 586 2556. Organized guided walks along Regent's Canal every first Sun of the month at 2.30pm from outside Camden tube station.

Streets of London 32 Grovelands Rd, N13, tel 822 3414. Wide range of walks led by informed guides, including Aristocratic London, Political London and Dickens' London. Send for programme.

BUS TRIPS

A guided bus trip round the tourist sights of London is a good introduction to the diversity of the city. Several companies run similar trips, they all take around one and a half hours (depending on the traffic), some have open-air seats, and all have informed guides giving almost identical commentary. They charge £6 for adults; children are half price. You should ring 222 1234 for a 24-hour information service about times of the London Transport version, although there are plenty of buses, leaving constantly between 10am and 5pm, from Victoria Station (opposite the tube station), Speaker's Corner at Marble Arch, on the east side of the Haymarket and Baker Street tube.

RIVER AND CANAL TRIPS

Viewed from the river, London looks (and sounds) entirely different. It is also a delightful, stress-free and quick way of getting from one end of the city to the other. The River Bus (tel 376 3676) runs from Chelsea Harbour (with plans to extend further up river) down to Greenwich and zigzags around the river stopping at all the major piers.

On a more touristic level, various cruiser boats with deck seats, bars and, in some cases, restaurants, operate trips up and down the river with tourist commentaries. On a bright sunny day, there is little to beat such a trip.

See also Getting Around, the River, p.26.

LTB River Service tel 730 4812 gives a 24-hour recorded information service about all sailings, weather and tide conditions.

Westminster Passenger Services Association tel 930 4721, gives information on return trips from upstream piers.

Similarly, **The Regent's Canal Information Centre** c/o 289 Camden High St., NW1, tel 482 0523, is a mine of information about their canal, including information about trips.

The organization responsible for London's canals and locks is **The Inland Waterways Association** 114 Regent's Park Rd, NW1, tel 586 2556, who also publish a useful booklet entitled *Canal Walks In London*, a map and cycle permit.

THE RIVER

Charing Cross Pier Victoria Embankment, opposite Embankment tube, WC2, tel 839 3572. Trips to the Tower of London (takes 25 mins) and Greenwich (takes 60 mins) every 30 mins from 10.30am–4pm daily (April to Sept) and every 45 minutes during the winter. Fares £2/£2.60, half price for children.

Greenwich Pier Cutty Sark Gardens, SE10, tel 858 0079. Trips to Tower Pier (25 mins) and Charing Cross Pier (45 mins). Hours as Charing Cross. Fares £2.20/£2.60, half price for children.

Also to the Thames Barrier (30 mins) and Westminster (60 mins). Fares £1.50/£2.60; £1/£1.20 for children.

Hampton Court Pier The Barge Walk, East Molesey, Surrey, tel 977 5702. To Kingston (45 mins) every 45 mins from 11.15am–5.30pm and Westminster (150 mins) at 3pm, 4pm and 5pm daily. Fares £2/£5.50; £1.50/£3.50 children.

Kew Pier Thetis Ter, Richmond, tel 940 3891. To Westminster (90 mins) at 3pm, 4.30pm and 5pm daily (April to 31 Oct only). Fares £3.50; children £2.50.

Kingston Thames Side, Kingston-upon-Thames, Surrey, tel 546 2434. To Hampton Court (30 mins) every 45 mins from 10.30am–5pm and to Richmond (60 mins) at 10.45am, 1.15pm and 3.45pm. Fares £2/£2.50; children £1.50/£2.

Richmond Pier Richmond Bridge, Richmond, tel 940 8505. To Hampton Court (105 mins) at noon and 2.30pm Tue to Sun (21 May to Sept only); Kingston (60 mins) at noon, 2.30pm and 5pm, and Westminster (135 mins) at 3pm, 4.30pm, 5pm and 6pm daily (April to 31 Oct only). Fares £3/£2.50/£5; children £2/£2/£3.50.

Tower Pier Tower Hill, opposite main entrance to Tower of London, EC3, tel 488 0344. To Westminster (25 mins) every 20 mins between 11am–5.20pm (April to 31 Oct) and every 30 mins until 4pm the rest of the time; to the Design Museum (5 mins) every 20 mins from 11.30am–6.30pm Tue to Sun; to Greenwich (25 mins) every 30 mins from 11am–4pm. Fares £2/80p/£2.20; children £1/60p/£1.10.

Westminster Pier Victoria Embankment, steps from Westminster Bridge, SW1, tel 730 4812. To Greenwich (60 mins) every 30 mins from 10.30am–4pm (April to 31 Oct) and until 3pm during the winter; Hampton Court (210 mins) at 10.30am, 11.15am, noon and 12.30pm (1 April to 31 Oct); to Kew (90 mins) and Putney (40 mins) 10.15am, 10.30am, 11am, 11.15am, 11.45am, noon, 12.30pm, 2pm, 2.45pm and 3.30pm (1 April to 31 Oct only); to Richmond (135 mins) 10.30am, 11.15am, noon and 12.30pm; Thames Barrier (75 mins) 10am, 11.15am 12.45pm, 1.45pm, 3.15pm (April to 30 Sept) and 11.15am and 1.30pm winter; to Tower of London (30 mins) every 20 mins from 10.20am until 5pm (April to 31 Oct) and every 30 mins until 4pm winter. Fares £2.50/£5.50/£3.50/£3/£5/£2.40/£2; children £1.20/£3.50/£2.50/£2/£3.50/£1.30/£1.

CANAL TRIPS

Jason's Trip Little Venice, 60 Blomfield Rd, W9, tel 286 3428. Round trips from Little Venice to Camden Lock. Season from 24 March to 9 Oct with several trips a day; journey takes 45 mins one way and fares £2.75 single, children £1.50.

Jenny Wren c/o 250 Camden High St, NW1, tel 485 4433. Round trips in a traditional canal barge that travels from Camden Lock to Little Venice; season Feb to Nov; journey takes one and a half hours and fares £2.50, children £1.20.

London Waterbus Company Little Venice, corner Warwick Cres and Blomfield Rd, W9, tel 482 2550. Round trip that can be co-ordinated with their schedule between Little Venice, London Zoo and Camden Lock. Season Mar to Oct; journey takes 35 mins to Zoo, Zoo to Lock 15 mins; round trip takes 1 hour 50 mins. Fares: Little Venice to Zoo £5.75 (includes admission to Zoo), Camden Lock to Zoo £4.85, Little Venice to Camden Lock £2.20. Children £3.45/£2.90/£1.20.

PARKS AND GARDENS

London is one of the greenest cities in Europe, blessed with 1700 parks and open spaces which add up to 46,000 acres. They range from small 'village' greens to lavish, landscaped parks with canals and rivers, pavilions, theatres, zoos, visiting funfairs, historic houses, cricket pitches, horse-riding paths, bandstands and boating lakes.

The Royal Parks (Regent's Park, Hyde Park, Kensington Gardens, Hampton Court, Bushey Park, St James's Park, Richmond Park and Greenwich Park) belong to the Crown and are administered by the Department of the Environment (tel 212 3341). All other parks and open spaces are administered by their appropriate local authorities and fully documented in leaflets kept at local libraries and town halls.

SOME LESSER KNOWN GREEN SPACES

Bostall Heath and Woods Bostall Hill Rd, SE2. Lovely woods with silver birch, beech and oak trees; in the spring, acres of bluebells and daffodils.

Chiswick House Burlington Lane, W4. Delightful grounds with 'river', woods, various stretches of grassland of different character, cricket pitch and well tended gardens.

The Gardens Paddington St, W1. Formerly a burial ground and still consecrated.

Highgate and Queen's Wood Muswell Hill Rd, N6. Delightfully unknown alternative to nearby Alexandra Palace.

Lincoln's Inn Fields WC2. The oldest square in Camden and the largest (seven acres) in London. Lunchtime band concerts, tennis courts.

Osterley Park off the Great West Rd, Isleworth, Middx. Delightful, country-style park that belongs to the 16th-century manor house home of Sir Thomas Gresham, which is now owned by the National Trust. Lakes, sweeping chestnuts and fine parkland.

Ravenscourt Park between King St and Goldhawk Rd, W6. Large areas of grassland, a stretch of water with wildfowl, tennis courts, bowls and adventure playground.

Rembrandt Park Warwick Ave, W9. Runs along the edge of Regent's Canal at Little Venice.

St George's Hanover Square Gardens, W1. Immaculately tended gardens with beautiful chestnut trees and surprisingly peaceful.

St George's Gardens Heathcote St, WC1. Surprisingly peaceful gardens just a stroll away from King's Cross.

St Giles-in-the-Fields St Giles High St, WC2. More paving stones than grass but lovely rose bushes and park benches.

St Mary Abbots Gardens Kensington High St, W8. A wooded grassland that provides a delightful retreat from Kensington High Street.

Tavistock Sq Woburn Place, WC1. Magnificent plane trees and flowering cherries (planted to commemorate the victims of Hiroshima), a copper beech (planted by Nehru) and a sculpture of Gandhi.

Victoria Park Victoria Park Rd, E9. Surrounded by canals, it's the East End's largest green space.

Waterlow Park Highgate High St, N6. The hillside setting gives views across London's skyline. Different levels, a terraced rose garden, tree-lined ornamental pond and grassland that leads down to Highgate Cemetery combine to make this a rather special place.

CEMETERIES

London's Victorian cemeteries are wonderful, eccentric and illuminating places that are full of surprises. Most are overgrown with ivy, brambles and gnarled old climbers that obscure much of their splendour, but there are plenty of famous names to track down on the ornate gravestones and lavish tombs. They are also uncharted wildlife sanctuaries, behind high walls. Most are open during daylight hours; at Highgate, London's most famous Victorian cemetery which holds 166,000 remains (including those of Karl Marx), there are tours between 10am and 4pm on the hour.

Abney Park Stamford Hill, N16.

Brompton Brompton Rd, SW5.

Bunhill Fields City Rd, EC4.

City of London Cemetery Aldersbrook Rd, E12.

Hampstead Cemetery Fortune Green Rd, NW6.

Highgate Swain's Lane, N6.

Kensal Green Harrow Rd, Kensal Green, W10.

Mortlake Roman Catholic Cemetery North Worple Way, SW14.

Tower Hamlets Southern Grove, E3.

PLACES AND EVENTS NOT TO MISS

There is so much to see and do in London. This is a personal selection of some of the obvious and not so obvious attractions.

Changing The Guard Buckingham Palace Forecourt, SW1. 11.30am April 1 to end July daily, and alternate days Aug to end March.

Chinatown area around Gerrard St, W1. London's Little Hong Kong.

Speaker's Corner Hyde Park, W2. On Sundays, at the Marble Arch corner of central London's largest park (340 acres), anyone can stand on a box and let off steam about anything; can be hilarious.

London Planetarium and **Laserium** Marylebone Rd, NW1, tel 486 1121. Open 12.20pm–5pm daily and from 10.20am during school holidays. Admission £2.65, £1.70 children under 16. Layman's guide to astrology with stunning projection (into a vast dome) of the celestial bodies.

Madame Tussaud's Marylebone Rd, NW1, tel 935 6861. Open 10am–5.30pm Mon to Fri, 9.30am–5.30pm Sat and Sun. Admission £4.80, children £3.15. Home of the famous collection of waxwork models that date from 1835 to the present day. Can be horrendously busy. The cheapest way of getting in is to combine a visit here with one to the Planetarium (*see above*) when tickets cost £6.10, children £3.80.

Nelson's Column Trafalgar Sq, WC2. A famous London landmark erected in 1840 to honour Nelson's victory over Napoleon at Trafalgar. But watch out for the pigeons.

Houses of Parliament Parliament Sq, SW1, tel 219 4272. House of Commons Visitors' Gallery open 2.30pm–10pm Mon to Thur, 9.30am–3pm Fri; House of Lords Visitors' Gallery open 2.30pm until debating ends Mon to Wed, and 3pm until debating ends Thur and Fri. Admission free; guided tours have to be arranged through your local MP.

The Old Bailey EC4, tel 248 3277. Open 10.30am–1pm and 2pm–4pm Mon to Fri. Admission free. London's most celebrated criminal court.

Royal Courts of Justice Strand, WC2, tel 936 6470. Open 10.30am–4.30pm Mon to Fri. Admission free. Fascinating neo-Gothic building, worth seeing even if you don't sit in on a court case.

Thames Barrier Visitors' Centre Unit Way, Woolwich, SE18, tel 854 1373. Open 10.30am–5pm Mon to Fri, and until 5.30pm Sat and Sun. Admission £2, children and OAPs £1.20, family ticket £5.50. See the largest movable flood barrier in the world, examine the scale models and tune into the audio visual displays that explain the whys and wherefores of the barrier.

Tower Bridge SE1, tel 407 0922. Open 10am–5.45pm daily April to Oct, and 10am–4pm daily Nov to 31 March. Admission £2.50, children and OAPs £1. Phone to find out bridge opening times (five times a day during the summer) and watch the original (1894) steam engine pump at work.

Tower of London Tower Hill, EC3, tel 709 0765. Open 9.30am–5pm Mon to Sat, 2pm–5.30pm Sun March to Oct, and until 4pm Nov to Feb. Admission £4.80, £3 OAPs, students, UB40 holders and the disabled, £2 children under 15.

A CALENDAR OF EVENTS

The Chelsea Cruise Takes place on the last Saturday of every month. Hot rods and souped up or customized old cars set out on a circuit that starts around 8pm and goes over Chelsea, Albert and Battersea Bridges. Join in or just hang in.

January

London International Mime Festival Performances at arts centres and fringe theatres around town. Details published in *Time Out* and *City Limits*.

February

Chinese New Year Exact date publicized in advance. The whole of Chinatown celebrates the new year with a lion dance, fireworks and special feasts.

March

Camden Festival and Jazz Week Celebration of the arts throughout Camden. Full details 278 4444.

East End Festival Celebration of locally-bred talent, details from 790 1818.

University Boat Race Rowing race between teams from Oxford and Cambridge Universities which begins at Putney Bridge and ends at Mortlake. Exact date well publicized in the press.

April

Camden Festival and Jazz Week Celebration of the arts throughout Camden. Full details 278 4444.

Easter Day Parade Battersea Park, SW11. An Easter Bonnet competition is the highlight of this colourful parade that takes place on Easter Monday. Traditional fairs also take place on Hampstead Heath and Blackheath.

May

Beating the Retreat Traditional ceremony performed by the marching and drilling bands of the Household Division. Takes place on Horse Guards Parade in late May, with evening performances lit by floodlight. Tickets must be applied for (from February) to Premier Box Office, 1b Bridge St, SW1, tel 839 6815.

June

Trooping the Colour Horse Guards Parade, SW1. The Queen's official birthday, when she inspects some of her guards from an open coach. First performed in front of King George III. Takes place at 11am, on the second Saturday in June.

July

Annual Festival of Street Entertainers Music, dance, theatre, magicians and performing artists of all sorts compete for a number of awards. Events take place around Carnaby Street, Soho. Details 287 0907.

City of London Festival Non-stop events throughout the City. Full details 606 3030 or 377 0540.

Clerkenwell Festival Street entertainment, concerts and events in venues throughout Clerkenwell. Details 354 7127.

London International Festival of Theatre Visiting companies from all over the world perform at venues throughout London. Details from 836 7433. Continues in August.

August

Notting Hill Carnival Centred around Portobello Road. A celebration of and for the West Indian and Caribbean community in London. Three days of dancing, street bands, processions and non-stop activity. Takes place throughout the August Bank Holiday.

Summer in the City Family-orientated festival organized by the Barbican Centre during the first week of August. Details 638 8891.

September

Covent Garden Clown Convention Covent Garden Piazza, WC2. Details from Alternative Arts 240 5451; planned for 11 Sept.

October

Annual Dance Umbrella Festival Organized by Riverside Studios. Details 741 4040.

Pearly Harvest Festival St Martin-in-the-Fields, WC2. A celebration of the Cockney tradition of the Pearly Kings and Queens. They assemble in their marvellous costumes covered in mother of pearl buttons.

State Opening of Parliament Palace of Westminster, SW1. A procession when the Queen and some of her family are decked out in all their regalia and are driven in gilded coaches from Buckingham Palace, along the Mall, through Horse Guards Parade to the Houses of Parliament.

November

Annual Dance Umbrella Festival Organized by Riverside Studios. Details 741 4040.

London Film Festival Hosted by the NFT and showing 1–26 November. Programme and ticket information 928 3232.

Lord Mayor's Procession and Show City of London (details 606 3030). Procession from the Guildhall to the Royal Courts of Justice.

Remembrance Sunday Whitehall. The Queen and State attend a ceremony and lay wreaths of poppies at the Cenotaph at 11am on the second Sunday in the month to remember the dead of the two world wars.

December

New Year's Eve Celebrations Crowds gather round Nelson's Column at Trafalgar Square to sing in the New Year.

SPORT

SPORTS CENTRES

The sports centres I have selected here tend to be run by local boroughs, often act as community centres and are almost free. Where there is a membership fee it is nominal, but all places are open to non-members. Often borough residents' membership is subsidized.

WEST END

Jubilee Hall Recreation Centre Tavistock St, Covent Garden, WC2, tel 836 4835. Open 8am–10pm Mon to Fri, and 10am–5pm Sat and Sun. The cost of membership is calculated on a unit system which relates to the various activities offered. The sliding price scale starts at £30 per year for one unit; under 16s, students and OAPs from £7.50 per year. Admission is free to members, but 75p to non-members and from £1.50 per class. Facilities include sports hall, weights room, sauna and jacuzzi. Activities include dance, aerobics, yoga, martial arts, keep fit, badminton, basketball, hockey, netball, climbing and fives.

NORTH LONDON

Britannia Leisure Centre 40 Hyde Rd, N1, tel 729 4485. Open 9am–10pm daily. No membership, admission 30p. Activities from £1. Facilities include sports hall, sauna, solarium and swimming pool. Activities include athletics, aerobics, martial arts, bowls, cricket, table tennis, tennis, trampolining, volleyball, football and squash.

Mornington Sports and Leisure Centre 142 Arlington Rd, NW1, tel 267 3600. Open 12.30pm–10pm Mon, 10.30am–10pm Tue to Fri, and 10am–6pm Sat. Membership £15 (residents), £30 non-residents, with reductions for the unwaged, but admission £1.50, £2 non-members. Activities £1.50 for non-members, with cheaper concessions during the day. Facilities include fully equipped sports hall, two weights rooms and equipment hire for badminton, basketball, cricket, football, lacrosse and table tennis. Also boxing, gymnastics, keep fit and table tennis.

Picketts Lock Leisure Centre Picketts Lock Lane, N9, tel 803 4756. Open 10am–10.30pm Mon to Fri, 9am–10pm Sat, and until 9.30pm Sun. Membership £15 adults, £7.50 under 16s, OAPs and during daytime. Admission free to members, 50p for non-members and from 55p for activities. One of the first custom-built London leisure centres that offers an extensive range of sport and fitness activities and is well equipped with an all-weather floodlit multi-sports area, combat rooms, swimming pool and dance floors.

Sobell Sports Centre Hornsey Rd, N7, tel 609 2166. Open 9am–10.30pm Mon to Fri, and 10am–9.30pm Sat and Sun. Membership £2 per year (residents), £18.50 non-residents; under 16 residents free, non-residents £6. Facilities include indoor ski slope, two climbing walls, an ice rink, weights rooms, squash courts and several activities rooms.

Swiss Cottage Sports Centre Winchester Rd, NW3, tel 586 5989. Open 8am–10pm Mon to Fri, 8am–7pm Sat, and 8am–1pm Sun. No membership or admission charges. Activities from 50p. Facilities include swimming pool, gym, squash courts and sports hall. Activities include aerobics, gymnastics, martial arts, sub aqua, netball, tennis and squash.

EAST LONDON

Finsbury Leisure Complex Includes Ironmonger Row Baths, Norman St, EC1, tel 253 4490. Open 10am–10pm daily. Membership £2 a year (residents), £15 non-residents. Admission free to members, 30p to non-members. Activities from 50p. Facilities include swimming pool, playing fields and sports pitches, squash courts and gym. Activities include aerobics, keep fit, martial arts, sub aqua, roller skating and trampolining.

Saddlers Sport Centre Goswell Rd, EC1, tel 253 2985. Open 11am–8pm (winter) and 9am–9.30pm (summer) Mon to Fri, 9.30am–5.30pm Sat and 11am–5pm Sun. No membership or admission. Activities from 50p. Facilities include swimming pool, gym, sports hall, squash courts and weights area. Activities include fencing, gymnastics, aerobics, racquetball, squash, table tennis, football and basketball.

SOUTH LONDON

Balham Leisure Centre Elmfield Rd, SW17, tel 871 7179. Open 7.30am–9pm Mon to Sat, and 7.30am–7.30pm Sun. Membership £12.50 per year, £5 to under 16s. Admission free to members, 50p non-members. Activities from £2, but cheaper swimming. Facilities include swimming pool, athletics track, solarium, table tennis and weights area. Activities include martial arts, dance and athletics.

Brixton Recreation Centre Brixton Station Rd, SW9, tel 274 7774. Open 9am–10pm daily. No membership, admission free. Activities from 30p. Facilities include two sports halls, sauna and solarium, gym, three swimming pools. Activities include archery, aerobics, keep fit, football, trampolining, climbing and basketball.

Chelsea Sports Centre Chelsea Manor St, SW3, tel 352 6985. Open 8am–10pm Mon to Fri, until 6pm Sat, and 1pm Sun. No membership or admission, activities from 35p. Facilities include swimming pool, sports hall, squash courts, tennis courts, football pitch and floodlit hard surface play area. Activities include aerobics, yoga, keep fit, spa baths and weight training.

Crystal Palace National Sports Centre Upper Norwood, SE19, tel 778 0131. Open 9am–10.30pm Mon to Sat, and until 5.30pm Sun. Membership £10 per year, half price for under 16s. Admission free to members, 45p adults, 35p under 16 non-members.

Facilities at this Olympic-standard centre include floodlit stadium and ski slope, athletics training area and numerous courts for tennis and squash. Activities include American football, diving, fencing, sub aqua and volleyball.

Elephant and Castle Leisure Centre 22 Elephant and Castle Complex, SE1, tel 582 5505. Open 7.45am–10.30pm Mon to Fri, and 9am–10.30pm Sat and Sun. Membership only applies to gym, £3. Admission 15p adults and 10p for under 16s. Activities from 80p, with reductions for usual concessionaries. Facilities include swimming pool, sports hall, martial arts area, squash courts. Activities include martial arts, keep fit, aerobics, trampolining, volleyball and cricket.

Queen Mother Sports Centre 23 Vauxhall Bridge Rd, SW1, tel 798 2122. Open 8am–10pm Mon to Fri, until 5pm Sat, and 9am–4pm Sun. No membership, admission 30p, activities from £1.15. Facilities include swimming pool, table tennis, basketball court and boxing rings. Activities include diving, keep fit, martial arts, trampolining and water polo.

WEST LONDON

Chiswick Sports Hall Chiswick School, Burlington Lane, W4, tel 995 4067. Open 6pm–11pm Mon to Fri, and 9am–9pm Sat and Sun. No membership or admission fee. Activities from 80p. Facilities include sports hall, training hall, multi-gym, squash courts and netball court. Activities include gymnastics, trampolining, volleyball, cricket, basketball and keep fit.

Jubilee Sports Centre Caird St, W10, tel 960 5512. Open 8am–10pm Mon to Fri, until 6pm Sat, and 9am–4pm Sun. Membership £7.50 per year, children free. Activities from 90p, concessions for children. Facilities include swimming pool, squash courts, sports hall. Activities include gymnastics, martial arts, trampolining, weight training, badminton and basketball.

MUNICIPAL TENNIS COURTS

These are the cheapest courts in London, and usually cost from 80p–£1.50 per hour. *See also* Parks and Gardens, p.179 and Sports Centres, p.187. All courts are bookable.

NORTH LONDON

Church Street Recreation Ground Church St, N9, tel 807 0113.
Clissold Park Green Lanes, N4, tel 254 9736.
Highbury Fields Highbury Place, N5, tel 226 2234.

EAST LONDON

Goosey Park St Alban's Avenue, E6, tel 471 1572.
Lloyd Park Forest Rd, E17, no telephone.

SOUTH LONDON

Battersea Park Battersea Park Rd, SW11, tel 871 7543.
Bishops Park Priory Bank, Bishops Park, SW6, tel 736 3854.
Rocks Lane Recreation Ground Rocks Lane, SW13, no telephone.

WEST LONDON

Holland Park Kensington High St, W8, tel 602 2226.
North Acton Playing Fields Noel Rd, W3, tel 993 6832.

MUNICIPAL SWIMMING POOLS

See also Sports Centres, p.187

WEST END

The Oasis 32 Endell St, Covent Garden, WC2, tel 831 1804. Open 9am–7pm Mon to Fri, and until 4.30pm Sat. Outdoor pool open May to end Sept.

Marshall Street Baths Marshall St, W1, tel 798 2007. Open 8am– 6.30pm Mon, Wed and Thur, until 8pm Tue, 5pm Fri and 4.30pm Sat.

NORTH LONDON

Cally Pool 229 Caledonian Rd, N1, tel 837 0852. Open 7.30am–7pm Mon, Tue and Fri, until 8.30pm Wed and Thur, 5pm Sat and noon Sun.

Clissold Rd Baths Clissold Rd, N16, tel 254 4272. Open 7.30am– 7.15pm Mon and Wed, 9am–8.15pm Tue and Thur, until 7.15pm Fri, 3.15pm Sat and 1.15pm Sun.

Highbury Pool Highbury Cres, N5, tel 226 4186. Open 7.30am– 8.30pm Mon to Fri, until 5pm Sat and Sun.

Kentish Town Baths Prince of Wales Rd, NW5, tel 267 9341. Open 8am–7.45pm Mon to Fri, until 4pm Sat.

EAST LONDON

Island Baths Tiller Rd, E14, tel 987 5211. Open 9am–5pm Mon, Tue, Wed and Fri, until 8pm Thur, noon–7pm Sat.

St George's Pool The Highway, E1, tel 709 9714. Open 9am– 4.45pm Mon and Tue, until 8pm Wed and Fri, 5.30am–6.30pm Thur, 8am–6pm Sat, 8am–11.45am Sun.

Whitechapel Baths Goulston St, E1, tel 247 3684. Open 8am–5pm Mon to Fri, until 6pm Sat.

SOUTH LONDON

Camberwell Baths Artichoke Place, off Camberwell Church St, SE5, tel 703 3024. Open 2pm–6.30pm Mon, until 8pm Tue, 8.30am–3.15pm alternate Weds, 9.30am–3.15pm Thur, 7.45am–2.45pm Fri, 8.30am–3.15pm Sat, and 8.30am–11.30pm alternate Suns.

Fulham Baths Normand Park, SW6, tel 385 7628. Open noon–8pm Mon to Fri, 10am–4pm Sat, and 9am–4pm Sun.

Richmond Baths Old Deer Park, Twickenham Rd, Richmond, tel 940 8461. Open 8.30am–6pm Mon, until 8pm Tue and Thur, 7pm Wed, 8pm Fri, 5pm Sat and noon Sun.

WEST LONDON

White City Pool Bloemfontein Rd, W12, tel 743 3401. Open 3.30pm–6.25pm Mon, noon–6.25pm Tue, Fri, and until 8pm Wed, 5pm Thur and 10am–4pm Sat, 9am–noon Sun.

SPORT FOR FREE AND NEARLY FREE

Consult the Sports Centres (p.187), Parks and Gardens (p.179) and River and Canal Trips (p.177) sections for locations that offer free sporting activities. *Time Out* publish a useful noticeboard section in their sports coverage which draws attention to free events and to private clubs that need members.

EMERGENCY SERVICES

HEALTH
HELP AND ADVICE

Ring **Healthline** 980 4848 which gives pre-recorded advice on many
common ailments with a referral advice.

PHARMACIES

The following chemists are open late and can deal with prescriptions:

THE WEST END

Bliss Chemist 5 Marble Arch, W1, tel 723 6116. Open 9am–
midnight.
Boots 44 Piccadilly Circus, W1, tel 734 6126. Open 8.30am–8pm
daily.

NORTH LONDON

Bliss Chemist 50 Willesden Lane, NW6, tel 624 8000. Open 9am–
2am daily.
Warman Freed 45 Golders Green Rd, NW11, tel 455 4351. Open
8.30am–midnight daily.

AMBULANCES

Dial 999.

ACCIDENTS AND CASUALTIES

24-hour walk-in casualty departments operate at the following hospitals. Be prepared to wait:

THE WEST END

University College Hospital Gower St, entrance Grafton Way, W1, tel 387 9300.

NORTH LONDON

North Middlesex Hospital Stirling Way, Edmonton, N18, tel 807 3071.
The Whittington Hospital St Mary's Wing, Highgate Hill, N19, tel 272 3070.
Royal Free Hospital Pond St, NW3, tel 794 0500.
Central Middlesex Hospital Acton Lane, NW10, tel 965 5733.

EAST LONDON

London Hospital Whitechapel Rd, E1, tel 377 7000.
Hackney and Homerton Hospital Homerton Row, E9, tel 985 5555.
St Bartholomew's Hospital West Smithfield, entrance Giltspur St, EC1, tel 601 8888.

SOUTH LONDON

Guy's Hospital St Thomas St, entrance Weston St, SE1, tel 407 7600.
St Thomas's Hospital Lambeth Palace Rd, SE1, tel 928 9292.
King's College Hospital Denmark Hill, entrance Bessemer Rd, SE5, tel 274 6222.
Greenwich District Hospital Vanbrugh Hill, SE10, tel 858 8141.
Lewisham Hospital Lewisham High St, SE13, tel 690 4311.
Westminster Hospital Dean Ryle St, Horseferry Rd, SW1, tel 828 9811.
St George's Hospital Blackshaw Rd, SW17, tel 672 1255.

Charing Cross Hospital Fulham Palace Rd, entrance St Dunstan's Rd, W6, tel 846 1234.
Hammersmith Hospital Du Cane Rd, W12, tel 743 2030.

DOCTORS AND DENTISTS

Lists of Local National Health Service doctors and dentists, chemists and opticians are kept at all libraries and post offices. A walk-in NHS surgery for anyone without a doctor takes place at **Great Chapel Street Medical Centre**, 13 Gt Chapel St, W1, tel 437 9360 between 12.45pm–4pm Monday to Friday.

DENTAL EMERGENCIES

Dental Emergency Care Service tel 400 0400/677 6363 or 677 8383. Open 24 hours daily; referral service for a surgery open for treatment.
Eastman Dental Hospital 256 Gray's Inn Rd, WC1, tel 837 3646. Open 9am–12.30pm and 1.30pm–4.30pm Mon to Fri. Dental casualty, no appointment needed.
Guy's Hospital Dental School St Thomas' St, SE1, tel 407 7600. Open 9am–4pm Mon to Fri, 9.30am–9.30pm Sat and Sun. Dental casualty, no appointments and no charges Mon to Fri.

ALTERNATIVE MEDICINE

The following organizations will put you in touch with registered practitioners; a large stamped addressed envelope is appreciated.
The Acupunture Association and Register 34 Alderney St, SW1, tel 834 1012.
British Chiropractic Association Premier House, 10 Greycoat Pl, SW1, no telephone enquiries, and £1 required for their register.

British Homoeopathic Association 27a Devonshire St, W1, tel 935 2163.
British Society of Medical and Dental Hypnosis 42 Links Rd, Ashtead, Surrey, tel 0372 273522.
Institute of Complementary Medicine 21 Portland Place, W1, no telephone enquiries.

DEPRESSION

Samaritans 24-hour helpline, tel 439 2224.

GAY AND LESBIAN

Lesbian and Gay Switchboard 24-hour helpline, tel 837 7324.

SEX

CONTRACEPTION AND ABORTION

British Pregnancy Advisory Service 7 Belgrave Rd, SW1, tel 222 0985.
Brook Advisory Centres 153a East St, SE17, tel 708 1234.
Family Planning Association 27 Mortimer St, W1, tel 636 7866.
Pregnancy Advisory Service 11 Charlotte St, W1, tel 637 8962.

STD CLINICS

St Mary's Hospital Special Clinic Praed St, W2, tel 725 1697.
London Hospital Special Clinic Turner St, EC4, tel 377 7307. No appointment is necessary at either of these clinics that specialize in sexually transmitted diseases.

RAPE

London Rape Crisis Centre PO Box 69, WC1, tel 837 1600. 24-hour advice, counselling and support service for victims of rape.

AIDS

Aids Helpline 24-hour free help and information service offering advice and support to anyone worried about any aspect of Aids.

Terence Higgins Trust 52 Gray's Inn Rd, WC1, tel 242 1010. Set up to support Aids sufferers, but also offers help, advice and counselling to anyone worried about any aspect of Aids.

HOME
GENERAL

Capital Helpline on 388 7575 will help with queries about anything; if they can't help, they'll know someone who can. Service operates between 9.30am–5.30pm Mon to Wed and Fri, and until 9pm Thur.

TELEPHONE

142 and 192 are the numbers for free directory enquiries in and out of London; 153 for international enquiries. 100 is the number for operator assistance, 155 for an international operator. 999 is the number for police assistance, the fire brigade and ambulance services. If you want to know the time ring 123.

GAS

If you smell gas, have a gas leak or loss of power, look in the telephone directory number 'G' for your local emergency number; if you don't have a book, ring 192 or 142 and ask the operator.

ELECTRICITY

If you have a power cut look in the telephone directory under 'E' for your local emergency number; if you don't have a book, ring 192 or 142 and ask the operator.

WATER

If you have a burst pipe look in the telephone directory under 'W' for your local emergency number; if you don't have a book, ring 192 or 142 and ask the operator. There is also a freephone plumbing helpline on 468 7767 and **Dyno-Rod Plumbing** operate a 24-hour plumbing service around London (but they aren't particularly cheap).

EMBASSIES

The telephone directory lists embassies, consulates and high commissions under their respective countries; directory enquiries on 142 or 192 will also give you numbers not listed here.

American Embassy 24 Grosvenor Sq, W1, tel 499 9000. 24-hour emergency telephone service.

Australian High Commission Australia House, The Strand, WC2, tel 379 4334.

Belgian Embassy 103 Eaton Sq, SW1, tel 235 5422.

Canadian High Commission Macdonald House, 1 Grosvenor Sq, W1, tel 629 9492. 24-hour emergency telephone service.

Chinese Embassy 49–61 Portland Place, W1, tel 636 5197.

French Embassy 58 Knightsbridge, SW1, tel 235 8080.

German Embassy 23 Belgrave Sq, SW1, tel 235 4142.

Greek Embassy and Consulate 1a Holland Park, W11, tel 727 8040.

Italian Embassy 14 Three Kings Yard, W1, tel 629 8200.

Royal Netherlands Embassy 38 Hyde Park Gate, SW7, tel 584 5040.

New Zealand High Commission New Zealand House, 80 Haymarket, SW1, tel 930 8422.

Spanish Embassy 24 Belgrave Sq, SW1, tel 235 5331.

ACCOMMODATION

ARTS CENTRES, GALLERIES, LIBRARIES AND MUSEUMS

LEISURE

RESTAURANTS, CAFÉS, ETC

INDEX

SERVICES

SHOPS AND SHOPPING

INDEX

THEATRES, CINEMAS, CLUBS AND PUBS

TOURIST ATTRACTIONS

TRAVEL